KILLING FOR
PLEASURE

KILLING FOR PLEASURE

THE GLOBAL PHENOMENON OF MASS MURDER

BILL O'BRIEN

JOHN BLAKE

Published by John Blake Publishing Ltd,
3 Bramber Court, 2 Bramber Road,
London W14 9PB, England

www.johnblakepublishing.co.uk

First published in paperback in 2002
This edition published in 2009

ISBN: 978 1 84454 798 2

British Library Cataloguing-in-Publication Data:

A catalogue record for this book is available from the British Library.

Design by www.envydesign.co.uk

Printed in Great Britain by CPI Bookmarque, Croydon CR0 4TD

1 3 5 7 9 10 8 6 4 2

Papers used by John Blake Publishing are natural, recyclable products made
from wood grown in sustainable forests. The manufacturing processes conform
to the environmental regulations of the country of origin.

CONTENTS

ACKNOWLEDGEMENTS

Preparing the manuscript for *Killing for Pleasure* has been an enormous task and was only possible thanks to the contributions of many people. Because some of the research material was gathered on my behalf it is impossible to personally acknowledge all those who have contributed to this work. Similarly there will be others whom I have contacted over the past two years who do not appear on these pages. If that is the case the omission is certainly unintentional and regrettable. I value the wide range of assistance given me to complete *Killing for Pleasure*.

Firstly I need to acknowledge the contribution of Bryan Bruce. Bryan is a television documentary maker who pointed out the pattern of behaviour in mass murderers which a lot of experts said was not there. Had Bryan had time this work would have been a joint project. With a Master of Arts degree in psychology and sociology, Bryan Bruce had the expertise to give me considerable guidance, help and encouragement. He also supplied field tapes and notes of interviews used in his television documentary *In Cold Blood*. That documentary compared the backgrounds of Gray, Bryant and Hamilton. This book began as an idea of Bryan's and I am indebted to him.

Others to contribute were: Dr Chris Cantor, Senior Research Psychiatrist at the Australian Institute of Suicide Research and Prevention for background material on mass murder; Margaret Vine at the Royal New Zealand Police College Library for considerable research material; Suzann Brown of the National University, San

Diego, USA who researched James Huberty's background; Detective Inspector Karen Trego, Thames Valley Police, England for homicide file statements relating to the Hungerford tragedy; Directeur Pierre Leclair of the Sainte-Foy Police Department, Quebec, Canada; John Myrtle, Australian Institute of Criminology; Amanda Phillips, State Coroner's Office, Victoria, Australia for statements relating to the two Melbourne tragedies; Tess Lawrence, Melbourne for material, advice and encouragement; Detective Superintendent David McWhirter, Thames Valley Police; Mike Cox, Texas Department of Public Safety; Sergeant Bill Horn, Austin Police Department; Deputy Chief Jim McCarroll and Lieutenant Dennis Baldwin, Killeen Police Department for access to the Luby's homicide file; Dr Ian Sale, Forensic Psychiatrist, Tasmania, Australia; Professor David Cooke, Forensic Psychologist, Glasgow, Scotland; Dr John Baird, Consultant Forensic Psychiatrist, Glasgow; Dr David Sime, Consultant Psychiatrist, Melbourne.

Others who provided assistance, advice or research material included: members of the Tasmania Police, in particular Deputy Commissioner Jack Johnston and Inspector Ross Paine; members of the Victoria Police, especially Inspector Chris Penno and Superintendent Pocock of the Freedom of Information Office; Laurie Atkins, Strategic Development and Melissa Tan of the Victoria Forensic Science Centre; Investigator Rockie Yardley, Edmond Police Department, Oklahoma; Jan Trygg, Polismyndigheten Dalarna, Falun, Sweden; Mrs Debbie Taylor, North Carolina; Dr John Blennerhassett, Professor of Pathology, Otago Medical School, New Zealand; Frank Scandale and Evan Dreyer of the Denver Post, Colorado; New Zealand Police colleagues, particularly Superintendent John Reilly and Constables Nick Harvey and Craig McKersey; Frances Vick and Charlotte Wright, University of North Texas Press and author Gary Lavergne for use of Gary's research material for his book *A Sniper in the Tower;* Dr Richie Poulton, Clinical Psychologist, University of Otago, New Zealand for help with the glossary; Anitra Kuiper, Tasmania; and translators Barbara Dineen, Michel Wisnewski and Dr Ted Nye.

Contacts around the world were arranged with help from Hannah Bianchini; Superior Court Judge Victor Bianchini, San Diego; Tom Green, National University, San Diego; Denis Nadeau (Royal Canadian Mounted Police), Dr Wally Graces (Texas), Jim Carroll (California) and Bob 'Ace' O'Hara (New Zealand) of the International Police Association; Detective Jaques Legros, United Nations, Rwanda; Inspector Mike Hill, New Zealand Police on attachment to the Surrey Police, England; Detective Inspector Larry Reid, New Zealand Police Liaison Officer in Sydney, Australia; Assistant Directeur Marcel Lemay, Montreal Urban Community Police Department, Canada; Jose Primera, Texas Alcoholic Beverages Commission; Paul deBomford, Tasmania Prison Health Services; Gustafsson Lotta, Swedish Institute, Stockholm. Other help came from Stuart Nicol, Picture Editor with *The Daily Record*, Glasgow; David McNie, Scotland; Craig Page and Gerrard O'Brien, *Otago Daily Times*, Dunedin, New Zealand; and Fuji Xerox New Zealand Ltd.

Thanks also to Jane Rumble and Tracey Borgfeldt of my publishers David Bateman Ltd, and particularly to Paul Bateman for encouragement and understanding when obstacles arose.

Special thanks go to my daughter Lauren for her help with psychological research and proof reading of the manuscript and my son Craig for pharmacological advice. Last, but by no means least, thanks to my wife Olwyn for the typing, editing and research she contributed to produce *Killing for Pleasure*.

Any work dealing in detail with tragedies is difficult, but it was easier for me after a 35-year police career. However for Olwyn it would at times be distressing to read many of the statements or to type out transcripts of interviews with family who lost loved ones. I do not underestimate Olwyn's contribution and am sincerely grateful for her work and encouragement.

PREFACE

On the morning of 13 March 1996, Thomas Hamilton drove to the Dunblane Primary School in Scotland and in a matter of four minutes shot dead a teacher and 16 young children. The following day a clearly distraught headmaster was interviewed on television.

'Evil visited us yesterday,' he said. 'And we don't know why: We don't understand it and I guess we never will.'

The actions of Thomas Hamilton, although rare, are still common enough to be not merely some aberrant behaviour and are not as isolated as they first appear to be. There are threads that bind mass murderers together. Although the features they possess are spread across the community making it difficult to predict their behaviour, they are nevertheless detectable. Professor Paul Mullen, a leading forensic psychiatrist based in Melbourne, Australia believes that by being more alert to the psychological and social needs of people, especially men, we may be able, quite by chance, to pick out those very rare killers. To do so, we do not look for the mass murderer but rather the lonely, desperate and suicidal men in the community.

Numerous personality traits and life events of the nine randomly selected subjects chosen for this book are shared by each of them. Each was socially ill, if not mentally ill, and by examining their lives we can build up a profile of the man most likely to commit this type of crime. *Killing for Pleasure* asks what makes a man (and it is always a man) become a mass murderer? Why is mass murder on the increase and why now? Is there a detectable pattern, and if so what can we do about it?

This book is about a particular type of mass murder. It is not about the political fanatic who kills large numbers of people for a 'cause'. Neither is it about the serial or family killer where there are multiple victims. It is about a phenomenon of the latter part of the twentieth century where angry, deranged men made spectacular suicides and in doing so took many victims with them. To distinguish them from other mass killers they are referred to in this book as pseudo-commandos.

The common question asked when these terrible crimes occur is: why? Not surprisingly the headmaster at Dunblane primary school is not the only person to say of mass murder, *we don't understand it!*

Professor Mullen interviewed Julian Knight, one of the few surviving mass killers. Knight went from his home in East Melbourne on to busy Hoddle Street where he opened fire on motorists and cyclists. After his arrest police took him on a 'tour' of his killing zone. Knight quite matter-of-factly spoke of his deeds.

'Can you tell us what happened?' the detective asked.

'The first one fell on the road . . . the second one, I don't know where he came from, so I dropped him as well,' Knight replied.

'Did they appear to be dead?'

'The one that fell back on the road wasn't.'

'What happened then?'

'Oh, I let off another two rounds.'

'For what purpose?'

'To finish her off,' he replied, answering the question as if it was an everyday occurrence.

Professor Mullen believes it is this coldness and the lack of frenzy during the outburst that has people so perplexed. Witnesses to mass murder often remark on the calm, deliberate and calculated way the killings take place, not an insane frenzy that one might expect.

Martin Bryant loaded his weapons and ammunition into his car and drove a considerable distance to Port Arthur then stalked his victims, including young children, in such a cold, calculated way it almost defies belief. He, like Knight, also survived and when psychiatrist Ian Sale interviewed Bryant he found there was something very wrong with the way he displayed his emotions or read other people's emotions. Dr Sale believes that is why Bryant could continue his rampage for so long. There was a complete disconnection between emotions and behaviour which allowed him to do what he did.

Thomas Hamilton was still in control when he stopped his murderous rampage. He was not under threat from police or anyone else. That would suggest he may not have had the same degree of disconnection as Bryant but he was the relaxed planner. When Thomas Hamilton walked in a semicircle around his young victims, as if herding them into his firing zone, he knew exactly what he was doing. Investigations after his death showed in-depth planning had taken place for weeks before the event and, on the evening before the rampage, that planning had been meticulous.

Before James Huberty killed 21 innocent people at a McDonald's restaurant in San Diego he told his wife he was 'going hunting humans', and like Huberty, David Gray of New Zealand had once remarked to a cousin, 'I don't like humans'. Each of the nine mass murderers featured in this book came from different places and committed different crimes, yet their personalities are remarkably similar.

What this book will not do is glorify the mass murderer. The murderers saw themselves as some kind of hero wanting to make a statement, looking for notoriety and needing to be seen as important and powerful. Branding these men as evil monsters may satisfy our immediate grief but it prevents us asking some painful questions, the kind of questions posed in this book. While people might see them as monsters, they are not - it is what they did that was monstrous - they are pathetic.

Professor Mullen provided a pre-sentence report on Martin Bryant. He told the Supreme Court, 'Almost all of them are men, almost all of them are young. The majority of them are people who are socially isolated and socially incompetent. They are often people with a really exaggerated sense of their own worth and ability, which is not shared by anyone around them, so they become increasingly angry and resentful at the world, increasingly distressed at their own failure and isolation.'

During an interview on the Bryant case Professor Mullen spoke on the Australian television current affairs programme *Four Corners,* 'People who do this kind of thing are inadequate, sad, silly people - not embodiments of evil, not dreadful monsters. The more we make them monsters, the more we make them evil, the more it will encourage people who want this kind of potency, that kind of power at any price. We have to remember that some people out there will accept gladly the label of evil and monster. They would be less willing to accept the label of wimp, weakling, inadequate, pathetic.'

The judge presiding over the hearing at Julian Knight's appearance spoke of the risk to the community posed by people such as Knight and Frank Vitkovic. 'I respectfully adopt the comments made by the State Coroner at the inquest into the Queen Street deaths to the effect that all the community can do is to understand why such horrors occurred and try to reduce the risks.'

This book aims to provide an understanding of the type of people with a proclivity to this offending and looks at why these tragedies happen. Knowing how these men lived and what led up to their crimes allows us to better understand and hopefully take steps to prevent or minimise future tragedies. There has been little study carried out on the reasons why mass murderers choose to do what they do. While it is true most die, thus denying researchers valuable material, a close comparison of their behaviour while they were alive shows a definite pattern. It is that pattern which forms the essential basis of *Killing for Pleasure.*

CHAPTER ONE
CHARLES WHITMAN

THE SOCIOPATHIC ACTOR
Austin, Texas – 1 August 1966
Victims: 15 dead, 27 injured

INTRODUCTION

Set on the rolling hills of central Texas, Austin has come a long way from the days when traders and buffalo hunters set up camp in what was then called Waterloo. Austin is very much a university city and the 'town/gown' atmosphere is evident. Today almost ten per cent of the population is enrolled for the wide range of courses available at the University of Texas. When the university was opened in 1883 the founders made a generous provision beyond the 94 hectares set aside for expansion. A further 800,000 hectares of West Texas desert were given to the university though few, if any, could have envisaged what a bonanza the land would prove to be. When oil was found in the desert in 1921 it provided a substantial income for the institution and royalties from drilling rights have enabled the University of Texas to display wealth. As well as having a campus that can cater for 50,000 students it also boasts a huge library, a research centre, an art gallery, two museums and a large special events centre.

As the State Capital, it is not surprising that the Austin skyline is dominated by the State Capitol building. This typically Texan building is not only large, but even bigger than the Capitol building in Washington D.C. When the Texas Capitol building was completed in 1888 it was reputedly the seventh biggest building in the world. Overshadowing the Capitol building is the 28-storey clock tower at the University of Texas, the site of Austin's darkest hour.

Texas has a rich, exciting history and observers of the Wild West days enthuse over the legends forged in those turbulent times. One hundred kilometres from Austin, nestled in downtown San Antonio is 'The Alamo', site of an incident that legends are made of. This most sacred shrine attracts three million visitors each year and is arguably the premier tourist attraction of Texas. The adobe and stone building dates from 1718 when it was the Spanish Franciscan Mission, San Antonio de Valero. Texas revolutionaries took it over in 1836 when 180 of them made a 13-day stand against a Mexican army. Self-appointed Mexican President Antonio Lopez de Santa Anna led an army of 5,000 that swept across Texas in an effort to wipe out the independence movement. Among the 180 rebels who took refuge in The Alamo were the legendary frontiersmen Davy Crockett and James Bowie. The army thrown at The Alamo by Santa Anna was repulsed only to attack again and again. With defenders' numbers thinning after each onslaught they were finally overcome and all 180 massacred. When Santa Anna counted his forces 1,600 of his men lay dead.

In 1954 Paul Horgan wrote *Great River: The Rio Grande in North American History*. Of the Texas defenders at The Alamo he penned: 'The Texan marksmanship, the speed, continuity and fury of their fire, were frightful.'

In late July 1966 Charles Whitman visited The Alamo. He, like the defenders of 130 years before, was an accomplished marksman. Two weeks after his visit to the shrine of The Alamo he would climb atop the University of Texas clock tower in Austin where he would display marksmanship that was truly frightful. But rather than leaving remnants of an army dead in his wake, dozens of unarmed, innocent Texans would be dead or dying at his hands.

THE BABE IN ARMS

Charles Joseph Whitman was born in Lake Worth, Florida, on 24 June 1941. He was the first son of his 18-year-old mother Margaret and named after his proud father Charles A Whitman. Four years later Patrick was born and a third son, John, arrived in 1949. The father's own dysfunctional upbringing would have a huge influence on the Whitman boys and, in particular, Charles.

Although spending his early years in a Georgia orphanage the self-made Charles A Whitman built up a successful plumbing contracting business. By 1966, assisted in the administrative tasks by his wife, he employed 28 full-time staff and had a fleet of 21 trucks. However the pursuit of success had been unsettling and by the time Charles jnr was seven his family had moved eight times.

A strict disciplinarian, 'CA' Whitman frequently used corporal punishment on his three sons and he wasn't too gentle on his wife Margaret either. By his own admission the Whitman patriarch had an awful temper, and the use of paddles, belts and fists was common punishment for misdemeanours. And, again by his own admission, the administering of physical punishment wasn't carried out often enough. CA Whitman provided well for his wife and sons but never let them forget it. In later life his generosity even extended to cars and some people believed he provided 'too well'. CA Whitman's hard work as a plumbing contractor had enabled him to buy a splendid upmarket home where he could show off his consuming passion - firearms. The home was adorned with guns and from an early age the Whitman boys were introduced to guns. A photograph taken of Charles jnr as a two-year-old, dressed in trainer pants, shows him holding two rifles, both of which were longer than he was.

The Whitman boys had a strong Roman Catholic upbringing, attending Catholic schools in Lake Worth. For a time Charles jnr was an altar boy in the family's church. Young Charles attended private kindergartens when he was three or four and in 1947 was enrolled at the Sacred Heart Catholic grade school. His formative years were unremarkable, but clearly Charles was pressured by his father to excel. At age eight he joined the Cub Scouts but couldn't wait to be a Boy Scout. Even before the enrolling age of eleven he tried to join and when he was finally admitted he showed phenomenal progress. In just fifteen months Charles Whitman earned 21 merit badges and received an award at a Scout Jamboree held in Florida in 1953.

When Charles became an Eagle Scout at age 12 years 3 months he was the youngest boy in the world to reach that rank, but his Scout master believed the results were due more to the constant pressure from the father than any raw ability the boy had.

Following attendance at a civic function, a photograph of young Charles and another boy, dressed in full regalia, appeared in a Lake Worth newspaper. The reporter was lavish in his praise of the boys. 'They made a fine appearance and reminded the public just why this nation is great.' Little over a decade later Charles Whitman would make a much darker impression on the media.

Charles Whitman excelled as a Scout and also as a musician. He took piano lessons at an early age and by twelve was an accomplished pianist. Again the father's dominance was present. CA was reported to have placed a belt on top of the piano to remind the youngster that perfection was expected. Music could have been an influence in the boy's life and for a while he played in a teenage band. However his dominating father was having nothing of it and forced his son to quit. Charles Whitman rarely played the piano again.

Perfection and excellence were bywords of CA Whitman. This even applied to the use of firearms and CA boasted that by age 16 'Charlie could plug a squirrel in the eye'. Young Charles was undoubtedly very proficient with a gun. He was also clearly gifted and in his middle school years, with an IQ of 139, scored in the top five per cent of his peers.

Even as a boy Whitman was preoccupied with making money, a trait that would remain with him, though not successfully, throughout his short life. He had a very large paper route in Lake Worth and though dependable, didn't take kindly to criticism and personalised customer complaints. Through his efforts he was able to buy a Harley Davidson motorcycle in 1955 when he was only fifteen. That same year Whitman entered St Ann's High School in West Palm Beach. He was popular but tended to draw attention to himself, usually by taking dares - some might say almost showing off. Although he dated girls he had no steady relationship while at school.

In his freshman and sophomore years Whitman was markedly

more successful than in earlier years. His grades were consistently high but began to fall away as he neared graduation. Even so, when he did graduate he was a creditable seventh in a class of 72 where the student accomplishment was above the national average.

Just before his eighteenth birthday an incident happened that dramatically changed the course of Whitman's life. While socialising with his peers the young Whitman got very drunk. When he arrived home his father reacted violently, severely punishing the boy before throwing him into their swimming pool. Whitman came close to drowning and, as an 18-year-old, was humiliated. In spite of his degree of drunkenness Whitman remembered the incident with bitterness. The humiliation was more than he could bear and instead of enrolling for university as planned Charles Whitman signed up for a career in the Marines. He never told his father and only confided in his mother. On 6 July 1959, at age 18 years and two weeks, Charles Whitman boarded a bus for Jacksonville, Florida and entered the United States Marine Corps.

Life with the Marines was going to be difficult. From an early age Whitman had been well provided for in a material sense but had been denied one essential element - an emotional support system. His father, who himself came from a dysfunctional family upbringing, had been relentless in instilling a sense of perfection and excellence in Charles jnr. As a result, the younger Whitman had never learned the art of accepting failure. Success was everything, failure was not an option. But the successes he had throughout life, despite his high IQ were due to constant supervision and a desire to please or to avoid his father's temper. Margaret would have been ineffective in trying to combat her husband's domination and excessively unrealistic expectations. In his desire to rid himself of his father's influence, Charles entered a domain where he was very much alone but had only managed to trade his father's discipline for an even stricter regime.

After basic training, Private Whitman was posted in December 1959 to a naval base in Cuba, one of the world's trouble spots. He stood 183 cm tall and within a short while bulked up to an impressive and muscular 90 kg. Whitman was fit and eagerly learned the art of combat. If he excelled at anything it was in the use of a rifle - where he was rated as excellent and placed in the sharpshooter category. He was particularly accurate shooting at moving targets and after a session with the 30 calibre M1 Carbine wrote in his notebook, 'World's finest'.

Charles Whitman was well regarded by his peers and would do anything for others in the squad. However, his cavalier attitude to danger and his disregard of road rules led him into trouble. He was involved in an accident where his jeep ran off the road and came to rest down a bank. Whitman's companion was thrown out and pinned under the vehicle but managed to crawl free only when Whitman lifted the jeep before collapsing unconscious. Charles Whitman was neither a safe nor prudent motorist. He had a number of traffic accidents and in two years was issued with five tickets for violations.

During the first two years as a Marine Whitman received a good conduct medal, a sharpshooter's badge and a Marine Corps Expeditionary medal for service in Cuba. He had a creed to live by and carried a card with him which read: 'Yesterday is not mine to recover, but tomorrow is mine to lose. I am resolved that I shall win the tomorrows before me.' Whitman tried to live by that maxim, as he did with numerous other things he wrote, but in the end he had to admit he couldn't.

While in Cuba Whitman heard of a scholarship for an engineering degree which on completion would grant the recipient a Commissioned Officer rank. The Marines only picked the best to go on scholarships and when Private Charles Whitman applied he fitted the 'best' category and was selected.

THE NEW TEXAN

In September 1961 Charles Whitman moved to Austin and enrolled at the University of Texas. Financially he was quite comfortable. Along with his Marine pay and an allowance from his father Whitman was given a position as a counsellor in his dormitory with free board. For the first time in his life he was free of authority and had to fend for himself. Despite being a Marine on scholarship and a dorm counsellor, Whitman didn't display the maturity expected of him. Very early in his time in Austin Whitman fell foul of authorities and was almost jailed. He and two student friends went into the hills west of Austin and poached a deer. Police were given the number of a car in which a deer was seen protruding from the trunk and when police and a game warden arrived at the dorm their job of locating the suspects was easy. They followed a trail of blood from the door all the way up to Whitman's bedroom where he and the others were busily skinning the animal in the shower. The game warden was taken aback by Whitman's charm and co-operation. So charming was the 'poacher' that the warden referred to him as 'a darn nice fellow'. Whitman was lucky he only had to pay a $100 fine.

Charles Whitman was a serious student. He had a fine physique, good looks and dressed well, and his personable nature made him appear more mature than others. But it was little more than a façade and Whitman, the consummate actor, had another side to him that he kept closely guarded. He believed he was a good bluffer and consequently would be a good gambler. During his time in the dorm he gambled - at times through the night - and often heavily. In one night alone he lost $400 and on another occasion $190 in a single hand. With insufficient cash to meet the $190 debt he wrote a cheque which bounced. The luckless student owed the debt went to Whitman's room intent on recovering his money and was told not to worry as Whitman's wealthy family would soon provide the shortfall. But the student quickly lost interest in recovering the debt. As Whitman spoke he was lying on his bed throwing a large hunting knife into a closet door. The much smaller man, intimidated by the large Marine, felt the debt wasn't worth following up.

Whitman's immaturity surfaced in a variety of ways. One night while drinking he tried to phone Soviet Premier, Nikita Khruschev, just to say he didn't like him. He also played pranks on people, some of them quite cruel. Whitman was out driving one night with a friend called Jim when they were involved in an accident. The bloodied and dirty Whitman made his way back to the dorm at 5 am and made the dramatic announcement that Jim had been killed in the crash. The others were stunned and sat about in disbelief and phoned Jim's sleeping girlfriend to give her the tragic news. Soon after Jim walked into the room sending Whitman into uncontrollable laughter. He thought it was very funny.

Before long, Whitman gained a reputation as an immature prankster and nothing he said or did was a surprise to his dorm mates. As a result Francis Schuck was not alarmed at Whitman's statement when they sat in a room looking up at the university tower. Whitman said someone could hold an army off from on top of the tower. He said he would like to go up the tower and shoot people from the observation deck. Four years later that's exactly what Charles Joseph Whitman would do.

The Goodall-Wooten dorm Whitman lived in was commonly known by students as 'Goody Woo'. The residence provided easy access to the campus, and passers-by had to be careful they were not bombarded from inhabitants of the 'party' dorm above. It was in that dorm in early 1962 that Whitman was introduced to attractive 18-year-old Kathy Liessner. Whitman was instantly drawn to her and so began his only serious romantic relationship. He went to great lengths to attract Kathy's attention. Once he phoned her in the females' dorm two blocks away imploring her to go to her window. By the time she got there he had run to his seventh floor balcony and was dangling perilously, holding on with one arm while waving to her with the other. Within days Kathy and Whitman were going steady. She was often in his company and was with him and three others in a car on their way to a firing range where Whitman wanted to try out a new pistol. When they stopped at an intersection Whitman couldn't resist the temptation to make disparaging remarks to an intoxicated man. He then produced his pistol and pointed it at the man, but rather than be intimidated, the pedestrian reached for what could have been his own weapon and the car with Whitman in, sped off. Kathy and her companions left Whitman in no doubt how stupid his actions were. They were frightened but Charles Whitman found the episode quite amusing. The incident didn't deter Kathy and after a whirlwind romance the two became engaged just five months from first meeting. The following month the 21-year-old Whitman and 19-yearold Kathy were married.

Kathy Whitman continued her studious ways and gained certification to teach science in secondary schools throughout Texas. She was a mature, professional young woman and was very popular. On the other hand, her husband's grades were dismal. Despite his IQ and being in the top five per cent at high school he failed to glow in the academic light of university. The Marine Corps expected a far better return for their investment. No longer did they regard Charles Whitman as one of their best and his conduct was not worthy of a commissioned officer. After eighteen months at the university the Marine Corps pulled the plug on Private Charles Whitman and returned him to active duty with the Second Marine Division at Camp Lejeune in North Carolina. Over 1,600 kilometres separated him from Kathy and he once again found himself back into the regimented existence that had dominated his life for so long.

Desperate to get back to his wife in Austin, Whitman tried to regain his scholarship status. He wasn't successful, and from then on developed a bitter hatred of the Marines. To make matters worse, Whitman was told his 18 months at university would not count as active duty, putting his discharge date from the Marines further into the future than he could bear. However, his service in Cuba and the fact he had been on a scholarship gave him a glimmer of hope to remain in the Marines. Private Whitman was promoted to Lance Corporal but his sudden rise in status was not matched with maturity. The trouble-making Whitman began to fall out of favour with the Marine Corps. Whitman was owed $40 by another Marine and when he went to collect the debt he demanded $15 interest and proceeded to threaten to kick the other man's teeth in if he wasn't paid. On 7 October 1964 Whitman and a friend were 'jumped' by four or five other Marines. In the ensuing fight Whitman was knocked to the ground and kicked in the face. Soon after, he was to have another scrape with authorities and faced a court martial on charges of gambling, usury and possessing an unauthorised, non-military pistol. Whitman was convicted and sentenced to 30 days' confinement and 90 days' hard labour. Rubbing salt into his wounds, the Corps reduced him in rank back to private. From that point the lonely Charles Whitman kept a diary where he could write down his thoughts about Kathy. He spoke of missing contact with her and confessed that she was 'pretty disgusted' with him. On 10 November 1963 Whitman wrote:

> Received a call from Kathy at 1510 hrs, it was fabulous, she sounds wonderful. I love her so much she sounded so pitiful when she cried that we were allowed to talk more than three minutes. It is so good to know that she loves and understands me. I will love her until the day I die. She is definitely the best thing I have in life, or as I say, "My Most Precious Possession".

The homesick Whitman no longer had a desire for Marine life. He wanted out of the service and made strenuous efforts to get an early discharge. Even his father tried to bring pressure to bear on influential people to get his son released. Unable to escape the Marines, Whitman turned more and more to his diaries for solace and to record his emotions.

> I have thought very much about the concept of death. When it overtakes me someday I must remember to observe closely and see if it is as I thought it would be.

He also wrote of the possibility that Kathy might be pregnant following a visit to the camp and about his brother Patrick's failings after being involved in a serious car accident:

> The boy has definite emotional and psychological problems but as far as I know he won't go to anyone for help . . . Until he puts forth some effort to make good I don't want anything to do with him.

This from a man who had his share of problems but couldn't identify them himself.

Whitman's isolation was starting to disturb his thinking: 'My mind is so broken up with thoughts, I never seem to consistently think of one plan for the future,' he wrote.

From February 1964 his diary notes were entered in a daily record book and began with:

I opened this diary of my daily events as a result of the peace of mind or release of feelings that I experienced when I started making notes of my daily events while in the Post Brig at Camp Lejeune, N.C. . . . At that time I seemed to have reached the pit of my life's experiences and it really relieved me to speak to myself in a diary. Unless it becomes a pain to uphold, I intend to make daily entries in this book or one similar continually in the future. Someday I hope to be in a brighter shade of life's light looking back on the drabness, with my wife, Kathy, sharing the pleasures and joys of life with me.

In his writings Whitman spoke kindly of 'daddy' yet considered himself to be undisciplined and lazy. His writings became increasingly depressed and he responded positively only following Kathy's lengthy letters and phone calls. He blamed the Marine Corps for all of his problems and resorted to keeping a diminishing record of the number of days he had to serve, as would a prisoner. Sometimes his diary entries were strange and he once wrote, 'Unless it is definitely advantageous healthwise, I see no need for a brassiere except that now they are an accepted and social necessity.'

The punishment of hard labour hadn't hurt him physically, but notes in his diaries clearly showed his unhappy time in the Marines was getting to him mentally. Only four days after being discharged from hard labour he was charged with failing to obey a lawful order.

He reflected on his unhappy year by writing about his predicament:

I wish so much that the Marine Corps would quit hindering my life and give me a discharge so that I could start leading a normal life. I have so much I want to accomplish. It seems I'll never get started. I hope I am able to discipline myself to keeping up with my correspondence courses. It seems like Kathy and I will never live together and have the troubles of normal people. God, I can't stand the Corps. My love for

Kathy and my sense of responsibility to our unborn children is the only thing that keeps me from going berserk. At times it seems as if I am going to explode.

At times Whitman did explode and despite loving Kathy he beat her during periods of leave causing her to become fearful of him. Charles Whitman was also starting to withdraw into himself and was leading an increasingly lonely existence.

I think so much of Kathy, but when I really start to concentrate on what we have done in the past and what I would like for us to do in the future I seem to explode. Or rather I seem to think I am going to explode. I wonder how long I can go on keeping to myself (I don't associate with very many people here now, and when I do I hardly ever discuss anything serious or my true feelings with them) without going nuts. I wonder if I will ever amount to anything in this world? I have great plans and dreams . . .

Finally, 6 December 1964 came and Private Charles J Whitman, First Class, was honourably discharged from the United States Marine Corps and he returned to Austin, Texas. Reunited with Kathy, and with the Marine Corps' experience behind him, Whitman enrolled at the University of Texas intent on studying architectural engineering. Between semesters, and in his spare time, Whitman tried a variety of jobs but nothing suited him. He also got involved in one way or another with Kathy's Methodist church, and she even got him to sing in the choir. Some of his behaviour was quite odd. On one occasion the minister visited their home to see Whitman but he didn't want to speak so ran out the back door.

Having been the world's youngest Eagle Scout should have made the ex-marine an ideal Scout leader and Whitman took on the role of Scout master to the Methodist church troop. But Whitman had little patience and had trouble controlling his anger. However, when it came to firearms' safety, he was well qualified and eager to show off his skills. On a camp he demonstrated the use of a .22 rifle by placing a clothespeg on a line some twenty metres away. When he shot at the peg he was able to make it spin before shattering.

Around this time Whitman's behaviour changed. He began to complain of persistent headaches, sweated profusely and nervously chewed his fingernails. He neglected his physical fitness and began to put on weight to the stage where boys in the Scout troop referred to him as 'Porky'. In January 1966 Whitman complained of work and study pressures and asked to be relieved of his scouting obligations.

DOWNHILL TO TERROR

Charles Whitman went into 1966 as an insecure young man. He was not achieving what he had hoped for. He struggled to develop any relationships in the Lions Club he joined and his engineering course study group found him increasingly difficult to deal with. Despite writing out his goals and making other lists for guidance, Whitman was unable to set priorities. Though he wanted direction in his life he found it elusive. Mid-course he decided he would like to become a lawyer, a dramatic change from his chosen career as an architectural engineer. Whitman reasoned that an engineering/law combination might help him achieve his life's ambition - wealth.

Patience and kindness were traits Charles Whitman found hard to adopt. One of his frequent fights with Kathy was so serious people close to her believed a divorce was imminent. Caring for Kathy didn't come naturally and he resorted to typing out a card of the things he thought necessary in a meaningful relationship:

Good points to remember with Kathy
1. Don't nag
2. Don't try to make your partner over
3. Don't criticise
4. Give honest appreciation
5. Pay little attentions
6. Be courteous
7. Be gentle

On the exterior Whitman appeared to be a nice, capable person but on the inside he was an uptight, nervous and highly-strung individual. He found it difficult to control his temper and several people witnessed his outbursts. Typical was an incident in Austin when he became annoyed at another motorist. When Whitman interpreted a gesture from the other man as a challenge he pulled the rings from his fingers and threw them on the dashboard before leaping from the car. The other driver drove off but the pumped up Whitman declared to his passenger that he 'was ready.'

In the spring of 1966 Kathy, Charles and their dog 'Schocie' moved from their apartment to a rented house on Austin's Jewell Street. From the time they moved in Whitman enjoyed the company of the children in his new neighbourhood. He tied a rope to a large oak tree and taught the youngsters how to climb it as 'Marines' do. Adults in the neighbourhood knew of Whitman's large collection of militaria kept in the garage and were not surprised to see him with firearms. They, like so many others, thought Charles Whitman was nice.

Kathy found employment as a first year teacher and worked part-time as an operator for the Southwestern Bell Telephone Company. While Kathy worked hard at two jobs, Whitman had given up ambitions he had selling insurance or real estate. Instead he got a job as an engineering laboratory assistant at the University of Texas. He kept up his studies but took on an academic workload that was realistically unattainable.

Almost 1,600 kilometres away in Lake Worth, Florida, the senior Whitman household was falling apart. Patrick Whitman had married and moved out of the family home. John's relationship with his father was virtually nonexistent and he too left. Without the children around, Margaret's tolerance of her dominating husband came to an end. After 25 years of a somewhat turbulent marriage Margaret decided it was time to leave. Lake Worth police were called to the Whitman home at 9.30 pm on 2 March 1966. The disturbance had quietened down by the time they arrived but at 11.20 pm they got a long distance call from a Charles J Whitman in Austin, Texas. He told police his father had threatened bodily injury to his mother and could they attend. The younger Whitman set off on the 3,200-kilometre round trip to get his mother. When he arrived at 4 pm the following day the Whitman family was in disarray. Police stood by for over an hour as Margaret and CA argued over the personal effects she could take. When Margaret left the matrimonial home, she headed directly for Austin with her son, who made the journey without any sleep.

Margaret soon found a comfortable apartment and a job as a cashier in a cafeteria. Patrick also moved to Austin, where he found employment and an apartment, but over the brief few weeks he was in Austin he felt neglected and believed his mother was showing favouritism towards Charles. Relationships became strained and Patrick returned to Florida. The dysfunctional Whitman family was in turmoil. CA was making constant calls to Charles imploring him to get his mother to return and to come to Florida himself. They wouldn't.

The combination of too heavy an academic workload, the parental break-up, constant calls from his father and a self-acknowledged lack of success and direction pushed Whitman into a depressed state. He believed his problems were all physical and that there was something wrong with his head. Rather than go for professional help, he wallowed in self-doubt and Kathy became concerned about leaving him alone. Late one night Whitman turned up unannounced at a teacher's home carrying a bundle of papers. Barton Riley greeted Whitman whose face was strained.

'I've got problems,' Whitman said. 'I just despise my father. I hate him. If he walked through that door I would kill him.'

Whitman meant what he said.

After a short while he calmed then suddenly said, 'I can't resist it any more,' walked over to a baby grand piano and played Debussy's *Clair de Lune*, not in the soft lyrical style intended but loud and strong.

His unusual rendition of the classical piece even woke Mrs Riley from her sleep upstairs. Soon after that episode and without consultation with Kathy, Whitman withdrew from the university and sold his books. He decided to become a bum and spoke of having 'something to settle'. Barton Riley, himself an ex-Marine, was having none of it and forcefully chastised Whitman, ordering him to continue his studies. Whitman, who had always responded when being told what to do, simply replied, 'Yes Sir!'

Whitman finally gave in to Kathy's insistence and sought professional help. A doctor he consulted prescribed the tranquilliser Valium and arranged for a consultation with Dr Maurice Heatly, a psychiatrist at the University Student Health Centre. He had one appointment and it was recommended he see a therapist for on-going sessions. However Whitman decided against the recommendation and never attended any follow-up. A week after speaking to Dr Heatly, when Whitman should have been having a session with a therapist, he went to the observation deck at the university tower, signed the visitor's book and had a look around. It is probable that in early April he had decided on what he would ultimately do.

Whitman was not addicted to drugs but certainly abused them. In his medicine cabinet he had thirteen bottles of pills prescribed by seven different physicians. The drug he used the most was an amphetamine, Dexadrine, which was capable of inducing insomnia, mood swings and extreme nervousness. Whitman, by virtue of the excessive study regime he had set for himself, resorted to drugs to stay awake and when studying did not sleep for several days and nights. Lack of sleep affected his reasoning with a resulting downturn in efficiency causing him to question his self-worth and creating doubts about his future.

Whitman was trapped in a vicious cycle. In order to compete he took Dexadrine to stay awake and Librium to help him sleep. His chosen combination of drugs was preventing him from functioning properly. He once took a 'nap' after a prolonged period of being awake but classmates had great difficulty rousing him. A calculation that should have taken fifteen minutes had Whitman working at it for four hours. He could 'drift', had difficulty hearing normally spoken voices and had to be shaken to gain attention.

Eleven days before the tragedy unfolded Whitman's brother 'Johnnie Mike' visited Austin. The brothers went to the observation deck at the university tower and looked at the expansive view from 28 floors up. Two days later the brothers and Kathy drove to San

Antonio to look over The Alamo, those last days together captured in photographs.

The final week of Whitman's life was uneventful. He went to classes and worked at his research assistant job. On the Thursday and Friday he was in good spirits and on Saturday relaxed at home taking an afternoon nap on the couch. Kathy took Whitman's photograph with their dog curled up at his feet. Sunday was very hot. Kathy had to work all day and Whitman went shopping. He purchased some food in one shop and in another bought a Bowie knife and a pair of binoculars. The uses he put these purchases to indicate he had already decided to become a murderer. At 1 pm Whitman picked his young wife up from work, went to a movie, then joined Margaret for a late lunch. Kathy was working a split shift so they decided to call unexpectedly on friends. While Kathy was her usual bright self her husband was surprisingly quiet. Kathy could not have possibly known that at the time Charles J Whitman was formulating plans to kill her and many others in a terrible orgy of destruction.

After Whitman dropped Kathy back to work he returned to their Jewell Street home. From then on his total focus was on the planning process to achieve his aim - Mass Murder.

THE TEXAN TERROR

Sitting alone at home Charles Whitman began to type his fare-well letter:

Sunday
July 31, 1966
6.45 pm

I don't quite understand what it is that compels me to type this letter. Perhaps it is to leave some vague reason for the actions I have recently performed. I don't really understand myself these days. I am supposed to be an average reasonable and intelligent young man. However, lately (I can't recall when it started) I have been a victim of many unusual and irrational thoughts. These thoughts constantly recur, and it requires a tremendous mental effort to concentrate on useful and progressive tasks. In March when my parents made a physical break I noticed a great deal of stress. I consulted Dr. Cochrum at the University Health Center and asked him to recommend someone that I could consult with about some psychiatric disorders I felt I had.

I talked with a Doctor once for about two hours and tried to convey to him my fears that I felt come [sic] overwhelming impulses. After one session I never saw the Doctor again, and since then I have been fighting my mental turmoil alone, and seemingly to no avail.

After my death I wish that an autopsy would be performed on me to see if there is any visible physical disorder. I have had some tremendous headaches in the past and have consumed two large bottles of Excedrin in the past three months.

It was after much thought that I decided to kill my wife, Kathy, tonight after I pick her up from work at the telephone company. I love her dearly, and she has been as fine a wife to me as any man could ever hope to have. I cannot rationaly [sic] pinpoint any specific reason for doing this. I don't know whether it is selfishness, or if I don't want her to have to face the embarrassment my actions would surely cause her. At this time, though, the prominent reason in my mind is that I truly do not consider this world worth living in, and am prepared to die, and I do not want to leave her to suffer alone in it. I intend to kill her as painlessly as possible.

Similar reasons provoked me to take my mother's life also. I don't think the poor woman has ever enjoyed life as she is entitled to. She was a simple young woman who married a very possessive and dominating man. All my life as a boy until I ran away from home to join the Marine Corps . . .

Suddenly the typing stopped. Visitors arrived as Whitman was mid-sentence in a letter detailing the forthcoming deaths of the only two people he was close to. Larry Fuess, a friend from the university dorm days had arrived with his wife. One might expect a man planning such horrific murders might be depressed, angry or nervous. But Whitman was engaging, funny and in good spirits. He recalled the fun times the men had together at 'Goody-Woo' and laughed with the Fuess couple. The Whitman demeanour in no way betrayed the shocking thoughts that were in his mind. In fact Whitman was remarkably calm. During an interview with author Gary Lavergne for *A Sniper in the Tower*, Larry Fuess recalled:

> . . . One of the more pleasant times we had with him in the preceding couple of months. We were with him and he had the whole plan in mind. He was writing the letter as calm as could be, he was funny and engaging. He was calmer than he had been in weeks, maybe even months before that . . . He seemed so together and calm that night.

When Whitman picked Kathy up from work he gave her no cause for alarm. About 10.30 pm Margaret Whitman phoned her son to let him know her whereabouts. She had gone to a friend's place and with the mercury earlier climbing to 101 degrees Fahrenheit, Whitman wanted to visit her air-conditioned apartment to cool down. Margaret hurried home to be there when he arrived. The two were close, even more so after her separation from CA. Margaret had nominated her eldest son as next of kin and they shared a joint savings account. Kathy had decided to go to bed and her husband left for his mother's apartment at midnight. When Whitman arrived at his mother's she was waiting for him in the lobby. He had a briefcase she assumed contained study documents Charles might work on in the air-conditioned comfort of her apartment. But the case contained a length of rubber hose and a large hunting knife. As soon as they were safely inside the apartment Whitman attacked his mother. The rubber hose was used to strangle her and a heavy object fractured her skull. Whitman took the hunting knife and stabbed her in the chest.

Having brutally murdered his mother Charles Whitman wrote a note:

Monday, August 1, 1966, 12.30 am
To Whom It May Concern:

I have just taken my mother's life. I am very upset over having done it. However, I feel that if there is a heaven she is definitely there now. And if there is no life after, I have relieved her of her suffering here on Earth. The intense hatred I feel for my father is beyond description. My mother gave that man the 25 best years of her life and because she finally took enough of his beatings, humiliation, degradation, and tribulations that I am sure no one but she will ever know - to leave him. He has chosen to treat her like a slut that you would bed down with, accept her favors and then throw a pittance in return. I am truly sorry that this is the only way I could see to relieve her suffering but I think it was best. Let there be no doubt in your mind that I loved the woman with all my heart. If there exists a God, let him understand my actions and judge me accordingly.

Whitman lifted Margaret on to her bed, covered her with the bedclothes and placed his note on the body. To ensure Margaret's body was not discovered until after he completed his mission he wrote another note and stuck it on the apartment door:

Roy,
I don't have to be at work today and I was up late last night. I would like to get some rest. Please do not disturb me. Thank you. Mrs Whitman.

When Charles Whitman left the building the security guard saw him. He was grinning.

Whitman got home to Jewell Street about 2 am. Kathy was sleeping peacefully and would not have known a thing as her husband took the hunting knife and plunged it into her chest five times. Kathy Whitman died instantly.

Whitman took the typed note he was working on when Larry Fuess called and he wrote in the margin: 'friends interrupted / August 1, 1966 / Mon 3 am / Both Dead'.

He then used a pen to complete the unfinished letter:

I was witness to her being beat at least once a month. Then when she took enough my father wanted to fight to keep her below her usual standard of living. I imagine it appears I brutally killed both of my loved ones. I was only trying to do a quick thorough job.

He put the letter in an envelope, marked it 'To whom it may concern' and placed it next to Kathy's body. Whitman tried to justify the killing of Margaret and Kathy, reasoning that he was saving them from embarrassment at what he would do later that day. He didn't give either of them a choice. In another note he wrote, 'Give our dog to my in-laws please. Tell them Kathy loved Schocie very much.' Whether the dog had witnessed the death of Kathy or sensed something would never be known, but the dog mysteriously disappeared the next day, never to be seen again. Earlier in the year he had made diary entries about how much he loved Kathy. He turned to those pages and scrawled in pen, 'I still mean it. C.J.W. 1 August 1966'.

Knowing that in a few hours he would be dead he was still preoccupied with money.

If my life insurance policy is valid please see that all the worthless cheques I wrote this weekend are made good. Please pay off all my debts. I am 25 years old and have never been financially independent. Donate the rest anonymously to a mental health foundation. Maybe research can prevent further tragedies of this type.

Although he had access to money from his joint account with Margaret, Charles Whitman only had $13.87 in his personal account. Finally he wrote notes to his two brothers and father along with one to have a film in his camera developed. One of those photographs was of himself and a smiling Kathy outside The Alamo.

From then on Whitman prepared assiduously for his spectacular suicide. Taking a green footlocker from his Marine days Whitman filled it with equipment for a siege. Water, gasoline, batteries, a radio, military paraphernalia, tools, food and even a set of ear plugs were carefully packed. His arsenal of high-powered guns and ammunition was made ready. Whitman must have thought he was in for an Alamo-type stand off. The footlocker contained a 35 mm Remington, a Sears 12-gauge shotgun which he purchased that morning and cut the stock and barrel down, a 6 mm Remington bolt action rifle with a scope, a 30 calibre M1 Carbine, a .357 Smith & Wesson revolver, a 9 mm Luger pistol, a GalesiBrescia pistol and the hunting knife he used to kill Kathy and Margaret. He took with him 700 rounds of ammunition. The bullets he selected were designed to kill by shock, flattening like a mushroom on impact with the victim. If the bullets don't kill the target they cause horrific wounds.

Kathy was due to start work at 8.30 that morning so an apologetic Whitman rang in at 5.45 am to say Kathy was unwell. He did not want anything upsetting his plan to get to the university tower. Unable to lift the heavily laden footlocker Whitman hired a two-wheeled barrow called a 'dolly'. From a hardware store he bought a supply of ammunition and at a gun shop he got more ammunition and a new shotgun. The cheque he offered for payment was going to bounce and Whitman knew it. While Charles was cutting down the shotgun the local postman went into Whitman's garage for a chat. The men spoke about guns for 25 minutes and, although what Whitman was doing was illegal he remained very, very calm. In the nearby bedroom Kathy lay dead in a blood-soaked bed. In his final preparation Whitman cleaned all of his guns, packed them into his footlocker and donned blue overalls. Before he drove away he turned to a page in his diary where he kept a list of basic things he called 'Thoughts to Start the Day'. At the top of the list he scrawled, 'August 1, 1966 I never could quite make it. Those thoughts were too much for me'.

Shortly before 11 am Whitman phoned his mother's workplace telling them she was unwell and would not be at work, then he left home and headed for the University of Texas. The relentless heat of the sun beat down through a cloudless sky. Already temperatures were in the high 90s and climbing. Twenty minutes after leaving home Whitman drove into a parking lot adjacent to the tower. He dragged the footlocker on to the dolly and hauled it up the steps to the entranceway. Dressed in overalls he looked like a maintenance man and was able to go unchallenged into the elevator. Although it was turned off, Whitman didn't panic but simply asked an attendant for help, and when the elevator was turned on he pressed the button for Level 27. As the doors closed he said, 'Thank you ma'am. You don't know how happy that makes me.'

The observation deck was one floor above the final elevator stop and Whitman had to haul his equipment up the flight of stairs, step by step. On the twenty-eighth floor receptionist Edna Townsley was alone and without warning Whitman attacked, striking her a savage blow to the back of the head and fracturing her skull. Whitman dragged the deeply unconscious woman across the floor out of sight.

A couple who were out on the deck taking in the expansive views came in to the reception area and saw Whitman holding two rifles. They said hello and Whitman smiled. 'Hi, how are you,' he replied. They thought a man that high up with a couple of rifles was a bit strange but Whitman's manner was casual and they walked down to the elevator. Whitman wanted to get on to the deck and the couple posed no problem so he let them go, but his well-laid plans almost came to an unexpected end. Coming up the stairs were the Gabour and Lamport families intent on taking in the views. Whitman had barricaded the door but the Gabours' two teenage sons forced the door open enough to get into the reception area. Behind them were Mrs Gabour and Mrs Lamport with their husbands further back. There was no way visitors were going to spoil Whitman's plans and he attacked them in a furious assault. With shotgun blazing the nearest family members never had a chance. As they tumbled down the stairs Whitman stood above them continuing to fire. Marguerite Lamport and Mark Gabour were murdered while Mary Gabour and her other son, Mike, lay critically injured. The two men, still some distance away on the stairs, were spared physical injury.

Whitman turned from the bloody scene and took his footlocker with him on to the deck. So began one-and-a-half hours of sheer terror.

If there was anything positive that might have come from the attack on the Lamports and Gabours it was having held Whitman up for a few minutes. He only just missed a change of class when the campus below would have been teeming with humanity. Even so, there were lots of targets, and the ex-Marine sharpshooter with a good conduct medal and an honourable discharge took aim. At 11.48 am Charles Whitman lined up his first target. Clair Wilson was walking through the campus with her partner Thomas Eckman when a shot rang out. Even from 71 metres high Whitman could see Clair was eight months pregnant. When he lined her up the cross hairs on his powerful scope were aimed at her unborn baby. The foetus died instantly as the bullet entered Clair's abdomen. Thomas turned to see what was wrong and as he moved a bullet hit him in the back killing him instantly.

From that moment people were falling in quick succession: Whitman was able to line up unsuspecting targets wherever he wanted. Initially no one knew where he was or what was going on. Some who fell were killed instantly, others were gravely wounded and could only lie on the fiercely hot pavement unable to move.

Panic didn't set in immediately. Given the size of the campus and the gunman's perch atop the towel, people were bewildered rather than startled. He couldn't be seen from the ground, just the puffs of smoke as he fired through rain spout vents. Whitman moved and fired quickly giving the impression there was more than one gunman. When he chose to fire over the parapet those on the ground only got a glimpse of his head.

Whitman's aim was deliberate and deadly. People in and around the campus were not the only ones in danger. In nearby streets people out shopping were oblivious to what was unfolding around them, but they too were targets. Whether walking, sitting or riding bikes anyone who moved became a target. Behind a wall, two police officers took shelter trying to see who was on the tower. The concrete wall they chose as cover had a range of balusters, the widest being just over 15 cm across. Officer Billy Speed was sheltering when a bullet from Whitman's powerful 6 mm Remington went between the tiny gap in the balusters, fatally wounding the unsuspecting policeman. Whitman's marksmanship was phenomenal.

Paul Sonntag was with his girlfriend at the entrance to a shopping mall some distance away. A bullet ricocheted off the pavement nearby and the couple dived for cover. In the distance Sonntag could see Whitman up in the tower and called his girlfriend to come and look. Paul was facing the sun and as he squinted he opened his mouth slightly. The young man wouldn't have known what hit him when Whitman's next bullet went into the 18-year-old's mouth. His girlfriend's frantic attempts to help were fruitless and she too was shot.

Despite being armed, police had no hope of getting Whitman from the ground. Their weapons were ineffective at that range and Whitman didn't present himself as a target. Strategically he couldn't have picked a better vantage point. The only way to end the tragedy would be to storm the fortress through the deck's door barricaded with the dolly but who could do it? The incident at the university tower was to see the birth of SWAT (Special Weapons and Tactics) teams but in August 1966 having to employ such groups against a sniper had never been envisaged.

Frustrated and frightened, some of the locals raced home and came back with sporting rifles. Soon a barrage of missiles was speeding at the tower and, while they were ineffective, they at least hindered Whitman's aim, slowing down the casualty rate.

When electrician Roy Dell Schmidt died, it emphasised just what police were up against. Roy was on a call but was unable to get to his destination due to "something" going on. He parked almost 500 metres away and was told of the sniper in the tower. Schmidt and his colleague took cover behind a Chevrolet car. Squatting down was uncomfortable and Schmidt stood up to move to a better position. As he rose a bullet hit him in the stomach and he slumped to the ground dead. Whitman's aim and weapons were incredibly accurate and thoroughly deadly. In a 500-metre radius of the tower dozens of people lay dead or wounded. People close to the tower took what shelter they could and stayed low. Others much further away were intrigued at the events unfolding. Billy Snowden was getting his hair cut in a barber's shop three blocks away. Snowden and the barber went to the half-opened door to see first hand what was happening. In the distance the tower seemed well out of range but looking back at them through his scope, 400 metres away, was Charles J Whitman. Almost immediately after the puff of smoke a bullet slammed into Billy Snowden's shoulder. At times Whitman put the Remington down and used the semi-automatic M1 Carbine to fire rapid volleys to the ground sending people scattering to safety.

Morris Hohmann was an Austin funeral director with a company-owned ambulance. He attended some of the seven wounded sheltering in a shop. To get to the victims safely he ran on the sheltered side of the ambulance as it drove towards the shop. He was there to rescue the injured but Whitman had no respect for anyone. A well-placed bullet felled Mr Hohmann who rolled under a parked car where he remained for 45 minutes. When he was finally rescued he was taken to hospital in his own ambulance.

To stop the terrible carnage the tower had to be stormed. There was simply no other way. Officer Ramiro Martinez had run the gauntlet over the campus grounds to get inside the tower building. He made his way to the observation deck along with Officer Jerry Day and the floor manager of the University Co-op, Allen Crum. Crum had retired as an Air Force Master Sergeant before taking on a job at the university and he knew the safest way to get into position. Armed with a rifle, Crum wanted to help guide the two police officers to the observation deck. Moments later the trio were joined by Officer Houston McCoy who had the only suitable weapon to bring the terror to an end. Armed with his shotgun McCoy followed the other men through the barricaded door. The metal dolly clattered to the floor but Whitman was on the other side of the tower and oblivious to the impending assault.

Officer Martinez, with pistol drawn, crept along the east side from the south end. Immediately behind him was Officer Houston McCoy, shotgun loaded and safety catch off. Allen Crum and Officer Jerry Day watched the south side looking towards the west. If Whitman left his position he would face a shotgun one way or a rifle the other. Suddenly Crum heard Whitman running along the west wall and in his panic fired a shot into the parapet. Whitman stopped and ran back to the north-west corner where he crouched with his back against the wall. On the east wall McCoy and Martinez continued but had to keep low as bullets from the ground slammed into the concrete wall above them. When McCoy and Martinez rounded the corner they saw Whitman crouched down, his eyes fixed to the south in the direction Crum had fired. Whitman hadn't seen them and Martinez took aim and emptied his revolver at Whitman. As bullets slammed all around him Whitman instantly looked to his left and saw the two policemen. Whitman spun around but fired too soon, the bullet going harmlessly into the air. As he was spinning, Houston McCoy levelled his shotgun and gently squeezed the trigger. The blast from the shotgun hit Whitman full in the face and as he fell Houston McCoy fired another shell. With Whitman on the deck twitching, Martinez reached up, grabbed the shotgun from McCoy, and ran over to the limp Whitman. Another blast from the shotgun at close range finished the saga. At 1.24 pm Charles Joseph Whitman lay dead.

PSYCHOLOGICAL PROFILE

Four months before the shootings Charles Whitman had seen a psychiatrist at the University Health Centre. Whitman revealed some of his innermost thoughts and it was those thoughts that were to plague the doctor for the rest of his life.

Dr Heatly's report reads:

This is a new student referred by one of the general practitioners downstairs. *This massive, muscular youth seemed to be oozing with hostility as he initiated the hour with the statement that something was happening to him and he didn't seem to be himself.* [Emphasis added]

Past history revealed a youth who was one of two [sic] brothers that grew up in Florida where the father was a very successful plumbing contractor without an education, but who had achieved considerable wealth. He identified his father as being brutal, domineering and extremely demanding of the other three members of the family. The youth married four or five years ago, and served a hitch in the Marines during his married life. He expressed himself as being very fond of his wife, but admitted that his tactics were similar to his father's and that he had on two occasions assaulted his wife physically.

He referred to several commendable achievements during his Marine service, but also made reference to a court martial for fighting which resulted only to [sic] his being reduced several grades to a private. In spite of this he received a scholarship to attend the University for two years, and remain a Marine at the same time. He said that his wife had become more comfortable with him and he says that she really has less fear of him now than in the past because he had made a more intense effort to avoid losing his temper with her.

The real precipitating factor for this initial visit after being on the campus for several years seemed to stem from the separation of his parents some thirty days ago. Although there has been gross disharmony through the years, his mother summoned him to Florida to bring her to Texas, and she is now living in Austin, but not with her son and daughter-in-law. The youth says that his father has averaged calling every forty-eight hours for several weeks petitioning him to persuade his mother to return to him. He alleges to have no intentions of trying to do that and retains his hostility towards his father. Although he identifies with his mother in the matter above, his real concern is with himself at the present time. He readily admits having overwhelming periods of hostility with a very minimum of provocation. *Repeated inquiries attempting to analyze his exact experiences were not too successful with the exception of his vivid reference to... 'thinking about going up on the tower with a deer rifle and start shooting people'.* [Emphasis added]

He recognises, or rather feels that he is not achieving in his work at the level of which he is capable and this is very disconcerting to him. The youth could talk for long periods of time and develop overt hostility while talking, and then during the same narration may show signs of weeping.

Observations: This youth told numerous stories of his childhood and of involvement with his father that were not repeated, and it was felt that this relationship together with the genetic feature is largely responsible for this present predicament. Although his father is semiliterate, he is a perfectionist in other respects and extremely expansive. The youth has lived for the day when he could consider himself as a person capable of excelling [sic] his father in high society in general. He long ago acknowledged that he had surpassed him in educational fields, but he is seeking that status in versely [sic] all fields of human endeavor. He is self-centered and egocentric and at the same time he wants to improve himself. The degenerated state of affairs with his parents plus his repeated recent failures to achieve have become extremely frustrating to him which he (and his father) would express his hostility; thus some of the experiences noted above.

No medication was given to this youth at this time and he was told to make an appointment for the same day next week, and should he feel that he needs to talk to this therapist he could call me at anytime during the interval.

M.D. Heatly

Dr Heatly's impressions of Whitman were one of the 'All American' boy. There was nothing the doctor saw in Whitman that day that could account, on a purely psychiatric basis, for the murderous actions of 1 August. The Health Centre is a voluntary operation and clients are not required to attend.

To be fair to Dr Heatly, Whitman did not present any symptoms that gave the doctor cause to enforce any compulsory treatment, even though Whitman was 'oozing with hostility'. Without legal grounds to commit Whitman for treatment at an institution there was no way follow-up treatment could take place unless Whitman wanted it. At the time, he didn't present a danger to himself or anyone else.

Texas Governor John Connally, wasted no time in setting up a commission to look into the tragic events at the university tower. The commission concluded that Charles Whitman was an 'intelligent, intense and driven man but someone who had been encased in internal and external predicaments causing personal turmoil'. He had an unhealthy obsession with outdoing his father. The separation of his parents and the subsequent family dynamics tended to make Charles Whitman the 'meat in the sandwich'. Everything in his world was falling apart. The commission concluded Whitman's frustrations had led to a 'profound personal dissatisfaction' and a poor self concept. He was, in his own perception, a failure. In an 18-month period during 1965 and 1966 he had held six different jobs, all of them menial. He wanted to be a mechanical engineer, a commissioned officer in the Marines, an architectural engineer, a real estate agent or a lawyer with an engineering degree. He knew a little about a lot but excelled at nothing.

Despite having some of America's eminent behavioural scientists and psychiatrists at their disposal the commission was unable to explain why Charles Whitman did what he did. He did have a history of prescription drug abuse. He wasn't addicted to drugs but did abuse them. The amount of amphetamines he may or may not have had in his system at the time of his attack could not be measured. Before a post-mortem could be carried out Whitman's body was embalmed and stomach contents and urine were washed down the drain.

For some time Whitman believed he had something wrong with his head and that his behaviour was caused by a physiological event. He wasn't wrong on one count. During the autopsy the pathologist found a well outlined tumour measuring 2 cm x 1.5 cm x 1 cm in the middle of Whitman's brain. However the pathologist who examined the tumour did not believe there was any correlation between the tumour and either a psychosis or the persistent headaches which plagued Whitman.

Charles Whitman was the first in what has become an increasing global phenomenon. Like the other killers profiled in *Killing for Pleasure* Charles Whitman was not a lunatic who ran amok with a gun. Had he been intoxicated, drugged or a raving maniac he could not have been so accurate in his aim. He, like the others, was calm, rational and ruthlessly efficient. The event was meticulously planned and he had ample time to change his mind but chose not to. The stark reality in the Whitman case, unpalatable as it may be, is that he *chose* the course of action he did.

Charles Whitman fits the definition of a sociopath and can be regarded as bad rather than mad. While many would think the Whitmans of this world are insane, they are not. Their actions are insane but in most cases mass murderers have a choice. And they *choose* to kill. They are typically self-centred, care little for others and have minimal empathy or compassion.

CONCLUSION

Charles A Whitman had a wife and three sons. His wife died at the hands of his eldest son who in turn died at the hands of the police. Some years later the youngest of the Whitman children, John Michael, was shot during an argument in a bar. Then in the 1990s AIDS was to claim the only surviving brother, Patrick. Charles A Whitman survived the entire family.

CHAPTER TWO
JAMES HUBERTY

HUNTER OF HUMANS
San Diego, California – 18 July 1984
Victims: 21 dead, 20 injured

INTRODUCTION

'I thought San Diego must be a heaven on earth . . . It seemed to me the best spot for building a city I ever saw.' So said Alonzo Horton, the founding father of 'New' San Diego, when he arrived there in 1857. And heaven on earth it is to many people.

Over 100 kilometres of beaches stretch along the coast, the pristine white sand gently lapped by the blue Pacific Ocean with sandstone bluffs hiding secluded beaches. Millions of vacationers flock to San Diego annually to enjoy the mild year-round climate. Rainfall is minimal, just enough to nourish the lush interior abounding with citrus orchards. Further inland, tall craggy mountains separate the ocean from the scorched desert plains.

Spaniards discovered San Diego a mere fifty years after Columbus set foot on the eastern coast of America. The Spanish influence is evident to this day, as is the distinctly Mexican flavour of a city only 30 kilometres from the border between California and Mexico. A million people live in San Diego with a further one-and-a-half million in the county. The beautiful San Diego Bay is home to the largest fleet of warships in the world. The sinister grey shapes of submarines, aircraft carriers and other fighting craft are an obvious and integral part of the city and contrast starkly with pleasure craft and yachts that shelter in the harbour.

San Diego also boasts its favourite sons. Dennis Conner the yachtsman of America's Cup fame, actor Gregory Peck, Dr Jonas Salk, inventor of the polio vaccine, and world famous children's author, Dr Seuss.

Perhaps one of San Diego's greatest attractions is the magnificent Balboa Park, arguably the world's finest zoo. Those who wander the tracks that meander through luxurious subtropical flora can marvel at the 900 species of animals living in 'manmade' natural surroundings.

On 18 July 1984, James Huberty, his wife and two daughters visited a McDonald's restaurant before spending a pleasant time at the San Diego Zoo. A few hours later Huberty went to another McDonald's restaurant and perpetrated an act so vile he turned 'heaven on earth' into a sheer hell.

THE INTROVERTED EMBALMER

James Oliver Huberty had an inauspicious start to life. Born on 11 October 1942 he grew up with his parents, Earl and Icle, and older sister Ruth in relative comfort on a farm southwest of Canton, Ohio. Earl Huberty was a mill worker and well-respected in the Canton community. Before he reached the age of one, James was diagnosed with polio and needed to wear leg braces for the early part of his life. As a youngster he was referred to by relatives as a nice boy but very quiet.

When Huberty was nine his parents divorced and Icle Huberty left Ohio for Tucson, Arizona to follow a calling as a missionary on Indian reservations. Earl Huberty remarried and James lived with his father and stepmother, but early indications pointed to a troubled existence for the youngster. He didn't get along well with his stepmother and it was Huberty's grandmother who had a big influence in his life.

As a child, James Huberty preferred his own company and had no real friends. Before long the introverted boy was being labelled as 'weird', 'a loner' and 'nondescript'. These adjectives became dominant descriptions throughout Huberty's life. At high school he was more of a hanger-on, tending to shy away from group activities. Tall, with a flat-top haircut, the bespectacled Huberty seldom said anything. Fellow teenagers at a barbecue remembered him as the only one of their peer group who wouldn't join in or even speak. He preferred to be alone.

The Huberty family was well regarded at the United Methodist Church, and classmates of Huberty thought he might enter the ministry and a life devoted to religion but were surprised at his chosen profession. Huberty attended the Pittsburgh Institute of Mortuary Service, training to be an embalmer. He successfully completed the course and was issued with an embalmer's certificate and later a funeral director's licence. Huberty relished his work, especially the technical aspect of his trade, and returned to Canton for his internship.

Don Williams was the funeral director Huberty worked for but the diligent intern lacked one essential ingredient - social skills. While Huberty was comfortable working with the deceased he had an inability to relate to grieving relatives. Don Williams summed up Huberty as one who didn't have the personality for his chosen profession. 'He was a very clean-cut chap but was very much the loner type. He would rather be by himself.'

When Don Williams suggested Huberty was in the wrong profession he took the hint and he moved to a job as a welder with Babcock and Wilcox.

In 1965 Huberty met and married Etna, a Californian substitute teacher in elementary school and part-time worker in a housing complex for the aged. The couple had two daughters, Zelia and Cassandra.

THE LONELY FATHER

Despite being married with a family, James Huberty was nevertheless a solitary person. Etna summed up her husband's lonely existence after the tragedy at McDonald's when she remarked, 'Jim had always been a nervous person who could not take pressure. He had a very unhappy childhood and came from a broken home. He was very sad. His only close friend was his dog Shep.'

When Huberty took on the job as a welder he shifted to nearby Massillon, an industrial town of 32,000, but he and his family were treated like pariahs, with neighbours generally keeping their distance. Huberty was paranoid about the imminent end of the world, either by nuclear war or disaster. He believed he and his family would survive by hiding out in the woods. He stockpiled food and weapons and took on a survivalist mentality with disastrous effects. His home in Massillon caught fire accidentally in 1971, the flames taking hold in the kitchen. Before the flames could be doused they spread to a cache of gunpowder Huberty had stored as he waited for the war to arrive. Tom Matthews, the Massillon fire chief, said the home was destroyed when the fire set off the gunpowder. The resulting explosion blew a window across the street leaving drapes hanging in the trees.

The Huberty couple worked hard, James at the welding plant and Etna at three different jobs. Their intention was to own a block of apartments as an investment for the future. The vacant land where their home once stood soon had a small apartment complex built on it which Huberty managed from his home behind the block. However Huberty did not get on well with the residents in the apartments. Two large, aggressive German Shepherd dogs Huberty owned were the cause of a lot of disagreements. The dogs regularly rushed at people or rummaged in refuse cans. Even Massillon motorcycle police were not immune from attention, with the dogs often chasing their bikes.

Sergeant Don Adams remembered the Hubertys as a problem regarding minor neighbourhood disputes. It got to the stage where officers would remark, 'It's the Hubertys again'. Police were called to numerous complaints either from the neighbours about the Hubertys or from the Hubertys about the neighbours. On one occasion police attended a call complaining that Huberty was using abusive language and when police arrived Huberty was belligerent and wouldn't calm down. He was arrested on a disorderly conduct charge - his only arrest during numerous incidents involving the police. Etna, too, met the full force of the law once when she threatened neighbours by waving around one of her husband's pistols.

Although Huberty was attached to his dogs he killed one for no good reason. One of the dogs jumped onto a car scratching the paintwork and Huberty responded by dragging the dog to the rear of the property and shooting it. 'There, I took care of it,' Huberty remarked.

His demeanour was that of a reserved man who always appeared to be angry and 'he was always frowning'. Others described him as antisocial with a 'chip on his shoulder', a man who did not like other people much. Along with his paranoid beliefs, Huberty also became quite territorial. One neighbour had seen Huberty sitting just inside a partly opened door of his home with a shotgun resting on his lap. On another occasion Huberty became embroiled in an argument with a neighbour over his daughters and other children, and he told the children's father, 'You just wait. I'm going to get you when you are alone sometime'. The threat, though serious, went unreported.

Huberty kept to himself at work and home but did attempt to better himself. Although it took 16 years of on-again-off-again study, he finally gained an undergraduate degree in sociology. James Huberty had ability and was quite intelligent but his introspective nature made it difficult for him to succeed.

Few got close enough to really know Huberty but two people did get into conversation with him over his passion - guns. One was Mike Mauger who operated a tavern/café close to the Huberty apartment. The bar trade gave Mauger an ability to judge people and his initial impression of Huberty was that of a strange, weird person. 'He would never look you in the eyes,' Mauger remarked. 'His mind was always somewhere else and he was so strange.'

Huberty regularly visited the café for coffee or a soft drink but seldom got into conversation with patrons. Neither did he talk much to Mauger, until the barman mentioned guns. That was the only time Huberty really conversed with Mauger and on that occasion he animatedly talked at length about his interest in automatic weapons.

Another to notice Huberty's passion for guns was co-worker James Aslanes. He and Huberty shared a mutual interest in guns that led to a short friendship. Whenever a colleague at the plant bought a gun Huberty would offer to buy it, especially if it was an automatic. But Huberty's fascination and knowledge of firearms was not matched by his practice. Once, while shooting with Aslanes, the supposedly knowledgeable Huberty began firing at a rock with an Uzi semi-automatic which, considering the chances of a ricochet, was an extremely dangerous practice.

Huberty and guns became synonymous. Some people claimed he kept loaded firearms in every room of his home, while other visitors to the house thought that was an exaggeration. Even so, it was clear that Huberty was fascinated with guns and he did have several loaded guns in the house. To take maximum advantage of his passion, Huberty erected a shooting range in the basement of his home and other residents heard the muffled thumps as he fired at makeshift targets.

Huberty, though not one to converse often, did at times express some of his more morbid views at work. He espoused theories such as his belief that rapists should have their hands cut off and be tied up by their testicles. The manner in which he expressed these views alarmed some of the co-workers he spoke to.

The Huberty marriage was punctuated by frequent quarrels that were equally divided between husband and wife. Etna said her husband had exhibited emotional problems as long as she had known him, and put his nervousness and trembling hands down to a traffic accident he had been involved in, but a visit to a neurosurgeon failed to solve the problem. Etna felt their marriage wasn't a 'typical' one and she gave Huberty ample opportunity to leave but he didn't want to go. If there was anything Etna tired of, it was her role of having to play the mother, if not the grandmother, figure to her husband. She felt as if she had become a substitute mother figure and didn't relish the role.

Huberty had a nice home in Massillon, and with a decade of employment with Babcock and Wilcox felt he was a worthwhile person. But his self-esteem was about to be dealt a severe blow. As utility rates soared and wages failed to keep up with inflation, financial circumstances for Huberty began to tighten. When interest rates rose and the economy contracted, the steel mill was forced to cut back and one of the first casualties was James Huberty. On 18 November 1982 Huberty's world came crashing down. He was one of the early ones to be laid off but others soon followed.

Huberty's paranoid views on capitalism had led co-workers at Babcock and Wilcox to laugh at him. While they considered him to be a communist, Etna had other views, believing her husband more of a Nazi. 'He believed he was a German,' she said. 'He even acted like one.'

He expressed views to co-worker Terry Kelly that pointed to what would ultimately follow. 'If this is the end of me making a living for my family I'll take everyone with me,' Huberty said.

Terry Kelly said Huberty was always talking about shooting somebody, so the threats were nothing out of the ordinary.

The loss of a job played on Huberty's mind, and soon after he had a nervous breakdown. For five-and-a-half months he remained on the unemployment list. Then he finally succeeded in getting a job with the Union Metal Manufacturing Company in Canton, Ohio. The position only lasted two months. The firm was sold to a foreign interest and all employees were given notice. Again Huberty faced the ignominy of being laid off. As his unemployed status bit into Huberty's self-esteem it also ate into his financial prospects, and he developed an even more bitter resentment. Huberty put his misfortune down to people who 'connived' against him, and to mismanagement by successive governmental presidents. Inflation was the cause of the economic problems besetting Huberty and he fervently believed the rich had conspired to create the oil crisis of the late 1970s. The working class, he decided, had caused inflation and would have to pay for their actions.

Unable to find work in Ohio, Huberty decided to leave the security of the place he grew up in and moved his family to Mexico. Etna had maintained their Massillon home well and the couple had spent a lot of time remodelling it. They had done a good job and expected to make a substantial profit when they sold it prior to heading for Mexico. The expected profit turned into a significant loss and some of the money from the sale of the apartments remained tied up in Ohio, further embittering the already troubled Huberty.

SOUTH OF THE BORDER

In October 1983 Huberty told acquaintances he was moving to Mexico where he would make a lot of money. Sometime earlier he and Etna had visited Mexico and enjoyed themselves, so they decided to swap the life they had known in Ohio for a totally different setting over 3,000 kilometres away. They headed for Tijuana, but found their vacation experience different from the reality of living and working there. The Huberty family lasted a mere three months in their new paradise.

The Huberty girls spoke fluent Spanish and settled well in Tijuana but Huberty found the city dirty and was unable to fit in with a new way of life. Etna crossed the US border daily to take her daughters to school in nearby San Ysidro. Huberty also regularly crossed the border and more than once fell foul of Mexican police who objected to the speed he got up to on his Honda motorcycle. They wouldn't have been amused either if they knew he referred to them as 'monkeys' and ridiculed their 'bird-like' whistles. Although Etna claimed her husband was not a racist he certainly showed disdain for many Mexicans.

In early 1984 Huberty decided to move to San Ysidro but problems continued to follow him. The Mexican government was struggling with its own financial crisis and was running very low on dollars. As a result, Huberty's investments in Mexico were effectively frozen. Dogged with unemployment and financial woes Huberty had to start afresh in the USA. The family moved into an apartment in San Ysidro, a poorer suburb of San Diego inhabited largely by a Hispanic population, less than three kilometres from the Mexican border.

On arriving in San Ysidro the Hubertys first moved into the Robinson IV apartments. Maria de Jesus Hernandez remembered her new neighbour as a very quiet man who never talked to her but she did see him react when two men tried to steal his Honda motorcycle. Huberty responded by shooting at them.

The neighbourhood disputes Huberty experienced in Ohio followed him to California, but to nowhere near the same degree. In mid-June of 1984, a month before the killings, Huberty and his family moved apartments to Averil Villas, half a block from a McDonald's restaurant. Huberty's views on capitalism and a growing dislike of the United States may well have been symbolised by an American icon, the McDonald's fast food chain. The new apartment overlooked McDonald's and he regularly took binoculars and looked down on the restaurant and its patrons.

Huberty, desperate for work, applied for a position on a security guards course. The federally funded scheme aimed to help unemployed and low-income people into work. Applicants had to be screened and Huberty experienced no problems gaining selection as security checks on him turned out negative. He had no criminal history and the FBI had no records of fingerprints either indicating felonies or any form of military service. There seemed to be simply nothing adverse about James Oliver Huberty. A widely-used personality test, the MMPI (Minnesota Multiphasic Personality Inventory), was given to Huberty - but this is not a sufficient test to identify those who display psychological illness or psychotic manifestations, a fact obvious in the Huberty case. He graduated near the top of the 27-student course and was given a licence to carry an exposed .38 or .357 Magnum pistol while on duty. Common to the theme of the James Huberty life, he graduated as a successful but nondescript member of the course. Soon after graduation he landed a security guard's job on a condominium building site, but his employment only lasted one week when he was dismissed for undisclosed reasons. Etna said he was philosophical about being dismissed but the effects of this latest loss belie her assessment.

The day before the massacre Huberty did something Etna had been trying to get him to do for eight years - he telephoned a family mental health clinic for advice. Huberty's sociological training allowed him to act as though he was calm and collected and, although he was seeking help, the screening questions did not indicate he was in desperate need of attention. He was told someone would phone him back with an appointment for the following week. Etna heard him make the call and when Huberty went out she tried to contact the clinic to tell them something her husband had omitted to say - that he was well armed and had been talking of killing people. He had also been hearing voices and had begun conversing with people who weren't there. Through a series of unfortunate coincidences, Etna was unable to pass on the vital information that might have seen preventative action taken immediately.

Huberty returned home after riding his Honda and sat down to lunch, but soon after unplugged the telephone. Although he was expecting a call for an appointment to attend the mental health clinic he didn't seem too keen on getting the message. Etna was unsure how to handle the situation but decided to reconnect the telephone so she walked into the lounge and plugged it back into its socket. 'Jim didn't say anything,' Etna said. 'He just looked at me.'

In any event, no call came in that day or the next and by then it was too late.

COUNTDOWN TO MURDER

On the morning of Wednesday, 18 July 1984, James Huberty had a date with a judge. Driving the wrong way around a traffic island and not displaying a current registration sticker on his car had seen Huberty issued with an infringement notice and an appearance in traffic court. Etna and the two girls went with him to the court appearance where he was pleased to be let off with a minor fine. Huberty left the courthouse in a better frame of mind, taking his family to a nearby McDonald's restaurant for a meal before spending an enjoyable time at San Diego Zoo.

According to Etna, the couple did not argue that afternoon; this was backed up by police Lieutenant Paul Ybarrondo of the homicide squad. However the Hubertys' neighbour was adamant the couple had argued in such a way that it frightened the youngest Huberty girl. Wanda Haseley said ten-year-old Cassandra came to her apartment saying her parents had fought, that her father was angry and that she didn't want to return home. Etna was aware Cassandra had gone to the Haseley apartment to babysit while Wanda went out on an errand. The fact Huberty and his wife may have fought suggests a possible catalyst for the deeds he was about to perform, but Etna Huberty stands by her story that her husband was quite calm. Over recent days Huberty had been exhibiting depression and delusions, but on the day of the murders he had been quite relaxed.

Etna, well used to strange comments from her husband, took little notice of him when he said, 'Society has had their chance, I'm going hunting humans.' He wasn't ranting or raving but acted quite calmly. 'I will not be going far,' he said as he turned and left the apartment to go to his car.

Huberty was wearing a short-sleeved maroon shirt, camouflage fatigue trousers and dark glasses. He gave no indication as to where he was going or what terrible things he had planned. Etna and thirteen-year-old Zelia made preparations to go shopping, unaware that Huberty was only a few hundred metres away.

People in the McDonald's restaurant at 522 West San Ysidro Boulevard would have had no reason to take notice of the black Mercury as it pulled into the parking space. Had anyone looked at Huberty's car the only thing that might have caught their attention was the selfishly arrogant bumper sticker 'I'm not deaf - I'm ignoring you'. If Etna Huberty had looked out her apartment window she might have seen her heavily armed husband walk towards the entranceway to the McDonald's family restaurant.

MASSACRE AT MCDONALD'S

It was a typically hot, sunny day when James Huberty strode into the McDonald's outlet. About fifty customers and staff were at the colourful restaurant, many of them children attracted by the offer of free ice cream cones. With birthday parties in progress, McDonald's was a place of laughter and enjoyment. Huberty should have been in his element. He often dined at McDonald's and, according to Etna, he loved children and would never harm them. Huberty carried a 12-gauge pump action shotgun, a Browning 9 mm semi-automatic pistol, a 9 mm Uzi semi-automatic rifle, and his pockets bulged with ammunition.

'I've killed thousands and thousands,' Huberty called out. 'Now I'm going to kill thousands more.'

Huberty ordered everybody to 'get down' and as mothers screamed and their frightened children cried, James Huberty began to shoot. So sudden and ferocious was the attack that most people were killed where they sat, slumped in the booths over their partly consumed meals. Huberty shot at anyone and anything. His victims ranged in age from 74 years down to an eight-month-old baby. Four young employees of the McDonald's franchise, that prides itself as a family restaurant, were killed.

Not content merely with killing, Huberty wanted to destroy what he saw as the bastion of capitalism and began to shoot at the lights, fittings and windows. Walking from one side of the dining area to the other, frightened survivors huddling under furniture saw him hover above the bodies of those he had slain and say, 'Come on, buy your burgers with ketchup on!'

He then turned his attention to those outside the building, hitting a motorist passing on the nearby freeway. Three 11-year-old boys, Omar Hernandez, David Flores Delgado and Joshua Coleman, had ridden their bicycles down to McDonald's for an ice cream, relishing the thought of some relief from the over 80 degree heat. Hearing the commotion inside the restaurant the boys tried to escape but Huberty saw them and opened fire. Joshua, shot in the arms, legs and back had to lie still for over an hour, pretending to be dead. His young companions had not fared as well and were killed by the fusillade aimed at them as they fled.

A few others were luckier. As Huberty entered the building a young mother ran out in panic but turned to see her three-year-old child inside, still sitting frozen with fear to the seat, crying. Huberty was looking in the other direction and didn't see the mother beckon her son, or see the child run from the restaurant to safety. Those left inside had little chance of escape and were summarily executed. Huberty's actions were calculated and deliberate. Police Commander Larry Gore later described the scene: 'Huberty acted with long, slow, methodical precision. He had lots of ammunition and took the opportunity to reload several times. It was awesome, just incredible. Young kids, adults, families.'

Those who died inside the restaurant were all killed at close range with every victim being shot in the head or chest. Huberty clearly meant to kill each and every victim, shooting some with multiple rounds. He was rational and calm and during the shootings and subsequent siege was seen to tune a radio to stations broadcasting the tragedy as it unfolded. Several times he helped himself to soft drinks to quench the thirst brought on by his terrible rampage. Two survivors who were huddled on the floor feigning death saw the gunman, reflected in a mirror, casually reload his weapons at least six times.

The first call for help to police was recorded a few seconds before 4.04 pm. Within moments other 911 emergency calls flooded the police Southern Division's dispatcher. Police responded immediately and the first officer to attend, who happened to be a SWAT primary response team member, pulled into the nearby post office parking lot. Before the officer could get out of the car two bullets ripped into his vehicle. Quickly driving to the rear of the post office the officer was able to put on body armour and take up a position to cut off Huberty's escape. As other officers arrived they stationed themselves around the restaurant. A fire crew arriving in their truck was sent scattering for cover as ten bullets from Huberty's rifle pierced the fire engine. Within eight minutes Huberty was completely surrounded.

Huberty, however, could not have picked a more opportune time for his attack. The build-up of traffic was at its worst between 4 pm and 5 pm, and to compound matters the interstate freeway ran right past the scene of the catastrophe. Police had to close off the freeway causing an even greater traffic jam. Each San Diego police patrol shift has a SWAT team that can be mobilised at short notice. Where ordinarily the SWAT team members might have assembled at McDonald's in ten minutes, the congestion tripled the time of their arrival. Police snipers at the scene were faced with another problem. The inside of McDonald's was semi-dark and Huberty had fired bullets through every window. The glass had cracked forming a giant spider-web effect on every pane, distorting the shadowy images inside. The late afternoon sun glinted off the crazy patterns making it virtually impossible to see into the restaurant. Looking out from the darkened interior was easier and Huberty was able to pick his targets. Throughout the ordeal he kept police pinned down. Huberty's Uzi rifle was similar to the military style M16 and the armour-piercing bullets he used flew from the restaurant with incredible speed. Rushing the gunman was not an option and police could only wait until they were provided with an opportunity.

One hour and 17 minutes into the ordeal Huberty at last made a mistake. He saw a police sergeant across the road in the post office and let rip with eight bullets, narrowly missing the officer. In his eagerness to kill the sergeant Huberty moved from the maze of shattered glass towards a window that had collapsed. As he stepped forward Huberty walked straight into the sights of a sniper hidden just 30 metres away. The SWAT officer squeezed the trigger on his .308 rifle and the speeding bullet slammed straight into Huberty's chest, piercing his heart and shattering his spine. Huberty fell to the floor, moved momentarily, then died.

James Huberty had fired almost 300 bullets in his rampage at McDonald's yet he still had 100 rounds in his pockets or in his nearby car. He had the weapons and ammunition to cause even greater harm.

In all he had killed 21 people, and another 20 lay injured.

PSYCHOLOGICAL PROFILE

There is no doubt that Huberty was concerned enough about his mental state to consult a mental health clinic the day before the attack. It is not unusual for people to seek help the way Huberty did. In the aftermath of the killings, survey findings revealed that 19 per cent of adult males in the United States experience psychological disorders in any given six-month period. While fewer than one in five seeks treatment there are still a lot of referrals to be screened.

Had Huberty revealed his delusions about killing people, or confessed to owning weapons, the clinic would have been bound by the Tarasoff ruling to act. The Tarasoff ruling came about as a result of a Supreme Court decision in Tarasoff v Regents of the University of California. Therapists have a duty to warn and protect people where a patient is deemed to be a threat to others, even if it means breaching doctor/patient confidentiality. Inherent in the Tarasoff ruling is the ability to predict dangerousness that, in the case of mass murder, is elusive.

Had the clinic Huberty contacted known of his threats to kill and his cache of weapons, it would have been bound by its policy to contact the police. Unfortunately an employee of the clinic had written his name down as 'Shuberty' so when Etna rang them to express her concerns they had no record of his enquiry. Etna talked to the clinic about her husband's threats and weapons and was advised to contact police herself which she failed to do.

The screening techniques used by clinics are designed to determine who needs immediate help and who can wait for an appointment. The president of the San Diego Psychiatric Society said that people who fit Huberty's psychological profile often make abortive attempts for help almost in the belief, and looking for confirmation, that no one wants to help them anyway.

Almost invariably the killers profiled in *Killing for Pleasure* are seen by health professionals and make comments to them about killing. They fit the pseudo-commando profile yet the screening techniques don't pick up their true level of dangerousness. Perhaps it is time to re-examine the screening techniques and try and develop indicators of potential pseudo-commandos that will mark them apart from the others referred for psychological assessment. Lessons learned from the Huberty case are lessons we should follow. When men of the Huberty mould make threats of killing they ought to be believed.

The post-mortem results on Huberty's body revealed he was not under any influence from drink or drugs. Nor was there any biological abnormality to his body or brain. In the latter part of his life Huberty's demeanour deteriorated. He became even more short-tempered and often beat his wife and children. He had attempted to commit suicide and threatened to kill Etna. The children were becoming increasingly fearful of him, this being confirmed by neighbour Wanda Haseley. Even more bizarre was Huberty hearing voices and often talking to people who were not there. He claimed to have seen God - a man who was two feet tall with a long beard. Based on the evidence of his behaviour soon before his death, several psychiatrists hypothesised that James Huberty was an undiagnosed schizophrenic.

Whether or not Huberty was schizophrenic is speculative, but one thing is clear. His delusions and fantasies and ideas of war became an obsession and he talked of having 'killed thousands and thousands'. A few months before the McDonald's massacre Huberty went up to a police officer in San Ysidro and turned himself in as a war criminal. After being interviewed at length he was released and sent home. Huberty had never been in the armed services and had never fought in a war, yet had delusions of having done so. Those delusions and fantasies were played out in the McDonald's massacre.

The only other possible abnormality that could be attributed to Huberty's behaviour was an excessive level of lead in his hair which could have come from his years as a welder, or from the frequent handling of guns and shooting in his basement range. Heavy concentrations of lead have been found in children with behavioural problems such as attention deficit disorder and other hyperactivity complaints. High levels of lead are significant in that the glial cells in the brain can be damaged. Glial cells serve the purpose of detoxifying harmful chemicals and also play a role in behavioural inhibition. Most biological theories concern themselves with the role of chemical imbalance that results in the failure of behavioural modifiers.

Both the lead theory and suggestions of schizophrenia have validity. But the lifestyle and behavioural traits of James Huberty, as seen in the comparative context of other similar killers, are the most likely keys to unlocking the mystery for his actions.

CONCLUSION

James Huberty's 74-year-old father was badly shaken when given news of his son's terrible deeds. The ageing man simply couldn't comprehend what his son did or what led him to do what he did. But Huberty's mother, Icle, had a more philosophical view. Though she had had the opportunity to, she hadn't seen her son in a couple of years. Icle had been in Ohio shortly before he moved to Mexico but didn't visit him as she got a message from God to return to Tucson. Icle, who described herself as a Pentecostal minister preaching the gospel around Tucson and on Indian reservations, believed her son's savage attack was the devil speaking to him.

'I recognised it right away,' she told Cheryl Clark of the San

Diego Union Tribune. 'Everything he did was the devil speaking to him. It was the killing evil devil, is what it was.'

Had Icle's theory or belief in the devil been accurate then Satan must have been very busy in the 1980s. The terrible tragedy caused by Icle's only son was just one of dozens of mass killings in the United States and around the world during that decade. Charles Whitman's attack in Austin, Texas in 1966 was the first of the pseudo-commando type attacks. But James Oliver Huberty's rampage at McDonald's saw the beginning of a rash of similar murders that has now become a global phenomenon.

CHAPTER THREE
JULIAN KNIGHT

DOLPHIN AMONG THE SHARKS
Melbourne, Australia - 9 August 1987
Victims: 7 dead, 19 injured

INTRODUCTION

Julian Knight is somewhat unique in the world of mass killers, being alive in a Melbourne prison. In a series of interviews with a journalist the year following the killings, Knight gave an insight into his persona, how he really sees himself.

'You might think I was an ordinary killer, but you would be wrong. I'm not like these guys. No way. Don't even put them in the same class. These guys are low life, know what I mean? Habitual criminals. Soon as they're out they'll be back in again. They can't help themselves.'

To illustrate the point Knight said, 'I'll tell you a joke, something that will make you laugh. One day I was waiting to make a phone call and one of the Russell Street bombers (referring to the bombing of the Russell Street Police Station in Melbourne where a policewoman was killed) was on the phone, chatting to his mother. He was gabbling on and I was getting impatient. She was asking him how he was and all that and I heard him say he was fine and okay and everything, and then he says, guess what Mum, I'm in here with the guy that done the Hoddle Street massacre. Well, you don't reckon that the shit hit the fan! She did her block! She was screaming out to him to go and speak to the Governor, so he could get moved to another part of the prison away from me. She was worried about his safety. What a joke! She was telling him, I want you to get away from that murderer, heaven knows what he might do to you. The joke is I'm nothing like those guys. Nothing. They've got nothing to be afraid of, not from me. They're the criminals, not me. I'm the one whose life is in danger in here. I'll tell you something. I don't know how long I'll survive in here because the truth is most of these guys are professional killers and I'm not. The truth is, that in here, I'm the dolphin among the sharks.'

Tess Lawrence is a freelance journalist working from offices in Melbourne, Australia. In 1990 she wrote a book, *Headlines,* in which she describes interviews with many famous people. She has interviewed Kirk Douglas, Bob Hope, Richard Attenborough, Cher, Joe Frazier, Zsa Zsa Gabor, the Dalai Lama, Mother Teresa and Nancy Reagan. But one interview she describes, and one that caused her a degree of angst, was with an infamous character called Julian Knight, a 19-year-old failed soldier who perpetrated the massacre on Melbourne's Hoddle Street on a peaceful Sunday evening. An experienced journalist and interviewer, Tess Lawrence couldn't help but be surprised at Knight's reaction to her visits. What angle would she go for? Knight asked her. How much did Lawrence know about the night? How much did she really know about the night? Had she seen the pictures of the victims? All the pictures? Furthermore he specifically asked her to send them to him along with news media clippings. He even supplied names and addresses of girlfriends who might be 'suitable' to give interviews about him.

Knight wanted to be sure this woman really understood, otherwise how could she interview him properly? 'You see, I'm not just a straight out killer,' Knight told her. 'Have you read about Son of Sam? Have you read about the McDonald's massacre? I'd like you to read up on them before you get back to me, so you have more understanding, so we can more thoroughly discuss this type of killing process.'

Several times Knight mentioned 'Son of Sam', the notorious murderer David Berkowitz who, in the summer of 1977, gripped New York in fear as he continued his orgy of random killings.

Knight also talked about James Huberty, who killed 21 innocent people at a McDonald's restaurant in San Diego in 1984. Just days after Knight's rampage on Hoddle Street, the English were sent reeling when Michael Ryan walked through Hungerford leaving 16 people dead in his wake. Julian Knight spoke of Ryan as if he was an old friend or a successful pupil. Throughout the interviews, Knight preferred to reflect on what he had done rather than show remorse for his actions.

While Julian Knight admires Ryan, he despises Frank Vitkovic who killed eight people in Melbourne four months after Knight's rampage. He took the limelight that belonged to Hoddle Street and Julian Knight didn't take kindly to that. Where Knight had been a soldier Vitkovic was unfamiliar with firearms and he only acquired his gun a short while before he committed his murders. He even had trouble operating it but managed to kill more people than Knight, much to Knight's chagrin. 'You shouldn't count Vitkovic,' Knight told Lawrence. 'The guy was an amateur, know what I mean? What did he know about guns? Just walked in and got one over the counter. Wasn't trained. It was a fluke he took out eight. A real fluke. Had to be.'

THE YOUNG DOLPHIN

Julian Knight reflects on the fact he was only 19 at the time of the shootings, when, in the space of less than an hour he went from being 'an average bloke' to a mass murderer. He was born on 4 March 1968 to a young Australian girl and given up for adoption when only a few days old. Knight's adoptive father was an academic instructor with the Australian Army and Julian, along with his mother and adoptive brother and sister, lived in bases around Australia, Hong Kong and Singapore.

Apart from disrupted primary school attendance caused by the many shifts, Julian Knight led a rather unremarkable life. The only significant incident was a schoolyard fight where he kicked another boy seriously enough to warrant an appearance in a youth court. Throughout his secondary school years Knight lacked motivation and was an under-achiever, despite being in the top three per cent of the Australian population with an IQ of 132.

In 1980 when Knight was 12 his parents divorced. Knight attended Fitzroy High, where he was regarded as a capable student who on occasions got into some 'stupid' behaviour but was not a difficult pupil. Knight was always polite and co-operative though reserved, and never showed signs of serious problems or violent tendencies. Knight's potential to succeed was not matched by his application. In English he was assessed as 'a clear minded, confident and articulate student but he should not be too complacent about his own abilities'. However his lack of concentration and commitment were noticeable. 'Julian is a most capable student but he appears to be both lazy and easily distracted,' his history teacher said.

Another said his attendance and level of commitment were poor and though he was a witty and intelligent boy he needed to push himself higher. After only a year at Fitzroy, Knight moved to Melbourne High School, apparently because he was not progressing happily or satisfactorily. Melbourne High provided a wider range of subjects and boasted an excellent military cadet unit, something in which Julian Knight was passionately interested. Knight kept a low profile; one teacher regarded him as 'a loner' with only one close friend. 'He seemed reserved and gave the impression of being self contained and able to get on by himself.'

Knight's geography teacher, however, had a different view: 'He was reasonably extroverted and open, not afraid to say what he thought and enjoyed saying things that made him the centre of attention.'

Julian enjoyed the popularity he got from his differences rather than by conforming with his peer group. The forced extroversion was attention-seeking and a way of making him more popular - and while this behaviour was eccentric, Knight was not regarded as mad or weird.

Knight's interest in the military clashed with school rules when he wore jungle greens on an excursion and took military magazines to school. Knight was interested in political classes and expressed his ideas.

'No matter how outlandish or outrageous the idea, and even if it was howled down or copped Knight derision from the class, he did not appear to be badly affected by this,' his teacher said.

Knight even asked the teacher if he could use a *Soldier of Fortune* article on a guerrilla group insurrection in a third world country as a reference. Throughout his years at Melbourne High, Julian Knight never achieved what he was capable of. Often outside interests, principally sport, get in the way of achieving potential, but in Julian Knight's case it was study versus the army reserve.

After leaving school Knight enrolled briefly at LaTrobe University but deferred. He then worked as a kitchen hand at McDonald's but was intent on joining the army as soon as he was old enough. Knight had girlfriends though only one long-term relationship. Over seventeen months Knight's girlfriend, Renee, got to know him well. She felt he had difficulty coming to grips with issues such as being adopted, never having been breastfed, and his parents being divorced. Where he could be an affectionate and witty person, he could also become violent and morose after drinking, often getting upset. 'In fact he cried a lot more than any other male I know,' Renee said.

It was Knight's reluctance to socialise with Renee's friends and his violent outbursts that saw the couple drift apart. On numerous occasions Renee witnessed sudden eruptions when Knight was drinking and brooding. Without warning he would lash out or throw a glass. During one party Knight began to argue about an ex-girlfriend he had never got over and began fighting with guests. During the outburst he punched and kicked Renee several times.

Knight was a regular customer at the Clifton Hill newsagency where he purchased magazines about paramilitary activity, among them *Soldier of Fortune* and *SWAT* magazines.

The newsagent remembered Knight for his purchases and also his dress. 'I've always seen him in some type of military clothing, in particular an army camouflage jacket,' he said.

On his eighteenth birthday Knight applied for a shooter's licence stating he wanted a firearm for competition shooting and hunting. Within six months of getting his licence Knight owned a shotgun and a Norinco .308 semi-automatic assault rifle. Early the next year he added a .22 semi-automatic Ruger to his collection, a present from an uncle. Knight was a gun fanatic and, after shooting at targets with Renee, was fastidious about cleaning his weapons. His bedroom walls were covered in military posters, some depicting dead people on South African roads. Renee believed Knight supported apartheid and had a hatred of black people and he talked of being a mercenary, even making enquiries with the South African embassy.

A KILLER'S TRAINING GROUND

A career in the army could have been the making of Julian Knight, but instead it heralded the beginning of the end. For years Knight had wanted to be a soldier and if he couldn't be a career soldier he fantasised about becoming a mercenary. Either way, the key to success would be discipline and that was something Julian Knight lacked.

Two of his army reserve comrades recalled a two-week course where they were trained in the use of rifles, pistols and machine-guns. The camps were highly concentrated where reservists ate, slept and talked army and killing as if it was an everyday thing. Having a self-loading rifle in their hands gave them a powerful 'Rambo'-like feeling, but when it was over they went back to being a plumber, or whatever. But Julian Knight was different. He was the one more dedicated to the 'cause', more so than anyone else Julian's reserve colleagues knew. They believed Julian Knight had only one ambition and that was to be a career soldier.

Knight was eventually selected to attend the Royal Military College at Duntroon in Australia's capital city, Canberra. Before being accepted he underwent psychological testing, the results of which are interesting.

In assessing applicants the Australian army uses an attributes rating scale system on a continuum from 'Good' to 'Very Weak'. If the applicant scores as weak, the weakness is not completely damning if it is offset with other very strong qualities. When Julian Knight appeared before the officer selection board he was assessed by four people and all rated him as weak for his intellectual potential - yet here was a young man with an IQ of 132. The president of the board rated Knight as marginal overall, as did the military and academic members. Only the psychologist differed by assessing Knight as adequate. Clearly, Julian Knight was lucky to make it into the Royal Military College. A comment from one board member summed up how Knight might do during training. 'He participated in, and directed group activities. However, I consider he may be over confident and his ability may not match his belief in himself.'

If the tests had concentrated more on clinical potential, Knight might have been rejected as unsuitable for military life. An army psychologist found Knight presented well but noted he was 'somewhat sensitive about his life, as if it had been all mixed up. He showed determination to take charge of his life and improve things. He is a bit sensitive about his family situation and may be a bit emotionally close to his mum. Socially seems okay but could be defensive and needs some sound development.'

Not everyone had faith in the selection board's processes or the psychological tests. Tim Watson-Munro is a prominent clinical psychologist in Melbourne and was sceptical of the tests given to applicants for entry to Duntroon.

'There are psychological tests with scales built in that can indicate disturbances. They look for violence, psychopathy or depression and as I understand it, in relation to the psychological input to Mr Knight, he had one test to do of brief duration. In retrospect they didn't look at those particular scales and may have looked more at leadership and management potential, not clinical potential,' said Mr Watson-Munro.

From Knight's army reserve experience he should have had an idea as to what to expect when he marched into Duntroon in January 1987. But he was unable to accept the discipline or hierarchical structure necessary in a disciplined force. Traditionally in military academies senior cadets instil discipline into their juniors, but Julian Knight didn't take kindly to it and hated being bossed about. At Duntroon Knight found he was on the lowest level of the pecking order and complained about the degree of 'bastardisation' (an Australian term for initiation ceremonies and bullying in a military unit). Making toast for senior cadets was one thing but having to crawl across furniture to deliver it to them was another, and for someone who is psychologically vulnerable such behaviour could be a flashpoint. For most junior cadets, the seemingly over-zealous attention to detail was part of accepting discipline, but Julian Knight saw it as being continually picked on.

In the first months at Duntroon, Knight was given extra parades for minor indiscretions such as equipment or clothing not being up to standard. May 14 1987 was a particularly bad day for him. He was pulled up twice for clothing being below standard, was late for instruction once, and was caught asleep in class three times, and to top it off was late for instruction the next day. Knight's disciplinary record was liberally sprinkled with more serious charges like being absent without leave, absent from duty (including exams), leaving his post, and prejudicial behaviour.

His desire to be a professional soldier was at odds with his disregard for the rules, conventions, and behaviour of the armed services, and within a short time his lack of maturity began to show. He was the one who asked 'stupid' questions and showed a tendency to prove to his peers an attitude of toughness. Where on one exercise he showed 'good aggression', on another he failed to 'stand to' during a night attack - opting to remain in his sleeping bag - and he failed to pass messages on to other cadets, forcing them to be late for interviews. His below-par academic results, low personal standards and poor discipline were counting against him, and by the end of April Knight was struggling. At an exercise on 6 May he was 'not digging with enough effort, did not take aimed shots in the line of fire exercise, did not use a correct fire position and made immature statements'. Two days later he was caught cheating in a map marking exercise, and on being interviewed by a senior officer, alcohol was found on his breath. When counselled by the CO, Knight was told he was the worst in his class.

The unpopular Knight was no longer being treated as an equal among his peers. In a peer group rating one cadet felt Knight was a character. 'He was a nice enough chap, very good-hearted but also very immature. He demonstrated immaturity by drinking too much if he thought he would be more readily acceptable.'

Others however had quite different views. 'Too young with no common-sense,' said one. Another said Knight had dug his own grave, making it worse for himself by talking back, with a further cadet claiming Knight didn't even attempt to fit in.

Knight's weapons instructor said he performed adequately with all weapons, and was above average for his peer group, but Knight had an unusual aspect. 'He expressed interests in the world's trouble spots and an unusual interest towards participation in combat,' the sergeant said. 'Several times Knight asked about the army's attitude to officers going into trouble spots in their own time.'

One of Knight's more mature contemporaries had served as a missionary in the Middle East and in 1986 was caught up in a military coup. He saw rioting in the street and shooting at close range. 'Julian Knight was particularly interested in those experiences,' he said. 'Where others would talk about it in a group situation, Julian would want it in detail, wanting to know what it was *actually* like to be shot at.'

Knight even contemplated taking leave to head for the Middle East to see first hand what it was like.

Soon after arriving in Canberra, Knight met and dated Meg. The content of letters Meg had written Knight showed clearly their relationship was very much an 'on again-off again' affair, but the pair regularly went night-clubbing together. Meg was with Knight one evening when an incident occurred that would herald the end for the man who so much wanted to be a soldier.

BEGINNING OF THE END

On Friday, 30 May 1987, Knight had gone absent without leave to the Private Bin Club wearing dirty denim jeans and scruffy shoes. After a parade rehearsal the following day, a lance corporal demanded an explanation as to why the orders of the commanding officer had been disobeyed. Jeans were not to be worn by cadets in the Private Bin Club. The corporal made an error of judgement by tapping Knight on the shoulder with a bayonet as he spoke, to which Knight responded aggressively. He pushed the corporal and headed off to the hall before he was dismissed from the parade ground. The cadet sergeant major confined Knight to the college grounds until the Monday, but in Knight's mind he had been illegally confined to the base so, dressed in jeans and sneakers, he made for the Private Bin Club with Meg. The sergeant major was at the club and was far from amused. He grabbed Knight by the jersey and started pushing him backwards. 'You disobeyed me and I fucking hate that,' he told Knight.

When a bouncer intervened, the sergeant left Knight and went back to his friends but as the night wore on the sergeant made repeated attempts to make Knight leave. At 1.30 am he approached Knight again saying, 'You disobeyed me, I hate that and you're leaving right now.'

A brawl began and Knight was struck heavily and thrown out of the club, his face covered in blood. Other cadets warned Knight to leave, saying the sergeant and five others were after him, and made it clear the boot would be put in once Knight went down. Knight wasn't going to leave and cleaned himself up in the public toilets.

Meg was determined to go back into the club and Knight followed. He sat in the corner drinking as other cadets continued giving him dirty looks until just before 3.00 am when Meg suggested they leave. The sergeant, who was by now well-affected by alcohol, was at the bar talking with a group of his friends. Knight went to walk past the group but hesitated. Still smarting from being roughed up, and believing the sergeant had hit him from behind, Knight took a knife from his pocket and stabbed the sergeant twice in the face. He fled from the Private Bin and kept running until he found a police patrol where he dropped the knife and told the police officers he had just stabbed someone. Knight claimed it was just an instinctive reaction, but he wanted to hurt the sergeant as much as he had hurt him. When asked why he chose that moment to stab the sergeant, Knight said he thought this was his last chance to get even. The incident at the Private Bin was to see Knight's career and lifetime ambition come crashing down. His overall performance, frequent indiscretions, and the stabbing incident, convinced the army they didn't need Julian Knight, and his career was over.

Soon after leaving the army Knight took Meg to Melbourne and visited Renee. 'Julian had changed and seemed to be an ocker, a yobbo, which was totally unlike him before. He had stopped using his brain and was inane,' Renee said.

She told Knight not to visit her again. She felt he wasn't stable, had become strange and frightened her. 'His lifelong dream of an army career had failed and his life was going wrong. When I was going out with him I thought then he needed psychiatric treatment and told him so.'

Following Knight's Hoddle Street rampage he was asked by various people whether he felt remorse for his actions and the answer he regularly gave was the regret that he took the lives of those very people he was trained to protect. That, said Knight, was to be regretted. It's an interesting point and in a book, *Mass Murder - America's growing menace* by Professors Jack Levin and James Fox (both PhDs in sociology), published in 1985, the authors talk about mass murderers who, in varying ways, help people but harm others.

. . . From a psychological viewpoint, both helping and hurting can have the same underlying motive, to control the fate of other human beings. Many people who have a profound lack of self esteem make themselves feel superior by attacking the weakness and errors, and in extreme cases the bodies of others. They are frustrated because they feel they have little power and control over their own lives. Something these people collect, and use, might be police and military uniforms or instruments of torture and guns.

The theory Levin and Fox propose has some credence in Knight's case. Not only did he regret killing those he was trained to protect, he also tried unsuccessfully to join the police. In his quest to gain employment in a uniformed body that would 'help' people, he enrolled in a security training course due to begin on 11 August, the Tuesday following the tragedy of Hoddle Street.

Family members never saw anything to indicate Knight suffered any form of mental disorder. After leaving the army he stayed with an uncle where he talked about his problems and how a few people 'had it in for him'. But there were no signs of irrational behaviour or thinking, only indications of being withdrawn and depressed. Knight's siblings had no idea about their brother's mental state. Younger brother Matthew said Julian was always quiet and withdrawn but was usually in good moods. Knight often confided in his sister, Sarah, and she never had ill feelings about him. The events on Hoddle Street would come as a complete shock.

After Julian Knight had left for Duntroon in January 1987 his mother, Pamela, turned his bedroom into a lounge, not expecting her son to return so soon. Knight's bedroom now consisted of a floral mattress on the floor, a pillow, and a radio placed between two lounge chairs. On an exercycle in the upstairs hall he placed his webbing belt holding camouflage army gear and water bottles, reminders of his failed army days. In a bookcase were a variety of books including *Alice's Adventures in Wonderland* and *Grimm's Fairy Tales,* but on the lower shelf, neatly arranged, were more than three dozen books on warfare.

COUNTDOWN TO DISASTER

On 27 July 1987 Julian Knight was employed as a storeman/driver by Cuggi/Rarity Stores in South Yarra. His supervisor, Barbara, found Knight to be always pleasant, punctual and easy to supervise, but also quiet and withdrawn, as if there was something else on his mind and he was just filling in time with Cuggi's. Ilaio was Cuggi's 17-year-old stockroom manager who worked closer with Knight than anyone else. He found Julian Knight to be a 'quiet guy' who kept to himself and despite trying to get to know Knight, found he wasn't very responsive. When Knight did talk it was usually about the army and particularly his liking for the training the army provided. When work finished on Friday 7 August, Ilaio told Knight to have a good weekend and Knight replied about going to have a rage of a weekend.

Knight went upstairs to the office. 'Goodnight,' he said to Barbara, 'have a good weekend.' But for many people in Melbourne, that weekend was going to be anything but good.

After leaving work Knight went home and later met up with his lifelong friend, Ben, at the Royal Hotel. 'To me Julian was a nice guy,' said Ben. 'He was a good friend, practically a brother, unselfish and always willing to help where possible. I believe if Julian had a particular problem or was upset I would probably know about it.'

Knight told Ben he'd found out his real name and where his mother was by using the Freedom of Information Act. 'I think he wanted to see what his natural parents were like but he wasn't really worried about it.' Ben also knew of Knight's ex-girlfriend Renee and saw him talk to her in the hotel on the Friday evening. 'I only saw him say hello to her and he didn't seem to be upset.'

But Knight was upset. Renee had planned a party and invited some of Julian Knight's friends but specifically told each of them that Julian was not to come along. When they left the pub without him Knight was hurt but said nothing to Ben. After a few drinks the two went back to Knight's home, arriving about midnight. They sat talking and playing cards for a couple of hours. 'Julian was in a normal mood and there didn't appear to be anything upsetting him,' Ben said.

They slept in until lunchtime on Saturday 8 August, and during the afternoon went to a nearby pub for a few games of pool. Neither was drinking as Knight was going to drive his car later on. After washing Knight's SLR5000 Torana they watched television and played cards until around 6 pm when Knight drove Ben home. The next time the two would meet, Julian Knight would be in custody on seven charges of murder.

On Sunday 9 August the extended Knight family gathered for lunch to celebrate Pamela Knight's birthday. Julian Knight's siblings, mother, uncles and aunts met at his grandmother's. He was in a good mood and seemed very relaxed and in good spirits. He talked about a security course he was about to start and seemed very pleased.

'His mood was the best he had been in for some time,' an uncle said. 'During the afternoon I remember him sitting reading a magazine and playing with my dog.'

Sarah Knight went to the family gathering in Julian's car and remembered him being in a good mood. Later Julian drove Sarah home, saying he would be going to the pub that night and perhaps taking a barmaid out. He dropped Sarah off and went straight to the hotel, had one beer then briefly visited a friend, Lisa. He went to her flat and gave her a magazine he had been reading at his grandmother's. Lisa had known Knight since their days at Fitzroy High School and had seen Knight 'go down the drain' following problem after problem with girlfriends. Knight often talked to Lisa about his problems, saying no one had been nice to him, and he would treat them the way he had been treated. Lisa had noticed Knight was quieter and keeping to himself after returning from Duntroon. She knew about his fascination with guns as he always talked about them, and claimed Knight's mother once confiscated the guns because he threatened to shoot his dog. When Knight visited Lisa on that fateful Sunday she noticed he was in a remarkably happy mood.

On the way home the gear-box in the Torana jammed and he couldn't get it out of second gear. Soon after arriving home Knight said he was going to the pub, said goodbye and walked to the Royal Hotel.

Sharon, the regular barmaid, had got to know Julian Knight. He had formed an attraction to her, but the feeling was not mutual. 'He used to bring me flowers and many times asked me to go out with him, but I didn't,' Sharon said.

Once, when she relented and had a cup of coffee with him, Knight told her about liking the army but how he wasn't mature enough. Knight often walked Sharon to her car and was always polite. On that Sunday Sharon was off duty and went to the Royal with friends. When she walked in Knight ran straight up to her.

'He told me he had been waiting for me and that I looked beautiful,' Sharon said. 'He asked me to have a drink but I was with friends so had nothing to do with him. He was stone cold sober and very bouncy.'

The only bar person working on that fateful night was Karlina, and 9 August was her first night at the Royal. She had worked in bars and restaurants for ten years and had met many different types of men, but Julian Knight made her uncomfortable. 'He was watching my every move and when I served him he started asking me about a scar on my face.' Knight asked Karlina if she had been knifed and she replied it was the result of a car accident. She tried to ignore him but he persisted, telling her he was fascinated with the scar on her face, and when she served other customers Karlina was aware Knight was still watching her. About twenty minutes later Knight began to apologise. 'I'm sorry that I offended you, I didn't mean to upset you,' he said repeatedly.

During the night the only person Knight spoke with was a 17-year-old apprentice sheet metal worker living at the hotel. They talked about Knight's car and his life in the army. Knight also opened up about Renee, their split-up and a claim he had five girlfriends in seven months in Canberra. He also spoke about talking to Renee on the Friday night and how she ignored him. Apart from small talk about football there was little else said, and although being a bit 'cheesed off' about the car Knight seemed quite all right. At closing time a 'regular' who had only ever said hello to Knight asked if he would make room at the bar so he could get a beer. 'He moved and when I ordered I noticed his glass was empty so I asked the barman to fill it. Julian said thank you and he was smiling,' the regular said.

Between Karlina and the licensee they estimated Knight had no more than eight glasses, about half what Knight believed he consumed, and they were adamant that when he left at 8.20 pm he was not drunk.

Julian Knight claimed later that, before he left the hotel, he had a vision of 'soldiers being ambushed' and felt this was 'a call to arms'. The catalyst for what Knight did next is as vague as his 'vision'. It could have been the problems he was experiencing with his car his failure to hear from his birth mother, rejections from barmaids and his ex-girlfriend, or the loss of his army career. Whether any of these factors or a combination of them caused Knight to become a mass killer will never be known. Whatever the catalyst, there can be no excuse for what he did next.

THE TERROR OF HODDLE STREET

When Julian Knight arrived home Sarah heard the door slam. 'I looked down the hallway and saw him standing by a wardrobe stuffing around in a box where he kept army things and clothing.'

Knight's firearms and ammunition were stored in his mother's upstairs bedroom and his army clothing hung over the exercycle in the hall. Sarah heard her brother go up and down the stairs and went to speak to him. 'Julian seemed in a weird sort of mood, he didn't seem happy and wasn't talkative. He had an expression on his face but I know he wasn't drunk.'

Julian Knight was well armed when he walked the few paces from his home doorway to Hoddle Street. In one hand he carried a Mossberg pump action shotgun, with 25 cartridges in a waist belt. In the other hand he carried a .22 Ruger loaded with a ten-round magazine. Three other magazines in his pocket gave him a total of 40 rounds. Slung across his shoulder was his high powered M14 loaded with 20 hunting rounds with 60 spare rounds in his denim jacket. As soon as he got to Hoddle Street he fired 40 rounds of .22 ammunition at people in their cars and although no one was killed in the initial onslaught, Knight created havoc.

Sarah had gone to bed and heard gunshots. Looking out the window onto Hoddle Street she saw a shape of someone carrying guns running towards the railway station. Although it was dark, the outline of the figure looked like Julian. Sarah ran to her brother's room but he wasn't there. 'Where's Julian? I heard some shots outside,' Sarah called to her mother.

The missing ammunition and guns were enough for Mrs Knight to suspect Julian was outside shooting and she phoned the police, but already they were fielding calls and the rampage on Hoddle Street was underway.

On the other side of Melbourne, Julian Knight's 16-year-old brother was staying at his grandmother's watching television when a news flash about a shooting in the Clifton Hill area came on the screen. Matthew saw Hoddle Street and the service station just fifty metres from their home in Ramsden Street, and for some reason thought his brother might be involved. He rang home to be told Julian was gone, and so were his guns.

After using up all his .22 ammunition, Knight discarded the Ruger in the bushes and turned his attention to the more lethal shotgun and M14. Moving along the nature strip between Ramsden

Street and the Clifton Hill Railway Station he was difficult to see. He moved quickly, running in a crouched position, occasionally stumbling but regaining his balance easily. He used the hedges, bushes and large decorative rocks to hide behind as he fired on the many pedestrians, motorists and cyclists in the area.

Vesna Markovska was Knight's first victim. The 24-year-old was driving alone towards her Clifton Hill home and directly behind her, in another car, was her fiancé Zoran. The windows of both cars shattered without warning. Injured, and unsure of what was happening, the couple stopped and got out of their cars. Vesna was instantly hit by another two bullets and died from a wound to the head. Zoran, unable to help Vesna, ran until he came across Constable Belinda Bourchier. Overcome with grief and anger at Knight's murderous attack, Zoran wrestled with the constable trying unsuccessfully to take her service revolver. Zoran had one aim in mind and that was to go after the man in the shadows who had taken Vesna's life.

Robert Mitchell, a 27-year-old company manager, was driving on Hoddle Street returning home from a social function when he saw Vesna on the road. Being a 'Good Samaritan' he stopped and ran towards the injured woman when he was felled with a single shot from the M14. Also driving along Hoddle Street was 21-year-old student Georgina Papaionnou. Seeing the chaos, Gina stopped and got out of her car. She was unable to see Knight in the shadows, but with street and car lights illuminating the scene Gina was an easy target. A bullet from Knight's M14 hit Gina in the lower side inflicting a terrible injury and she fell to the road helpless.

Like moths to a light, others came to help, thinking the scene was a motor accident. Peter Curmi and John Muscat heard the commotion from a nearby house and went to investigate. Stephen Wight was at work preparing to close the Collingwood swimming pool. Attracted by the noise he ran to the shelter of a large elm tree and saw the two men approaching from the other direction. He called to them to keep away but Curmi and Muscat couldn't resist the urge to help and kept going. Before they could offer help to the three people on the road they were downed, Peter Curmi shot in the back and leg, and John Muscat hit by a shotgun blast to the head. From behind the elm tree Wight waited and, thinking Knight had moved away, came from cover and ran towards the group of dead and dying. He was wrong. Knight was in the shadows and a blast from the shotgun stopped Stephen Wight in his tracks and he fell to the road with serious head and chest wounds.

Dusan Flajnik was driving to work at the Carlton and United Breweries when he came into the gunman's sights. Two bullets from the M14 struck Dusan in the chest and shoulder causing massive, fatal injuries. Also driving on Hoddle Street was Kevin Skinner, who was returning home after celebrating his birthday with his family. In the passenger seat his 23-year-old wife Tracey was nursing 18-month-old Adam, when they saw the group of casualties.

'When I saw the bodies on the road I thought it might have been an accident so slowed to a crawl,' Kevin Skinner said. 'Then the passenger window seemed to explode and I yelled to Tracey to get down. I felt her head hit my knee and thought she had done what I said. The first shot was followed by four or five more and I tried to accelerate but the car coughed and spluttered, nearly stalling. I drove past and started to slow down, when I looked at Tracey she had no face left. Adam was sitting against the door just staring at her.'

Kenneth Stanton, unaware of the danger before him, rode his motorcycle heading for work in the city. Out of the darkness a bullet ripped through his left thigh into the petrol tank and he fell to the road screaming in agony from his massive wound. Knight approached from the shadows, took aim at the injured young man and, in Knight's own words, 'finished him off' with another two bullets.

Knight found cover by running along the railway lines towards Merri Creek, a kilometre from Hoddle Street. The driver of a passenger train was horrified to see the armed Knight, illuminated in the train's headlights, walking along the tracks straight towards him. He and his twenty-five passengers were in danger and as he began to reverse Knight suddenly veered away towards the shelter of the creek when a helicopter passed overhead. Knight crossed the knee-deep water and climbed a bank under a bridge. Constable

Colin Chambers was directing traffic on the bridge and did not see Knight take aim with the M14. He felt an impact on his back followed by an explosion and dived for cover. A high calibre bullet had torn through his duty jacket, burning his skin. Chambers could easily have been Knight's eighth fatality.

Constable Keith Stewart and his crew in the police helicopter above switched on their Nitesun searchlight and saw a shadowy figure run across the creek to a hiding place under the bridge. Suddenly the 3400 kg craft lurched and a strong burning smell and the unmistakable odour of jet fuel filled the cockpit. Stewart made an emergency landing in a nearby reserve and the crew scrambled out. A hole the size of a fist had torn through the skin of the helicopter and jet fuel poured from one of the punctured tanks. The chances of an in-flight fire or explosion were seriously high and would have meant certain death for the crew.

The departure of the helicopter disappointed Knight who fully expected a Special Operations Group (SOG) marksman to be on board. His wish to be fired on would not be fulfilled. Knight, low on ammunition, made his way along McKean Street towards his ex-girlfriend's home but his progress was hindered when he heard a police car approaching at speed. Two constables, directing traffic on Rushall Crescent, had seen a crouched figure run across the road and gave chase. Knight turned into an alleyway and dropped down out of sight. The car driven by Constable John Delahunty came to a screeching halt with the headlights pointed to the alley. As Constables Delahunty and Ralph Lockman got out of the car, Knight let off a dozen rapid shots, the muzzle flashes so great that Knight couldn't even see his target. The constables dived for cover but the explosions were so loud they thought the gunman was right above them. Delahunty, with blood trickling down his cheek from shrapnel wounds, returned a single shot from his revolver, narrowly missing Knight's head. Out of ammunition, Knight felt in his pocket for the bullet he kept for the 'final solution' but could not find it. Unable to take his own life he held the rifle in front of him and let it drop.

'Don't shoot, don't shoot,' Knight called out.

'Get out in the light where I can see you,' Lockman shouted back at the pleading gunman.

'I've had military experience,' Knight kept saying as he was manacled and bundled into the back of a police car.

Following Knight's capture, paramedics were finally able to attend some of the 19 wounded victims. Already Vesna Markovska was dead as were Robert Mitchell, Dusan Flajnik, Tracey Skinner and Kenneth Stanton. Of those who ran to Vesna's aid, only Stephen Wight and Peter Curmi would survive their injuries, with John Muscat dying of head injuries the next day.

Ambulance officer Noel Shiels attended to Gina Papaionnou and was horrified when he lifted the police coat covering her. The huge wound to her hip looked for all the world like a shark bite, such was the type of ammunition Knight had chosen for his powerful M14. Gina was conscious and followed the paramedic's movements with her eyes.

'Can you tell me your name?' Noel asked.

'Gina,' she replied.

'Can you tell me your surname?' but Gina was too weak and just shook her head.

Noel felt her skin - it was very cold. She had lost a lot of blood and was in deep shock, her pulse was rapid and thready, and her blood pressure was unrecordable. Gina was appearing to drift away so he asked, 'Can you tell me what happened?'

She looked up at Noel and said weakly, 'I got out to help.'

Gina looked as if she wanted to say something else but didn't have the strength. Eleven agonising days later Gina Papaionnou died.

THE DOLPHIN IN THE NET

In the world of mass murderers Julian Knight is a rarity. He is one of the few survivors, and in the hours following his capture he gave a fascinating insight into the mind of a mass killer when he took detectives on a tour of his 'killing zone'. Knight's composure and matter-of-fact answers, coupled with a seeming total lack of emotion, were chilling.

Excerpts from transcripts of Knight's lengthy interview with

Detective Senior Sergeant McCarthy and Detective Senior Constable Kent of the Victoria Police Homicide Squad reveal some interesting thought processes.

McCarthy: OK. Would you start off telling me what caused this thing tonight?

Knight: I dunno.

McCarthy: Why did you go and get those firearms out and ammunition?

Knight: 'Cos I was going to go out with them - out into the street.

McCarthy: Yeah, all right - and why did you want to do that?

Knight: I wanted to see what it was like to kill someone, and I knew as soon as I killed someone the police would arrive, and then the SOG, and they would finish me off.

McCarthy: Right - did you want to be finished off?

Knight: Yes.

McCarthy: Why?

Knight: I don't know [*upset*].

McCarthy: Was it something you'd been thinking about through the afternoon or was it a sudden decision you made?

Knight: [*Crying*]

McCarthy: Is it painful for you to think about it?

Knight: [*Crying*] Been thinking about it for years. [*Crying*]

McCarthy: What have you been thinking about for years?

Knight: What it would feel like to kill someone - and get killed in return.

McCarthy: What age were you when you started thinking about that?

Knight: [*Crying*] Only about 16 or 17.

Knight talked about his intention to kill people, to keep on shooting until he ran out of ammunition and displayed his fantasies to fight.

McCarthy: You said from the age of 16 you had a desire to kill?

Knight: Desire to fight. I thought about East Timor, Irian Jaya, Philippines, Thailand, Burma, Afghanistan, Iran, Iraq, Beirut. Specially wanted to go to South Africa, Central America - anywhere there was a shit fight on.

At 7 am the interview was suspended. Knight then asked for newspapers to see how the incident had been written up. Alone in the room, but still being videotaped, he eagerly rushed to the papers and appeared not to be able to read them quickly enough. After a break, Knight went with the detectives to retrace his route and though handcuffed he was otherwise free to move about. All around Hoddle Street police emergency tape sealed off the scene. Cars and a motorbike were left where they stopped, eerie reminders of the terror unleashed by Knight the evening before. What was striking about the reconstruction, recorded on video, was Knight's unbelievable calmness and matter-of-fact answers. When Knight was asked what his intentions were towards the people in the cars, he answered without the slightest hesitation. 'Kill them,' Knight said in a clear voice.

He then described what happened next. 'The first one fell on to the road and the second one, I don't know where he came from but I dropped him as well,' Knight said.

The detective asked him if the victims appeared dead.

'The one that fell back on the road wasn't . . . I let off another two rounds,' Knight said, still showing no emotion.

'For what purpose?' the detective asked.

'To finish her off,' Knight replied.

Knight was asked about the motorcyclist and pointed to where the rider had swerved and fallen. 'He was moaning in agony so I put another two rounds in him,' Knight calmly continued. 'It was always impressed on me it's better to be killed than to be seriously wounded and this bloke sounded seriously wounded.'

In Knight's mind he was justified in killing the man in a kind of warped sense of compassion.

PSYCHOLOGICAL PROFILE

Forensic psychiatrist Dr Allen Bartholomew interviewed Knight and it was immediately apparent Knight was of at least average intelligence and was not clearly psychotic. The first brief interview elicited information such as Knight's court appearance for a schoolboy assault, his views on discipline at Duntroon and how a senior cadet had fondled Knight's girlfriend's breasts in front of him. He talked of being 'illegally' confined to barracks in the incident leading up to the fracas and stabbing at the Private Bin.

A longer interview, later that same Monday morning, was far more revealing. Knight told Dr Bartholomew he had been fighting 'almost as long as I can remember, much of it at primary school where I would stick up for others being bullied.'

Knight recalled incidents at Fitzroy High School, claiming to have been hit once or twice by what he termed 'ethnics'. Over the hour-and-a-half Knight talked about his life at university, the army reserve, the Royal Military College and of thoughts of wanting to join the Victoria Police.

'He spoke of his family and this area of enquiry would seem of some real importance,' Dr Bartholomew said. 'Every time the matter was touched upon he became very tearful. His natural mother was an Australian girl now living in South Africa, and to this end he claims a love and fascination for South Africa and wants to be a soldier there, especially in towns like Soweto.'

Dr Bartholomew gained the impression that Knight clearly had much affection for his parents, not least his father, who was an instructor in the army with the rank of Major. But Knight was very angry his adoptive parents lied to him over their divorce intentions. However, Dr Bartholomew could find no evidence that Knight's family background played any important part in his behaviour of 9 August. What did markedly impress the psychiatrist was how Knight's mental state changed from tearfulness (when speaking of family matters and his ex-girlfriend Renee) to elation and exaltation when speaking of killing and being in a combat situation. *Then his eyes lit up, he sat in a more upright manner and his tearfulness cleared up.*' [Emphasis added]

Dr Bartholomew went to the hospital wing of Pentridge Jail, where Knight was held for his protection, on Saturday 15 August 1987. His mental state was the same as previously, except when speaking of his adoptive parents, his ex-girlfriend, and shooting his victims, he not only cried but wept hysterically.

'I could only catch odd words and phrases as he wept in this manner rocking on his mattress,' Dr Bartholomew said. 'His hands were over his face and he was pulling his hair. He said disjointedly "everything was moving fast . . . very fast . . . the face did not exist . . . just white . . . not people, just targets like we were trained . . . noisy . . . everything coloured . . . unreal . . . I must be a fucking cunt . . . shit . . . shit."'

To snap him out of his despair the doctor told Knight to 'stop that', then asked a neutral question (about the mattress). Knight stopped weeping and continued a sensible, coherent conversation.

After watching the cold clinical approach of Knight on the police interview tapes, and the rather odd request of Knight for the newspaper accounts of the tragedy, the doctor concluded Knight was not insane. 'He has moments of depression or disdain of a reactive type but then is "normal". If a diagnostic label has to be affixed it is Personality Disorder,' Dr Bartholomew remarked.

Another to evaluate Knight was Dr Kenneth Byrne, a forensic psychologist. He believed Knight had several very serious difficulties. 'Knight is overwhelmingly self-centred and immature,' he said. 'He can see things from his point of view and only from his point of view. He tends to get on other people's nerves causing them to become irritated with him without having any idea that he personally has produced this. He then feels like a victim. He collects causes and injustices that other people have done this or that to him. Then all of this builds up a lot of rage, resentment and anger.'

Following several lengthy interviews, Knight's defence psychiatrist, Dr David Sime, prepared a comprehensive report. It was clear to the doctor that Knight had a low tolerance to stress, and subsequent overreactions saw him turn to violence, exacerbated when drinking. Although intelligent, Knight was emotionally unstable, and had a strong, compulsive obsessive streak indicating a serious personality disorder.

The months leading up to the rampage were times of escalating environmental stress in Knight's life, heightened by a series of rejections. His forced removal from the army, thwarted attempts to contact his birth mother, and rejections from girlfriends, coupled with his parents' divorce left Knight vulnerable. Contributing to his downfall was Knight's pathological sensitivity to rejection. However, it was Knight's commitment to things military that was the most fundamental influence in the whole situation. Knight's fantasies all revolved around imagining himself in battle situations, particularly where he became the hero/anti-hero. He would not die but be wounded. Fantasies ranged from being a Roman legionary to a French paratrooper, or a German tank commander at some particular historical battle. Much of his thinking was military-based. When asked to write a list of feelings or strong opinions Knight listed apartheid, civil unrest, martial law, subversive elements in society and racism. For sounds he liked to hear he listed gunfire, helicopters, shouted commands and heavy boots marching.

Before Knight left the hotel on the Sunday night he had a vision of men in combat. This created an impulse to get his guns and go out onto Hoddle Street. There seems little doubt from studying his background, coupled with the opinions of psychiatrists and psychologists, that Julian Knight fits quite comfortably into the category of 'pseudo-commando'.

CONCLUSION

When Knight was sentenced to life imprisonment on each of the seven counts of murder, and ten years on each of the 46 counts of attempted murder, the judge said Knight would not become eligible for parole for 27 years. However, he offered a glimmer of hope to the 19-year-old mass killer:

> Your prognosis is undoubtedly better than that of someone with brain damage because it appears that your condition is likely to improve as you mature over a period of years when you will cease to be a danger to the public. It was common ground among the doctors that in 20-25 years' time the degree

of change, and therefore the degree of danger which you present, can be assessed. In that sense it is thought that your prognosis is reasonable, particularly as you are bright and have a desire to better yourself.

So what has happened to Julian Knight in the 12 years he has been in maximum security? Soon after he began his 27 years' incarceration a neuropsychological assessment was made, testing him with the 'Wechsler Adult Intelligence Scale'. His IQ score of 132 placed him in the very superior range on the Wechsler classification, a range shared by a little over two per cent of the population. Taking advantage of his opportunities he has pursued an educational path, having a Bachelor of Arts degree from the Deakin University conferred on him in May 1996. While his grades do not indicate a superior intellect, they were nevertheless sufficient to gain the degree. Knight chose papers on media studies, psychology, political rights, and modern industrial society, and majored in strategic and defence studies. His highest mark was for a study of Asian defence policies, clear evidence that Julian Knight has still not rid himself of his all-consuming interest. Knight has also pursued a wide range of other studies as diverse as French, forklift operation and cooking.

Knight's interest in military matters was referred to by Professor Mullen in his report prepared for the parole board, dated 25 September 1997. Professor Mullen's report (which Julian Knight sent to the author) records:

> Mr Knight continues to be invested in an image of himself as part of the military and martial world. Even his academic studies centred on strategic and defence studies. Given the nature of Mr Knight's offence the continuing preoccupation with things military, and with himself as a soldier, cannot but raise concerns. In fairness to Mr Knight his psychological and emotional survival have to date probably owed much to his self-image as a disciplined soldier surviving in a hostile environment. No alternative structures, personal or intellectual, have been available to replace, for Mr Knight, the sustaining imagery of the military.

In the two years following Professor Mullen's assessment, courses of study undertaken by Knight have all been directed towards law subjects.

At Knight's trial, suggestions were made that he might have been in the early stages of a schizophrenic-type illness but the passage of time has proven those suggestions to be unfounded. Knight shows no evidence of any psychotic illness. At his trial he was variously described as being immature with a disordered personality, anti-social, narcissistic, self-centred, and hysterical. During his confinement Knight has been regarded as aloof and arrogant, which fits with the evaluations of him being self-absorbed.

Professor Mullen also writes:

A serious personality disorder was considered to have played a part in the tragedy. In the intervening years there is evidence Mr Knight has matured and a number of aspects of his then personality have been replaced by more adult ways of understanding and responding to the world.

It would be hoped that Knight might not only display more adult ways of responding, but that he also puts some of the Hoddle Street fascination behind him. While researching material for *Killing for Pleasure* the author made contact with Knight. In his reply Knight referred to a range of references: 'Given that you have made a detailed study of mass murder I assume you have obtained most of the main published material on the subject.'

He recommended a number of publications and supplied names, addresses and phone numbers of academic authors in the United States of America. What was perplexing was an extract from a draft research file on the Hoddle Street shootings. In the covering letter Knight wrote:

The research file I have enclosed is an extract from a draft paper I have compiled on my case. It should provide you with a good base for an examination of my case.

The information on Knight gathered for *Killing for Pleasure* came from police reconstructions and statements from victims and witnesses listed on the police homicide file and the coroner's inquest file. The police version differs slightly from Knight's recollections. However, it is interesting how he himself sees the events as they unfolded. From his own perspective, some parts of his 3,500-word summary are reproduced as follows. By substituting the word 'I' for 'Knight', the reading of the following extracts graphically illustrates the predatory nature of Knight's action, a nature so characteristic of pseudo-commandos.

It was now 9.39 pm and numerous police units were rushing to the scene. Knight dropped the empty Mossberg shotgun on the ground and took up a prone firing position with his M14 rifle. At this point Vesna Markovska broke cover from behind her car and made for the footpath on the eastern side of Hoddle Street. As she stepped on to the footpath she was spotted by Knight who fired a shot which seriously wounded her. When she fell back on to the roadway Knight fired two further shots which killed her . . .

Immediately following this shot Robert Mitchell, who had driven through the ambush zone unscathed and parked his car further down Hoddle Street, ran up the eastern side of the street in an attempt to render assistance to the fallen Markovska. As he reached her and came to a halt, Knight quickly fired a shot at him which hit him in the right side of the head and killed him instantly . . .

Immediately afterwards Knight fired at the rider of a motorcycle, Kenneth Stanton, who was hit in the left leg and fell on to the roadway. As he lay there Knight shot him a further two times and he eventually died . . . . Knight continued to reload and change position as he continued to fire at the passing cars. The next car Knight fired at was a car containing Kevin Skinner, his wife Tracey and their son Adam. Tracey was killed instantly by a blast to the face and Adam, who was on her lap below the window sill, received minor glass wounds . . .

At this point Knight, who was surrounded by at least forty armed police officers, decided to withdraw from the area and begin 'hunting' police officers. It was just after 9.45 pm and he'd expended 40 rounds of .22 calibre bullets, 25 rounds of 12-gauge buckshot and 32 rounds of 7.62 mm calibre bullets in the preceding 15 minutes. Five people lay dead, two were fatally wounded and a further 17 had been wounded. In addition to the expended ammunition, Knight had lost his 'suicide' bullet and another 7.62 mm bullet as he had moved up the nature strip. Knight had also lost his knife on the nature strip. He now retained only his M14 rifle and 17 rounds of ammunition.

Knight's matter-of-fact descriptions, terms used such as 'ambush zone' and 'hunting' police are rather disturbing. He describes the events in an intricate but somehow detached way. The murder of Tracey Skinner was particularly disturbing, yet Julian Knight describes her death in a dispassionate way, devoid of feeling.

To seek a balanced view of Knight's actions he was invited to respond to a series of questions. Again, in the interests of balance and fairness some of those answers are referred to.

Tess Lawrence, the journalist who interviewed Knight in the early part of his sentence, is adamant Knight despised Vitkovic and spoke of Ryan as if he were a 'pupil'. Another journalist who interviewed Knight claimed he spoke of Charles Whitman as if he were an old friend. Twelve years on, Julian Knight rejects these inferences. He claimed to have had a limited knowledge of Whitman's and Huberty's exploits, and says they are not, and were not, 'heroes' of his. In regard to Vitkovic and Ryan, Julian Knight wrote:

It disturbs me that both of them apparently viewed my actions as an incentive for their own actions. Apart from that I don't really have any views on them.

The 31-year-old Knight said, 'I am certainly not the same person I was in 1987, but surely this is to be expected, given that I was only 19 then.' One hopes that Julian Knight has matured and that he will be able to put his militaristic tendencies behind him. When he reaches the age of 46 he will be eligible for parole. It would not bode well for society if, in the interim, the dolphin became a shark.

Footnote: In March 1998 Knight attacked a fellow murderer inmate using a snooker ball in a sock and a hand-made baton. For that assault he was sentenced to six months jail to be served concurrently with his life term. In October 1999 he allegedly used a screwdriver to stab another inmate following an altercation over the use of a computer.

CHAPTER FOUR
MICHAEL RYAN

HUNGERFORD'S MYTHOMANIAC
Hungerford, England – 19 August 1987
Victims: 16 dead, 15 injured

INTRODUCTION

Nestled in the Kennet Valley in the English Midlands is the picture postcard market town of Hungerford. Surrounded by beautiful English countryside, the township of 5,000 inhabitants seems idyllic, not just for the quiet, slow pace of life, but the low crime rate. Living conditions are predominantly of a high standard and the valley is rich in history dating back centuries. The law-abiding traditions of the area are such that prior to 19 August 1987, the act of murder last occurred in December 1876. The Tilbury brothers, a couple of poachers, killed two police officers. The brothers were convicted and hanged for their despicable crimes.

But 111 years later the peace and tranquillity of Hungerford was to be torn apart when Michael Ryan walked the town's streets leaving 16 people dead in his wake and the lives of hundreds in ruins.

MAKING OF A MURDERER

To the casual observer, Michael Robert Ryan was a fortunate young man. Having left school at the age of 16 without qualifications, and despite having few employment opportunities, he was destined to become wealthy.

Whilst working as a gardener, on one of his sporadic forays into employment, Ryan came across a dog that had strayed from its home. Being familiar with dogs, Ryan returned the lost animal to its grateful owner. Instantly a friendship grew between Ryan and his new found friend, a retired colonel in his 90s. It may have been an odd friendship, for the two used to dress up and play soldiers. But it seems the elderly gent was grateful for the company and began to bestow upon Ryan some of his considerable wealth. With a tea plantation in India, a large hotel in Eastbourne, and a mansion near Hungerford, the colonel was in a position to reward those closest to him.

The five-bedroomed mansion was signed over to Michael Ryan, and he and his widowed mother were able to use it whenever they chose to. Through the colonel's generosity Ryan was able to take flying lessons in fixed wing aircraft as well as helicopters. Ryan and his mother were invited to visit the tea plantation and to take holidays at the hotel. And Michael would be able to drive his mother to Eastbourne in the Ferrari bought for him by the colonel.

Ryan was not only a beneficiary of the colonel's wealth but also the favourite of the colonel's nurse, and soon the couple became engaged to marry. But tragedy intervened. The nurse fell from a horse and was admitted to hospital, forcing the wedding to be called off. This was the second engagement for Michael Ryan, the first being called off when his fiancée refused to buy Mrs Ryan a birthday present.

Ryan's association with the colonel was dogged by other misfortunes. A trip to India was called off because of a bad storm, and the colonel's housekeeper died suddenly of food poisoning after eating crab meat. Dorothy Ryan was so distraught at the news that tears welled in her eyes as she related the story to friends and relatives. Clearly Dorothy Ryan believed the stories of the colonel and related Michael's fortunate turn in life to many people.

But that is all they were - stories. The colonel never existed. The cars, plantations, flying lessons and fiancées were all elaborate creations woven into Michael Ryan's mind. Whether his mother genuinely believed the stories, or for some reason colluded with her son to keep the fantasy alive, will never be known. Friends and relatives were in no doubt that Dorothy had convinced herself the colonel was real.

A mythomaniac is a psychiatric term used to describe someone who has a tendency to lie, exaggerate or relate incredible imaginary adventures as if they had really happened. This occurs with some mental disorders. The imaginary colonel, and other fanciful tales Ryan wove, place him in the category of mythomaniac.

Michael Ryan was the only child of Alfred and Dorothy, and when he was born on 18 May 1960, his parents were already older than the average age for starting a family. Dorothy was 36, but considerably younger than Alfred, then aged 53. When Alfred Ryan died of cancer at 78, his death had a profound effect on his son, then aged 25.

Dorothy and Michael were left together in the council-owned terraced house at 4 Southview, Hungerford. Michael Ryan had lived there all his life, and it would be from there that he would begin his reign of terror in the town. Alfred worked as a building inspector for the Hungerford Borough Council and was regarded as a perfectionist and strict disciplinarian. Some people said there was no love lost between Alfred Ryan and his son, while others believed the opposite. Relatives said Alfred was 'Michael's life' and the young man seemed to change following his father's death. While they regarded Michael as moody and self-centred, with an introverted personality, he suddenly became more outgoing and relaxed after his father's demise. Regardless of how the pair got on, Michael Ryan took great care of his father during the man's prolonged illness. The suffering of a drawn-out death got to Alfred Ryan and he once asked his son to leave a loaded firearm nearby so the end could be hastened.

'No,' his son replied, refusing his father's request, 'that's not what guns are for.'

The relationship between Dorothy Ryan and her son was more clearly defined. Dorothy simply doted on her only son. This could have been in part due to Dorothy giving birth to a stillborn child two years prior to Michael's birth - after this event she gave up hope of rearing any children. Throughout Ryan's life his mother would ensure he had whatever he wanted, be it toys as a child, motorcycles as an adolescent, or motor cars as he headed towards adulthood.

Relatives and acquaintances, however, were divided over their beliefs about the relationship. On one hand, it was thought Dorothy over-mothered her son, while others claimed she henpecked her boy to a degree where he didn't like going home. The truth is probably somewhere in the middle, but it is an inescapable fact that Mrs Ryan lavished her son with anything he wanted. That alone did not make Dorothy Ryan strange. She was popular and well-regarded around Hungerford, and were she to have lived would have been devastated by the shame her son was to bring on the family.

Michael Ryan was ill-equipped to work at anything that would bring in a high pay packet, but he didn't have to. His mother maintained two jobs. During the day she worked as a dinner lady at the nearby primary school, and on evenings and weekends she was employed as a silver service waitress at the fashionable Elcot Park Hotel. Dorothy was able to buy her son a car as soon as he had a licence, and she updated it every two years. While she could afford her son's indulgences, she was left with little for herself. When Michael and his mother met their deaths on that dreadful August afternoon, the unemployed Michael left a thousand pounds in his building society. Conversely, his hardworking mother had just 25 pounds in her building society account and was overdrawn by 800 pounds at the bank.

Some aspects of the relationship between Ryan and his mother were quite unusual. On occasions, when Mrs Ryan was without her car, Michael would pick her up from the hotel.

'She used to become agitated when Michael picked her up,' an acquaintance, Pamela Sculler, said. 'She would say things like, "I must go because Michael's waiting," it was as if he didn't like to be kept waiting.'

Dorothy mostly drove herself to work and on every occasion telephoned her son as soon as she arrived. She would let the phone ring three times then hang up, 'to let Michael know I've arrived safely'. The strange ritual would be repeated just prior to leaving work.

Michael Ryan's childhood lacked one vital ingredient - the company of his peers. The boy was always alone and had very few friends. As a pupil he was unremarkable, an 'anonymous sort of lad', and 'a rather awkward loner', according to teachers. Even when picked on by other boys he never stood up for himself. Other children, finding him moody and sulky, tended to leave him alone while some, sensing Ryan's isolation, made him the target of their bullying. The unpopular and lonely boy's life at school was quite miserable. Ryan was not academically motivated, preferring to be a truant and ride his motorcycle than gain qualifications. This was a source of disappointment and irritation to his parents, particularly Alfred, who had hoped the boy would amount to something. Clearly the father was irritated at this failure and his annoyance increased as he watched his wife spoil the lad.

There was speculation that Alfred Ryan was overly strict with discipline regarding both his son and wife. Michael never complained about being bullied or assaulted by his father, but the attention Alfred sometimes directed towards his wife seemed more obvious. Close relatives believed Alfred was a violent husband who tended to knock his wife about. There was speculation that Michael may have adopted his father's attitude towards his mother. In early 1987 Dorothy arrived at work with bruising and swelling to an eye and she claimed she had fallen over a neighbour's dog but in the same conversation mentioned their garden shed. It was in this shed that Michael Ryan kept his formidable arsenal. If Alfred Ryan did in fact beat his wife, it is quite possible that, through learned behaviour, the eye injury may well have been the result of Michael lashing out in anger at his mother going near 'his' shed.

Relatives and neighbours regarded Michael Ryan as a loner and a remote and inadequate person. His Aunt Nora found him to be very quiet. 'He was the sort of person you couldn't get very close to,' she said. 'He seemed to behave the way a person that was older than he was would.'

This was hardly surprising, as the only people he regularly associated with were his ageing parents. But where Nora found Ryan to be a poor mixer with no friends, his Aunt Constance found her nephew to be a kind and gentle boy. She would often visit the Ryan household, taking the train from London for regular visits. Constance made all the visits, never the other way around. Michael would pick her up at the station and drop her back for the return home. Ryan's 'Walter Mitty' persona was also obvious to Constance. On each visit it seemed that Michael had another girlfriend and the aunt was invited to one of his pending weddings. She was never told who the lucky girl was or the reasons why the marriages were called off.

The weather around Hungerford was overcast and showery when Constance made one visit. Ryan wanted to show his aunt the countryside, so took her and his mother for a ride in his car. They drove to an area overlooking Hungerford, a place Ryan confessed to visiting regularly. He liked the spot as the clouds gave him a strange feeling. He pointed out a building saying a murder had happened there a few years beforehand. This was yet another of Ryan's fantasies as no murder had occurred in the town for more than a century. The next murders in that small settlement would be at his hands.

It was obvious to Constance that her nephew rarely worked, as he was always at home whenever she visited. His occasional jobs had been as a gardener at a nursery and as gardener/handyman at a girls' school. He also worked as a handyman on a large estate in nearby Newbury. Ryan's history of sporadic employment was unspectacular and he would have remained anonymous except for one occasion when he shot a green woodpecker, an action that offended his workmates. At other times Ryan signed on with the Department of Health and Social Security to draw an unemployment benefit.

Ryan's relationships with women were generally dismal. His mother often remarked how she wished Michael would find a girlfriend and employment so he could settle down. The so-called fiancées he had were figments of his imagination. He simply lacked the skills to maintain effective relationships with the opposite sex. He was often seen in local bars having a drink and one thing was constant - he was always alone. He did meet a waitress and made a nuisance of himself by persistently asking her out. Ryan couldn't take 'no' for an answer and was finally warned off by friends of the waitress. He didn't take kindly to the warning and, as is common with mass killers, stored the rejection and caution as a grudge.

Ryan was neither a homosexual nor a misogynist. He was simply a loner. His fantasies about marriage tend to rule out a hatred of women. After Ryan's death a supposed gay lover came forward and told the media about the pair's love affair. This was simply a ploy whereby the 'lover' would make money from selling his sensational story to the highest bidder.

The feeling of power when holding a gun is a significant feature in the makeup of mass murderers. Ryan enjoyed that sense of power, and told his Aunt Constance about an incident in the countryside. When he came upon a 'stroppy' man out shooting rabbits, Ryan produced a handgun and pointed it at the stranger, forcing him to run away.

From an early age Ryan had a fascination with things military, not that he was into modern gun collecting. That was to come later. His only hobby was an impressive collection of antique firearms and swords. Ryan was known to walk around Hungerford with the air of a soldier but he never belonged to any military organisation. He may have wanted to pass on the air and mystique of the military life, but any connection was only in his mind. He once boasted to a youngster that he was an ex-paratrooper and told others he was kicked out of the army for fighting. He was regularly seen wearing camouflage or combat clothing and paratrooper-style boots. Several people remarked on his style of clothing. At times he played out his fantasies by telling colleagues he would camouflage himself and creep up on picnickers in the local forest. He would watch for a while then disappear, enjoying the fact he went undetected. Other people were told of Ryan's four trips to Africa where he fought as a mercenary. Again, this was a fantasy, conjured up in his mind. Ryan had never been issued with a passport and had never left the British Isles. His descriptions of African expeditions and an elaborate trip on the Orient Express simply never happened.

For most of his life Michael Ryan was a shadowy figure who never gave away anything about himself. He was often seen out and about, distinctive in the sunglasses he always wore, regardless of the weather. Yet people who knew him didn't really know much about him at all.

TOWARDS THE END

While Michael Ryan had an avid interest in guns in the months leading up to his rampage, it had not been a life-long obsession. Through his earlier interests in antique firearms, Ryan became a frequent visitor to dealers and spent a lot of money on 'feeding his habit'. Where he might pay £100 for an antique naval sword, he was also prepared to pay well over £1,000 for a pair of silver mounted Queen Anne pistols. As late as March 1987 Ryan was still buying antique weapons. He paid £250 for a nineteenth-century percussion pistol, but his cheque bounced. The cost of his habit outstripped his ability to pay and the cheque was returned to the dealer marked 'refer to drawer'.

During his many negotiations with antique dealers, some of Ryan's odd behaviour and Walter Mitty lifestyle emerged. Edred Gwilliam was one dealer with whom Ryan did business. Two of Ryan's more elaborate stories were told to Mr Gwilliam. Ryan had said he was married to an Irish girl who had got pregnant to him. They had bought an old cottage near Hungerford and were in the process of renovating it. While the renovations were going on he lived with his wife and child at the Southview home. Ryan's wife couldn't get on with his mother so moved out. The marriage subsequently disintegrated when he found his wife in bed with an elderly uncle. The wife and baby returned to Ireland while Ryan continued to work for the uncle.

There wasn't a shred of truth in the story, as was the case with another tale he wove for the dealer. Ryan explained that, when his father died, he left Michael a considerable amount of money which he used to set up a partnership with a friend. The two had supposedly set up a house renovating business in London, employing a dozen workmen. The business folded because the partner had taken all the money and run off to Australia.

Gareth Vincent dealt solely in antique weapons, armour and uniforms. Exactly a year before the killings at Hungerford, Ryan phoned Mr Vincent offering a collection of swords for sale. Ryan dictated a very detailed list of swords he had available, quoting book references for similar items. He knew exactly what amount he wanted for each item but said if the dealer would buy the entire collection Ryan would be prepared to reduce the prices. Ryan confided to Vincent that he had previously had bad deals from auctioneers, had become fed up with the whole antiques scene and wanted to sell everything. Mr Vincent visited Ryan at his Southview home. After some small talk about the dealer's Rover car, Ryan showed off his Vauxhall Astra and said the car might have to go as well. The men went inside where negotiations took place. As they went into the lounge Ryan called out to his mother in the kitchen, asking her to make coffee. The swords, all very attractive well-decorated weapons, were laid out on a table.

'They've all got to go,' Ryan said.

He went through each item, sword by sword, and haggled over each price. A supposed pending marriage and the purchase of a cottage were, according to Ryan, going to take all of his cash. Later on he said he needed money for a business venture. Each time the men differed over a price Ryan would raise one or other of the reasons he needed money for. The negotiations took most of the afternoon and the men drank several cups of coffee. During these breaks Ryan's behaviour was odd.

'It seemed strange that his mother never came into the room,' Gareth Vincent said. 'Each time she would knock on the door he would open it just wide enough to accept the coffees which were passed through one at a time.'

The two finally agreed on a price for the swords, and then Ryan showed the dealer a collection of books and framed pictures of antique guns. 'He began going through the books one by one at which point I said I didn't deal in books.'

Ryan asked if Mr Vincent would give him £50 for the books to which the dealer reluctantly agreed. The transactions ended up totalling a substantial £3,000. Ryan wasn't convinced the price was correct. 'That can't be right,' he said and got his own calculator to check the figures.

The calculator worked by light and kept fading out in the middle of Ryan's calculations. It took almost half-an-hour before Ryan eventually came to the same total. The negotiations had taken some hours. With several cups of coffee inside him and the prospect of a drive home, Mr Vincent asked if he could use the toilet. Ryan made an excuse and refused, pocketed the cheque for £3,000 and bade Mr Vincent farewell.

Those transactions saw an end to the only hobby Ryan had. His interest in weaponry changed and soon after he began collecting the modern day pistols and rifles that he was to use with such deadly effect.

Following the Hungerford killings the *Sunday Mirror* ran a story entitled 'Ryan sold guns to underworld'. The report said, '. . . he was a key figure in an illegal gun dealing network and handled "hot" guns used in hold ups.'

Such reports might have been nurtured by Ryan's boasting about being able to get weapons for people. Police enquiries into these, and other stories about Ryan, showed they had no basis. The guns Ryan owned were all legally owned and registered.

Community beat police at Hungerford deal with the majority of firearm applications. On 30 November 1986 Constable Ronald Hoyes went to Ryan's home at 4 Southview to make enquiries into the granting of a firearms certificate. The constable found Ryan to be a quiet individual who was extremely polite. The home was untidy and cluttered with furniture. The constable was shown Ryan's membership card to the Dunmore Shooting Centre at Abingdon. Ryan said he was a keen pistol shooter and that he would be joining other shooting clubs. Ryan had held a shotgun certificate since his 18th birthday, but required another certificate to possess rifles and pistols. His initial application was to own a Smith & Wesson .38 pistol he said was for target and competition shooting. He had a Chubb purpose-built firearms cabinet secured in the front bedroom. Police did not find anything to the detriment of Ryan in character enquiries, and a certificate was issued. The constable returned to see Ryan in early 1987 to update the certificate when Ryan sold the .38 and bought two target pistols. Nothing was untoward in either the character references or storage facilities. The constable visited Ryan for the final time in June 1987 for another update. Again he found Ryan extremely polite, but commented he felt Ryan was a loner.

A Czechoslovakian target pistol Ryan bought in 1986 came from a dealer who advertised in a target gun magazine; nothing that passed between Ryan and the dealer gave cause for concern. Less than a week before the killings, Ryan bought an AK47 Kalashnikov with a cash deposit, intending to pay the balance with his Visa card. The following day he bought an Underwood carbine rifle. Only five days later he would unleash mayhem on Hungerford with chilling effect.

Michael Ryan honed his shooting skills at two clubs. He was a frequent visitor to the Dunmore club from August 1986 but was always alone. Visits would last an hour, with half the time on the range and the rest browsing in the shop. Occasionally he shot well, but more often than not his performance was below average. Apart from minor conversations with staff, Ryan kept to himself. Despite telling police he was going into competitive shooting he never did. Ryan showed a worker at the club a 9 mm Bergman gun that was lying loose in the boot of his car. Ryan was trying to get a magazine for the gun, and remarked in passing that he also had a Thompson machine gun and a Scorpion pistol. During 1987, he bought and sold several pistols and shotguns and purchased over 1000 rounds of ammunition.

Michael Dingle managed the Dunmore shooting centre, remembering Ryan as a quiet individual who never socialised with other members. On each visit, Ryan was distinctive in the camouflage jacket he wore. He never expressed any interest in club activities, saying he was content just to shoot for pleasure. A month before Hungerford, Ryan joined the Wiltshire Shooting Centre and purchased weapons from them. The day before he rampaged through the town, Ryan took his Kalashnikov to the range. Normally he would have had a brief conversation with the centre manager, but on that occasion he left without speaking.

The months leading up to the Hungerford disaster saw Ryan in a number of verbal confrontations with people. In April that year he began work at the Newbury District Council. He was employed clearing footpaths and mending fences on an environmental improvement scheme. At the time Ryan had been unemployed for a year but agreed to begin work on 7 April. He did not turn up for work either on that day or the next. When the scheme manager phoned Ryan to check on his whereabouts, Ryan said he was wondering whether to bother turning up but decided to the next day. Despite his initial reluctance to work, the manager found Ryan respectful and polite, though lacking in ambition. Ryan was introverted, usually working on his own, and during breaks would sit alone reading the paper. His work was satisfactory but his attendance wasn't. He came close to being fired when he failed to turn up for work on six occasions.

Charles Amor was one of the leading operatives on the work scheme and got to know Ryan. 'I must say that when I gave him a job he was a damned good worker. As far as Ryan is concerned I'd describe him as moody and surly,' said Amor. 'He was also a liar and I used to pick him up on it. Afterwards he said he liked me because I was straight up with him.' Amor also noticed how Ryan would take the 'mickey' out of other workers but didn't like it when the roles were reversed, and friction arose.

Ryan began to talk of his interest in guns, and during one lunch break said he always carried guns with him. Amor didn't believe him and thought it was just another lie. Ryan insisted and took his workmates to his car where he produced a pistol from under the passenger seat. Ryan removed the magazine and showed the others. It was loaded with ten rounds of ammunition. Amor was surprised, telling Ryan he could be imprisoned for carrying a loaded gun around. He told Ryan never to bring a gun to work again. Ryan was undaunted, saying he always carried a gun, then reached around to the waistband of his trousers and pulled out a small black pistol, fully loaded. He showed the men how to stand when shooting, raised the pistol to shoulder level, then simulated firing at targets.

'Ryan said whenever he went out at night he carried the Beretta pistol with another gun locked in his car,' Amor said.

Ryan bragged that he could get the men any kind of weapon they wanted, giving rise to subsequent claims he was an underworld dealer. Later, Ryan turned up to work with two shotguns, one a Russian model with animals beautifully engraved on the metal. The gun was new and had its identification numbers scratched out. Ryan was quite reckless in his display of weapons to virtual strangers. Had he been reported his gun licence might have been revoked but nothing was said to authorities. Ryan boasted about shooting road signs but Amor told Ryan they were just more of his lies. 'If you doubt me go and look for yourself,' Ryan had said. 'Sure enough,' said Amor, 'the signs he told me to look at had holes in them.'

A couple of days before Ryan finished on the community work scheme, he began to misbehave, hoping to get fired. He became abusive to Charles Amor and was generally slacking on the job. Had he been fired he would have been eligible to draw the unemployment benefit, but if he resigned he would get nothing. Eventually he did resign, saying he had another job arranged. He apologised to Amor for his behaviour. Ryan's time with the scheme was unhappy but could have been worse for fellow workers. After one particular ribbing by two colleagues Ryan said to Amor, 'If those two keep having a go at me I will shoot them.'

Ryan was fuming and Charles Amor sensed he really meant it. In hindsight, it was fortunate for the workmates that they ceased the taunting. Ryan had the weapons to carry out his threats and certainly had the mentality to do it.

It was evident that all was not well around Southview either. Dorothy Ryan had not been happy with neighbouring children picking her fruit and flowers. She also complained that the next-door neighbour's dog was a problem, regularly pulling her washing from the line. While this annoyed Mrs Ryan it made her son angry.

Arthur Whiting lived in a semi-detached cottage at the end of the road next to an open field on the Hungerford common. People frequently used the road as a thoroughfare to the common. Mr Whiting got to know the regulars on the road, including the Ryans. Over the years he had become friendly with Michael Ryan, whom he often saw with his dog Blackie. Ryan appeared quiet and civil but he did not approve of the bad language some of the kids in the street used. A week before the tragedy Whiting met Ryan on his way to the common. Ryan talked of having bought a new firearm and boasted of how he could hit a coin off a wall 100 metres away. Whiting never had difficulty conversing with Ryan and regularly discussed the neighbours.

'He told me he didn't like any of the neighbours,' Whiting said. 'He specially didn't like the ones at number 13, they were a wild bunch, always cussing and swearing.'

Arthur Whiting had his problems too. One of his hobbies was raising chickens, but these tended to stray on to adjacent land. A black mongrel dog owned by Ryan's next-door neighbours, the Lepetits, had killed a number of chickens. Whiting met Ryan on the common.

'Have you shot that dog yet Michael?' Whiting said jokingly. 'It's not the dog that wants shooting,' Ryan replied angrily, 'it's the bloody owner, he wants his head blown off!'

Several days later, Ryan was to shoot and injure Alan Lepetit during his random shootings in Hungerford. The next time Arthur Whiting saw Ryan it was at the height of the rampage.

Ryan's threats about the Lepetits were not the only ones he made to neighbours. Other abuses, though quite serious, were not reported to police. Ryan's only transgression with the law at that time was a minor infringement for speeding.

Sometime in the weeks leading up to Hungerford, Ryan was alleged to have had an altercation with Ivor Pask, another neighbour. The men had argued over an incident where Ryan's dog was fouling the Pask garden. While Mr Pask was reluctant to mention the incident, it was widely reported in newspapers following Ryan's death. In one paper it was reported that Ryan threatened Mr Pask saying, 'The next time I see you it will be with a knife'. Another report said Ryan held a knife as he taunted Mr Pask to 'come in here and fight'.

It seemed out of character for Ryan to be outwardly confrontational; usually he kept things to himself and built up grudges. However, it is clear that some threat was made, and Ryan was known to carry flick knives as well as firearms.

Another potentially more serious incident arose between Ryan and neighbour Mrs Reagan, who argued over children playing on the Ryans' driveway. He didn't like people encroaching on to his territory. Some days later, as Mrs Reagan was hanging washing on the line, Ryan fired pellets at her from an airgun. This wasn't the first time he had used an airgun to frighten people, it occurred in the past when he was a schoolboy. Now that he was in his mid-20s the act towards Mrs Reagan had sinister connotations.

When mass murderers begin to rampage there is rarely an obvious reason as to why it happens at the chosen time. There is always a steady build-up but the catalyst is usually unclear. In Ryan's case it could have been related to his mother's employment. About a fortnight prior to the Hungerford killings, the hotel where Dorothy Ryan had worked for 12 years was becoming busier. It was their policy to employ more full-time staff. Casual staff would still be needed but not as often. As a consequence, Dorothy Ryan's hours were to be cut, and though she was disappointed, she accepted the situation. On 9 August she began two weeks' holiday saying she was going to Eastbourne, no doubt to stay at the hotel of her son's mythical friend, the colonel. She was due to return to work on 16 August, but found another more stable job and tendered her resignation.

The day before the tragedy Dorothy seemed quite settled. She was quite excited at the prospect of a new job, and was reported to be in high spirits. Michael Ryan's welfare was very much dependent on the income from his mother's two jobs. It is possible the pending changes posed a threat to his lifestyle.

Ruth Goodman worked at the hotel and was one of Dorothy Ryan's closest acquaintances. Mrs Ryan told her friend she had been badly treated over the staff changes and that she had resigned. On the morning of 19 August Dorothy visited the hotel and asked Ruth to say goodbye to some of the staff. At 11.35 am Mrs Ryan left the hotel intent on going shopping at Newbury, and almost exactly one hour later her son began the killing spree that would catapult this insignificant man into the annals of criminal infamy.

MARKET TOWN TERROR

In comparison with other mass killings, the rampage by Michael Ryan was long-lasting. His first victim in the township fell at 12.47 pm and the last at 1.45 pm, a total of 58 minutes.

Because of communication difficulties and an unarmed police force, Ryan was able to move around with impunity. He had ample time to stop his carnage but chose to carry on.

The reign of terror began in the late morning of that autumn day. Eleven kilometres west of Hungerford is picturesque Savernake Forest, a popular spot for people to picnic or take strolls. On the morning of 19 August, 33-year-old Sue Godfrey took her children, aged four and two, on a picnic. Ryan, armed with his Beretta pistol, abducted Sue Godfrey, forcing her to walk 70 metres from her car. He had a groundsheet with him that he spread on the forest floor. From a scene reconstruction it seems that Ryan chanced upon the woman and decided on a sexual attack. It is just as likely that Mrs Godfrey attempted to escape and that Ryan shot her as she fled. Sue Godfrey's body was found ten metres from the groundsheet with 13 bullets in her back. Her four-year-old daughter heard the shots and saw Ryan run to his car and speed away.

Ryan fled the scene and headed for home, stopping first at the Golden Arrow petrol station. He was a regular customer there and would always buy £4 worth of petrol. On this occasion Ryan came from the opposite direction and filled his car's tank as well as a five-litre can. The cashier could see Ryan fiddling with something in the boot but took little notice until he raised a rifle to his shoulder and fired a bullet through the window, narrowly missing her. He entered the service station and fired again from three metres but missed, so moved right over to the cashier and fired again. The weapon jammed and the cashier, cowering on the floor, heard several clicks then Ryan's footsteps as he left to go back to his car.

By the time the frightened woman contacted the police Ryan was almost home. His car screeched to a halt in the driveway of 4 Southview. A neighbour watched him get out of the car and storm into his house, slamming the door after him. He had a peculiar look on his face later described as fierce.

Soon afterwards Ryan emerged from the house. He was wearing a bullet resistant vest and carried his Underwood carbine and Kalashnikov AK47. The Beretta pistol was in a holster. He threw a bag of survival gear into his car. In it he had packed a first aid kit, respirator and military clothing. It was obvious he was making his escape, but for the people of Hungerford there was to be a cruel twist of fate. Ryan's car refused to start. Enraged, Ryan poured petrol into his home and set it alight. Going back to his car he fired bullets into it, turned around and aimed his gun at the first of his Hungerford victims.

Mr and Mrs Mason lived a couple of doors from Ryan. Oblivious to what was unfolding, the couple were easy prey for Ryan. Both were murdered, one with the AK47 and the other with the Beretta pistol. Running eastward towards the common, Ryan shot at anyone he came across. People in the street were gunned down while other people had bullets screaming through their windows. Two young girls who knew Ryan watched him jogging along the road. When he saw them he stopped, turned to them and bent his legs to crouch. He brought the rifle to his shoulder and fired. Fourteen-year-old Lisa Mildenhall was struck in the leg but managed to escape.

'I looked straight in his face,' Lisa recalled, 'then he smiled at me before he fired.'

Kenneth Clements was briskly walking along Southview. His son Robert was trying to keep up when they came upon Ryan who was pointing the barrel of the rifle skyward. When he saw Clements, Ryan lowered the gun, took aim and fired, killing the defenceless man but allowing just enough time for Robert to escape. Not content with having felled Clements, Ryan was seen to take aim and fire another three or four rounds into his body.

Confusion had arisen at the police communications centre. Some police had been sent to the Golden Arrow petrol station to respond to calls from the cashier. As they sped there calls began coming in to say a man was going berserk in Hungerford. Unarmed police responded to the Hungerford calls and Constable Roger Brereton drove at speed into Southview. He came to a sudden halt when he was confronted by Ryan, who had stepped out from a garden and was firing shots into the police car. Constable Brereton only had time to call for help, saying he had been shot. Moments later he was dead. Ryan hadn't given the constable a chance, firing 24 bullets into the car.

A sergeant and two constables arrived at the scene and tried to assist, but when they came under fire from Ryan they had to retreat. Police control issued warnings for staff to take extreme care. They knew there was at least one gunman and that he was on the move and unable to be contained. The situation was desperate.

By now, Ryan had slowed to a walk, but he was still picking out targets with a deliberate aim. He fired on an ambulance crew responding to the tragedy. The crew saw Ryan in front of them raise his rifle before the windscreen exploded. The driver quickly reversed, saving herself and her wounded comrade from certain death.

Ryan's next victim was neighbour Alan Lepetit whom he lined up from over a hundred metres away. The first bullet Ryan fired hit Lepetit in the arm, knocking him to the ground, and as he got up a second bullet thudded into his thigh. Despite his injuries Lepetit ran to the refuge of a nearby shop.

At the very beginning of Ryan's rampage Mrs Marjorie Jackson had been one of his first victims. She was inside her home when Ryan fired a volley of shots through her window. Mrs Jackson was wounded in the back but managed to get to the phone to call her husband. Ivor Jackson and his friend George White responded to the call and as they turned into Southview their car was raked by a dozen bullets fired in rapid succession. The car crashed into the police car in which Constable Brereton had died shortly before. Mr White died instantly, but the seriously wounded Ivor Jackson remained in the car making out he was dead.

Moments later, Dorothy Ryan drove into Fairview Road where she was flagged down and told not to go further. Ignoring the advice she accelerated into Southview. There she saw her home on fire and the crashed cars on the road. She alighted from her car and walked past George White's Toyota. Ivor Jackson was still inside the car feigning death when Mrs Ryan walked past. He heard her say, 'Oh Ivor!' before she started running after her son.

She began shouting, 'Michael, Michael, stop it!'

But Michael didn't stop. He turned his gun on his mother. Witnesses heard Mrs Ryan call out, 'Don't shoot me,' but her anguished plea for mercy was followed by two loud bangs and a loud scream and she fell to the ground.

Ryan's final farewell to his mother was to put two more bullets into her back from point blank range. After killing his mother Ryan walked along the footpath. Behind him he left seven people dead and another seven injured.

Ryan took to nearby playing fields and passed 68-year-old Betty Tolladay. The elderly lady, unaware of the carnage, rebuked Ryan for making so much noise and swore at him. With that Ryan turned the gun on her, inflicting serious injuries.

Several children were playing on swings and slides near the memorial gardens and as Ryan approached them he fired on Francis Butler who was walking his dog. The man fell instantly to the ground, fatally wounded. Ryan could have easily killed the children but chose other targets instead. It could have been that, as he knelt near Mr Butler's body to reload, the youngsters had time to flee. It was at this point that Ryan discarded the carbine rifle.

Ryan continued his massacre unabated. His next victim was Marcus (Barney) Barnard who died in his taxi from head wounds. Inexplicably, Ryan threw his AK47 to the ground in disgust and turned to walk away, but after a few steps returned and retrieved it. At that moment it is possible Ryan had had enough of killing. If so the moment passed quickly and he resumed his horrible orgy of destruction using both the semi-automatic pistol and the lethal AK47. His aim was deliberate and calculated and he was taking his time.

Trevor Wainwright is one of the community constables stationed at Hungerford and knew Ryan. On the day of the massacre the constable's parents were arriving to stay with him. They entered the town unaware of the drama unfolding and came upon Ryan. The gunman pumped ten rounds into their car and Mr Wainwright died almost instantly. His wife, suffering serious injuries, screamed hysterically beside her dying husband and could only watch Michael Ryan reload his weapons and casually walk away.

Ryan was in total control and calmer than ever. At one stage he knelt to reload when an unsuspecting woman walked by. He simply looked up then went on reloading.

Ryan changed tack in Priory Road when he stopped outside the home of an elderly couple, Victor and Myrtle Gibbs. Until now, all of Ryan's victims had been fired upon from the street but at the Gibbs' house Ryan decided to invade their sanctuary and kicked in the glass panelled door.

Mrs Gibbs called out, 'What the hell do you think you're playing at?' Her protestations were followed by the sound of gunfire and soon after Ryan emerged from the broken door, pausing on the driveway to reload his pistol. Inside Mr Gibbs lay dead with his mortally wounded wife close by his side. Myrtle Gibbs was to die of her injuries the following day.

A milkman in Priory Road, suspicious of several loud thumps he heard, thought someone was interfering with his milk float. When he went to investigate he saw a 'Rambo' figure walk through the broken door of the Gibbs' house opposite. Ryan aimed his pistol but didn't fire and the milkman made his escape.

A resident in Priory Road wasn't so lucky as the gunman with a 'crazy' look fired a bullet into the man's leg. Another to notice the 'crazy' look was 77-year-old Dorothy Smith. She had known Ryan for 20 years but hardly recognised him. 'Is that you making all that noise?' she asked him. 'You're frightening everyone to death, stop it.'

Ryan just turned his head towards her. 'He had a terrible, vacant look in his eyes,' she said, 'and this funny sort of grin on his face. It looked as if he was brain dead.'

Almost an hour had passed since Ryan fired his first shot in Hungerford when he claimed his last fatality. Thirty-four-year old Ian Playle was driving his wife and two children through the town, and as they rounded a bend Mrs Playle heard the engine whine in their car as the power diminished. At the same time there was a crack as though a stone had gone through the windscreen. She turned to her husband and was horrified to see him bleeding profusely from the neck. Mr Playle died instantly and their car swerved and struck a parked vehicle. A witness had seen the Playle's car come into range. Ryan never stopped walking, fired a single shot through the windscreen, paused, shrugged his shoulders and continued walking towards the John O'Gaunt School. With a half-grinning smirk on his face and the pistol in his hand pointed in the air at head height, Ryan strolled on as if he was on patrol.

Perhaps the luckiest person in Hungerford that day was Jeffrey Broadhurst, who was in the front room of his Priory Road house. He pulled back the net curtains to see what was happening and came face to face with Ryan. The Kalashnikov was brought up to the aim position but Ryan didn't shoot. Instead he grinned at Mr Broadhurst and continued on.

The final person to be wounded by Ryan was George Noon who was walking with his son further along Priory Road. He had heard shooting in the distance and a helicopter hovered overhead warning people to take cover. As he went to push his son inside their house Mr Noon felt a bullet slam into his shoulder and as he fell back a second bullet hit him in the right eye.

The hovering helicopter was probably the reason Ryan chose to take refuge in the nearby school. Ryan began to run, firing at houses as he went. The only time he stopped was to confront Thomas North who was in the front porch of his house. Ryan lifted the revolver and said, 'bang!' then turned away and ran into the school grounds.

Around Hungerford 16 people lay dead or dying and another 15 were injured, most of them seriously. Countless others were traumatised as the hour-long ordeal came to an end. Ryan had fired at least 119 shots in Hungerford, 84 from the lethal AK47, 34 from the Beretta but only one from the carbine. Mrs Godfrey and seven of Ryan's other victims died from the Beretta while eight died from the Kalashnikov loaded with bullets that had the ability to pierce armour plating. Ryan had been prepared to face police return fire. The bullet-resistant waistcoat he wore would have protected him from all but the most powerful weapons available to the police.

THE END IS NIGH

With difficult communications, a lack of available firearms and an emergency 999 system completely swamped with calls, it took police some time to comprehend exactly what they were dealing with. In the aftermath of the tragedy the local police came under severe criticism from people who had the benefit of hindsight. Some calls on the emergency phone lines reported Ryan's location, but often these calls were made well after Ryan had moved on. Other callers gave wrong locations and it became impossible to know just where he was.

Ryan chose to lay siege in an upper storey classroom at the John O'Gaunt School. Once police confirmed he was inside, the Tactical Firearms Team was able to seal off any escape routes. He could not escape, but because police were unsure as to whether Ryan had hostages, or had booby-trapped the building, they would not take an offensive role, instead opting to talk him into surrender.

Ryan may have thought surrender was the best option. He tied a white rag to the barrel of the AK47 and poked it through a broken window. The rifle was then thrown from the window, clattering to the ground below. Sergeant Paul Brightwell, a trained negotiator, finally engaged Ryan in conversation at 5.29 pm. Over the next hour and 23 minutes the sergeant and Ryan spoke. Apart from firing occasional shots, and saying he had a hand grenade, Ryan remained calm and rational.

Ryan must have known he had killed his mother, yet during negotiations kept asking how his mother was, and wouldn't surrender until police could tell him. In all he mentioned his mother 14 times.

'I must know about my mother. Tell me or I'll throw the grenade out the window,' Ryan shouted. 'I want to know. I must know.' He asked about his dog. 'Has anyone found that?' he asked. 'I shot it. I had my eyes shut the first time and I just winged it.' He asked Paul Brightwell to look after the dog and to give it a decent burial.

It was not until the two were well into the negotiations that Ryan spoke about the carnage. 'What are the casualty figures?' he asked. Sergeant Brightwell said he didn't know, but told Ryan he would obviously be aware a lot of people had been shot, to which Ryan replied, 'Hungerford must be a bit of a mess . . . It's all like a bad dream.'

In the context of having just shot so many people, Ryan was somehow concerned about others. He referred to the discarded carbine rifle with a magazine in it. 'It is just that there were some kids nearby - I don't want them to find it,' he called to police below.

At 6.24 pm Ryan shouted out, 'If only the police car hadn't turned up. If only my car had started.' He asked again about his mother, saying it was all a mistake and how he didn't mean to kill her and that he should have stayed in bed. Sitting alone in the barricaded classroom, Ryan had time to reflect on what he had done. The contemplation of suicide was present but it frightened him.

'It's funny,' he shouted to Paul Brightwell, 'I killed all those people but I haven't got the guts to blow my own brains out.' The realisation of the mayhem he had caused, coupled with the fact he would be without his mother and would face a miserable life in prison, must have been a worse option than suicide. At 6.52 pm he sat in the corner of the classroom, placed the barrel of the pistol to his temple and pulled the trigger.

Sergeant Brightwell heard a single muffled explosion. He called several times to Ryan but got no reply. When police forced the barricaded door open they found Ryan slumped on the floor, the 9 mm Beretta attached to his wrist with a lanyard. The bullet he saved for himself went through his right temple, exiting out the left side of his head. That single bullet brought to an end a terrible rampage.

PSYCHOLOGICAL PROFILE

Michael Ryan was never known to have consulted a psychologist or psychiatrist. While experiencing the normal viruses or infections most of the population succumbs to, he was never seriously ill. Ryan did however suffer from a persistent problem with a syndrome, 'globus hystericus', which is a sensation of a lump in the throat. Globus is sometimes associated with stress and causes difficulty with swallowing. The syndrome was persistent over a long period of Ryan's life and became more prominent at times of tension, such as a few days after the death of Alfred Ryan. He was treated with Diazepam (a mild tranquilliser) but a month later opted to discontinue taking the tablets even though the globus was still a problem. An ear, nose and throat specialist could find no abnormality, and the conclusion was that Ryan succumbed to the effects of stress.

If there was anything Ryan showed paranoia over, it was his

belief that he was prematurely going bald. When he consulted his doctor over the supposed hair loss the doctor concluded his hair pattern was in fact normal. One acquaintance, Steven Wells, noticed Ryan's self-consciousness not only about his stature of 167 cm, but especially the belief in his potential hair loss. David Gray, who perpetrated a similar massacre in New Zealand three years later, had the same imagined hair loss problem as Ryan and went to extraordinary lengths to cover his head.

CONCLUSION

Michael Ryan was a nondescript individual who never seemed destined to achieve. Had it not been for the Hungerford massacre he would probably have led a life of anonymity. Instead, he killed 16 innocent people and himself, ensuring his name and dreadful deeds would be remembered for a long time. He plunged a peaceful town into chaos and created a legacy people would want to forget. But someone had a final thought for the callous murderer. A few hours before Ryan's family attended his funeral a blonde woman in her 20s called into the undertakers.

'These are for Michael Ryan,' she said, leaving a bunch of sixteen red roses behind. She walked out, got in her car and drove away. She disappeared as quickly and mysteriously as she had appeared.

CHAPTER FIVE

FRANK VITKOVIC

AN INSULAR ENIGMA
Melbourne, Australia - 8 December 1987
Victims: 8 dead, 6 injured

INTRODUCTION

The tennis tournaments that sort the 'best from the rest' are the four 'grand slam' events comprising Wimbledon, the French Open, the US Open and the Australian Open. The Australian Open is held at the magnificent Melbourne Park Stadium where thousands of fans flock each January to watch the best in the world.

In 1982 the names at the top of the men's tennis world were Borg, Connors, McEnroe and Lendl. At the same time, a young man named Frank Vitkovic took up tennis as a casual sport. His early attempts were on a school court where he and a friend would hit a ball to one another across a wooden bar placed on a couple of chairs. The naturally talented youth went from those humble beginnings to become an accomplished and promising player. He modelled himself on the Swedish greats - Bjorn Borg and Mats Wilander. Vitkovic wanted to achieve perfection. With his natural ability and fierce desire to succeed, the world of professional tennis beckoned him. But it never happened.

In October 1984 he felt a pain in his right knee. The injury, though relatively minor, became a huge obstacle in the mind of Frank Vitkovic. He ceased playing tennis and gradually withdrew into himself. He gained weight and lost the fitness he was once proud of. His passions changed from studying and sport to self-centredness and paranoia. Any chance of fame as a tennis professional deserted him. Where his name could have been linked to Borg, Sampras or Becker, it was instead to become synonymous with Knight, Ryan, Whitman and Bryant.

In December 1987 Detective Sergeant John Hill of the Victoria Police wrote of the scenes of Vitkovic's Queen Street shootings:

In twenty-one years as a member of the Victoria Police Force and eight years as a member of the homicide squad, I have never seen a more horrific example of wanton, deliberate and callous multiple murders and woundings carried out by one person against other totally innocent, trapped and defenceless human beings. One can only speculate about the absolute fear and terror that the victims and survivors of the shootings experienced as Frank Vitkovic coldly and deliberately chose his victims and shot them.

In a prison cell, not far from the killings, Julian Knight found out about Vitkovic's rampage. Knight was quick to label Vitkovic an 'amateur'. And he was right. Unlike Knight, Vitkovic had never been trained in firearms use or the art of killing. During his spree Vitkovic had trouble operating his semi-automatic rifle, using it as a single shot that kept it jamming. If the young man had the knowledge and experience of Knight the death toll in Queen Street, Melbourne could have been enormous.

In many ways, Vitkovic was a 'dormant volcano'. No one, least of all his family, knew that the man who had never had an interest in firearms had secretly purchased an M1 carbine and hundreds of rounds of ammunition. No one was aware of his mental state, his paranoia and intrusive thoughts of hatred. The only person who knew about the murderous intent of Frank Vitkovic was himself - and he wrote volumes of notes in diaries indicating a deeply troubled and paranoid mind that would one day exact terrible vengeance on his perceived enemy.

Vitkovic could have played out his ambitions on the

tennis courts of Melbourne Park in front of thousands of admiring Aussie fans. Instead he acted out the fantasies of a deranged gunman in front of a nation and world already reeling from a string of senseless killing sprees.

NORMALITY TO NOTORIETY

For most of his 22 years, Frank Vitkovic led an unremarkable life. He was a diligent student who worked extremely hard to achieve high academic standards. Vitkovic was seen as a quiet, passive and inoffensive boy, but his writings in the elaborate diaries revealed a darker side. Most mass murderers took their secrets to their graves, not so Frank Vitkovic. He left many clues to his thinking, including his views on what makes a mass killer.

Born on 7 September 1965, Frank Vitkovic was the only son of immigrant parents. His mother, Antoinetta, was Italian and emigrated to Australia around the same time Drago Vitkovic left Yugoslavia for a new life 'Down Under'. The only other member of the Vitkovic family was Frank's older sister, Liliana.

Where Antoinetta worked at various jobs, mostly in the domestic areas of hospitals, Drago was a self-employed painter and worked at that trade for most of his life. The family unit was, by most accounts, normal and easygoing but some people, health professionals included, believed there were cracks in what appeared to be a harmonious relationship. Certainly, the young Frank found some tension, once telling a counsellor of problems, but then recanting the suggestions. When he wrote his suicide note to his parents and sister he spoke of them in glowing terms.

Before his death, Frank Vitkovic was very much a loner, preferring his own company. In his earlier days, however, he had a small circle of friends - and not one of them had a bad word for him. He was remembered as a quiet, shy boy who was also witty and intelligent. As a schoolboy he was a keen cricketer. He also had an exceptional memory, especially for football scores and statistics. Other kids would question him on any match and Frank was able to come up with a range of statistical information. He even memorised things like the heights of buildings, and was so keen on figures they called him 'The Stats Man'. Most people know the date they were born but few would know the time of their birth. Vitkovic did. 'Born Tuesday, 7 September 1965 at 3.45' he wrote on the cover of his diary.

Being shy it was difficult for the young Vitkovic to make friends, especially those of the opposite sex, and he confessed in his diaries that he could not talk to girls, always getting tongue-tied when he tried to make conversation. Worse still was his belief that he lacked sexual prowess and that others were ridiculing him for it. He was convinced there was something wrong with his penis and that's why kids at school had called him 'Vic the Prick'. He didn't say anything about the taunts of others that he took very much to heart. School friends said most of the other kids were called names, it was just part of growing up. Vitkovic was no different and the name given him was just because it rhymed. But he saw sinister intent at the slight and this was to play on his mind for a long time.

Throughout Vitkovic's early diary entries he talks often of friends like Craig and Con. Together they played tennis and snooker or went to discos. Frank Vitkovic never gave any of his friends the slightest indication that they had done wrong or had fallen out with him. On reading his diary entries of the final 12 months the reverse is evident.

Vitkovic's own family was unable to detect the serious problems simmering in Frank's mind and none of them were aware that inside his wardrobe, along with hundreds of rounds of ammunition, were newspaper cuttings referring to Julian Knight's rampage on Hoddle Street. Neither could they know the significance of six lines in one of Vitkovic's notebooks:

'M14 automatic, automatic carbine, pump action' were written at the top of the page. Knight had a pump action shotgun and two semi-automatics. At the bottom of the page Vitkovic had written Kalashnikov, Beretta and M1 carbine, the three weapons used by Michael Ryan to terrorise the residents of Hungerford. It appears that Vitkovic was collecting weapons and ammunition for a similar reign of terror.

This then was a young man who was a far cry from the boy

growing up with his sister Liliana. She recalled her brother with affection. Her memories of him were of a quiet, gentle boy who studied hard, intent on being a lawyer. He wanted to do well to make his parents proud of him. He never claimed he was being harassed and his moods never changed; he was always happy with a smile on his face. Any depression he showed was due to his inability to get back to university or tennis after a knee operation. Such periods of depression were mild and short-lived.

'I couldn't say how many hours he spent studying,' Liliana said. 'He was always in his room, possibly six or seven hours at night studying.'

Vitkovic's diaries revealed he did study hard, well into the night, but then would watch late night movies until the small hours. He put a lot of pressure on himself, believing his parents expected him to achieve, though they would have been content for him to just reach his potential.

The Vitkovic household seemed fairly representative of the time and place. Frank Vitkovic had once confided in a friend that his parents were very strict. 'On one occasion when I went to his house he gave me a drink and then washed the glass immediately,' Craig said. 'I got the impression from this and what he said that they were strict.'

Vitkovic's diaries, written at the time he was supposedly happy and relatively carefree, give indications that he was the classic enigma. A week before the killings Liliana had an engagement parry at the family home. 'During the night Frank was very happy and having a good time. He spent a lot of time with my girlfriends, cracking jokes and making them laugh,' Liliana recalled.

That was the Frank Vitkovic on the surface. Deeper down he was full of hatred and seething about how he believed people treated him, especially his friend Con. Yet to Liliana and her fiancé he seemed completely normal. 'He showed no signs of depression and said nothing ill of Con. He always thought Con was a nice guy,' Liliana said.

He also had a compassionate side, raising money for charities such as the Australian Birthright movement. He held strong urges to help underprivileged people and often said if he could, he would help ease the suffering of Ethiopians.

One of the closest people to Frank Vitkovic was his future brother-in-law Gino. 'My first recollection of Frank was that he was a really pleasant guy,' Gino recalled. 'He made me feel as though I had known him for years.'

Gino had met Con, of whom Frank Vitkovic spoke highly. 'I never heard Frank speak badly of Con and I've never known of any arguments between them,' said Gino.

On the night of his engagement Gino also saw the lighter side of Frank Vitkovic. 'You should have seen him that night,' Gino said, 'he was so happy.'

When Vitkovic killed eight people a week later he shocked many people. His devastated family had no idea what he was planning. 'The last time I saw Frank, on the night of 7 December, we all watched television together,' Liliana said. 'He stayed up till 3.30 am watching the Masters. Frank didn't give any indication he was preparing to do what he did.'

To his friend Craig, one of the men whom Vitkovic would blame for the tragedy, the mystery is as deep. 'He was too quiet,' Craig remembered. 'A mother's perfect kid, never out, never in trouble. He's the last guy I would have thought would do the shooting on Queen Street. I never once saw him display any temper.'

So how could such a quiet, shy young man turn into the monster of Queen Street without a hint of trouble brewing?

The diaries he had kept since a 12-year-old contained simple details of what he did, where he went and what he watched on television. He had a passion for the film *King Kong,* which he saw over and over again. As he got older the diary entries began to show his growing interest in sport, with detailed entries of cricket matches, Aussie Rules football, and particularly tennis. He talked in depth of his performance, scores, and the shots he made or missed. He was almost fanatical about the game. If he wasn't watching tennis on television he was out playing.

Vitkovic appeared to be a fairly normal teenager. Several early entries however gave an insight into what some might consider a rather fragile adolescent. 'I watched King Kong (1976) film,' he wrote. 'It was a great movie, the fifth time I've seen it but I still love the film. The ending is very sad though.'

The next day Vitkovic played tennis but that night wrote in his diary, 'Today I was still sad over King Kong but I went and played tennis.' Here was a 16-year-old who had seen a film five times but was still troubled the next day about the ending. A week later he was still making references to the film, wishing it would come on television again. He rarely made his feelings apparent in his writing but there were a few exceptions, like on 15 March 1982:

> Today I got very angry when we did not have the English test, especially after studying for so many hours. It was a waste. Then I got even more angry when Miss Cunt Romano deliberately stopped me from reading. It has gone far enough. Soon I will complain for I haven't been picked once to read in over a month's school.

Young Vitkovic was keen on achievement.

> Today I was disappointed with my maths mark. Only 80% which has dropped my average by 3%. Then we went and played tennis and I came back from 2-5 set point to win 7-5. Now I'm going to watch Ben, about the killer rats.

Problems for Vitkovic during his adolescent years were to shape a lot of his thinking. The journey of confusion from childhood to adult life can be a very difficult one, and for young Vitkovic that was the case. The 14-year-old fell head over heels in love with a teacher. From then on, for almost a year he wrote of nothing but his intense love for Helen McLeod. The year before he had made a reference to her, saying she had told him he had no class spirit. He wrote how he hated her, but the following year developed a crush that became an all-consuming passion. In March 1980 Vitkovic wrote of his burgeoning interest:

Of course I can set no specific date for this event in my life because I don't even know when it all actually started or for what reason. My old teacher of 1979 who frankly I showed very little interest in now turned me on. It was not just puppy love, I really liked her but was scared to say so. I watched her all day, Mrs McLeod was her name - Helen McLeod. It's a story that would be good for a motion picture I suppose. After a while I decided there was no future in it and tried to forget about her but I couldn't. I hoped that she would tell me off so that I wouldn't like her any more but I kept on liking her, I just couldn't stop. Me, just a 14-year-old boy in love with my teacher. I got all confused, wild, I didn't know what was happening to me. I tried to tell Mrs McLeod so she would tell me to get lost but I was scared that I might be expelled. I think about her every day. I had dreams. I lost interest in my schoolwork my grades went down. I wanted to get it off my chest. It was too great a problem for a boy of my age. I constantly fell asleep in the classroom, would it never end. That's why I write this to get it off my chest. She changed my life, work became secondary. This goes on.

From that point he went to extraordinary lengths just to be seen by her or to get her to speak to him. Twelve months of diary entries revolved around his infatuation culminating with his biggest thrill of the year when he got a lift in her car. Then in September of 1980 he suddenly changed, with an unusual and out-of-character entry:

I don't hate all girls, in fact about 60% of girls are OK. It's just those women's lib moles who shit me the most.

He then said his favourite 'sheila' was Mrs McLeod but then referred to her as an 'old bag' and a 'bloody moll'. Changes in his personality were becoming clear and on 23 March 1981 he wrote:

Everything I do goes wrong so I hate life. Sometimes I think nobody loves me, and I don't blame them for this after the things I do. But I know that I love myself, but I feel as though the world is against me especially the foolish women molls. One day everyone will pay for their sins. I believe in anti racist ideas and I believe in the superiority of animals that have no foolish emotions, feelings, or religions. So I am just a mixed up person and seem to have two totally different personalities one good which is trustful and the other half which is bad and offers plenty of deceit.

Vitkovic was now only 15-and-a-half. His 'love' for his teacher had not only waned but he wrote of her in the most derogatory way, and the final entry where he mentioned her concluded:

Oh yes it's been a bad year 1980. Not as I predicted but it happened anyway. I lost the teacher I <u>love</u>.

The next time Vitkovic wrote in his diary he headed it up:

Dear Janet. I love my mother very much. I adore her, she is the only type of person I like and one of the few persons in the world who loves me.

Young Vitkovic seemed to be struggling with adolescence and wrote some quite disturbing entries in June and August 1981:

Dear Janet,
Today I got up at 10.30 and watched a 60 Minutes special on Ian Botham. The time now is 8.30 and I'm going to watch the cricket all night. I'm getting desperate my mission worries me at times and I'm simply getting old. I must survive and the mission will be carried out. I get the strange feeling that they all hate me. My mind is changing a lot.

Me and my Mum had a bad argument. She hit me hard with a spoon, so hard that it broke. She may hate me I'm not sure, but I know one thing for certain I am hated very much by many people, but they don't know anything of my hatred which is twice as much as theirs. I'm cracking up under a lot of pressure. I love to get on the bus and get to school. For my family often treat me badly. I still love my mother, even though at times I hate her. I love her for one basic reason. She gave me life. So far I haven't used my life well enough. I haven't done enough bad things yet but I seem to have developed a few bad habits. I love playing jokes on people. And I hate rich people and drop spit on their cars. The silly turkeys have got too much, they need a bit of fixing. Anyway they're just a pack of hypocrites. I did the wrong thing today, now I was almost in tears. This incident started when I was doing some work for Dad then I made a mistake and Pops hit me. I stormed out. Mum said she was going to hit me. I said come on try. First she hit me with her hand then she pulled out the spoon and hit me. I resisted and she bit me on the arm. Then she called me a bastard and threw the spoon at me and went back into the lounge room. At first I was angry but now I've cooled off. FV signing off, it's 9.39 pm on Saturday.

Suddenly Vitkovic stopped writing about his feelings and reverted to his earlier style of just recording what he did, where he went and what he watched on television. Gone were the vitriolic statements about hate, and gone too was any mention of his lost love.

If Vitkovic had stumbled on rocks on the road through adolescence he was about to trip on a boulder. In 1983 the 18-year-old visited the Coles New World store in the Northland Shopping Centre where he was caught looking up a woman's dress and police were called. He told police he saw the woman looking at clothing so got on his back and crawled backwards as close as possible to look up her dress. When interviewed in the presence of his mother, Vitkovic conceded a need for professional help. The police agreed that if he sought help they would take no further action, thus avoiding the public humiliation of a court appearance.

From the outset Frank Vitkovic had shown remorse and great shame for what he had done. There was no indication of violent or aggressive behaviour; he had never attempted to touch the woman, and he appeared quite rational. Vitkovic saw Dr Sood, a consultant psychiatrist who gained a good insight into the adolescent. Vitkovic came across as a shy, immature youngster who spoke hesitatingly. He showed no sign of thought disorder, perceptional abnormality or marked mood change, apart from his sense of shame. Dr Sood couldn't find any evidence of the violent fantasies that would become apparent to a university psychologist three years later.

The psychiatrist did however believe Frank's mother and father had a rather distant relationship. The doctor surmised that Frank was under pressure from both parents to achieve and that, according to Vitkovic junior, his father did not think much of him. Dr Sood arranged a family assessment session to look at the differences between the mother and father but acknowledged any attempts to bring them together might be unsuccessful. During the assessment Frank was seen to be the 'baby' in the family and any attempts on his part to separate seemed to cause distress to Mrs Vitkovic. Various issues were raised with the family but they showed no interest in following them through. In the end the psychiatrist concluded that Frank had suffered a 'minor adjustment reaction to adolescence' in the setting of a dysfunctional family. The minimum number of sessions needed to satisfy police that a prosecution need not follow were completed and the matter ended there.

The dress incident happened in August 1983 and coincided with Vitkovic's most academically challenging time. To ensure a place in the university he aimed for excellence in his Higher School Certificate examinations. During that year he studied harder than ever, pouring all of his spare time into his studies and gaining quite exceptional marks which put him into the top five per cent of students that year.

If ever there was a noticeable change in Frank Vitkovic it was at the end of that year - and it was dramatic. The last diary entry before the 'change' read as follows:

Nov 10 - today I studied for eco, went to the house then I came home due to the birds being too noisy. I kept going till 11.20

when I watched *Twilight Zone*. *Children of the Damned* was tops, it was a terrific film.

This was a typical, matter of fact entry but on Friday 13 January 1984 his writing suddenly became expressive and adopted a totally different style to anything previously:

Today I became more and more nervous and worried about my forthcoming HSC results which should arrive on Tuesday. I hope and indeed pray for resounding success not merely a minimal pass which I would find profoundly disappointing. To fail would simply be incomprehensible. Certainly I would react savagely to such a remarkable turnaround in my intellectual ability which reached its pinnacle by the October exams. Only time will reveal my fate. The new year has been quite enjoyable aside from my tennis form which has reached an absolute nadir, albeit last night's doubles clash indoors at Epping where I struck the ball exceedingly well though my volleys could do with a good deal of improvement. A second disappointment of these holidays has been the blatant absence of any adroitly made science fiction films or horror movies or movies of any nature in general. Instead I have been forced to perpetuate exceedingly boring American soap operas and comedies which are at best addle brained. At least some relief is forthcoming with the EP masters being telecast from Sunday. An early election is now inevitable and I purport to enrol at the electoral office as soon as possible. So as to assist the NP in its quest for a second term of government.

Wednesday, 18 January. Today at approximately 12.10 I received my HSC results for 1983. I had been waiting all morning for them and even went to the extreme of asking an old lady across the road if she had received her mail whereupon I engaged in an amiable chat with the old lady. Finally at 12.10 I saw the postman leave our house. I opened the letterbox and there it was, amongst two other letters. Nervously I opened the letter and the contents revealed startled me. I had acquired three A's and two B's. I went delirious and almost reached the point of crying such was my uninhibited ecstasy. I kissed my dad a few times and immediately rang up my sister who was also elated. I rang David who previously informed me of his results by phone earlier that morning, he had got 283. I rang Con with my results and he passed too. After a game of tennis I went to a party and had too much to drink with the result that I became nauseated and Leeson paid for my taxi trip home. I got home at 12.00 and vomited outside on the lawn before I got inside and went to sleep to mark the end of a thoroughly unforgettable day.

THE BUDDING LAWYER

In 1984 Frank Vitkovic enrolled at the University of Melbourne intent on studying law. He had few close friends and rarely joined in with campus activities but did team up with one young man the same age as himself. Paul, studying law and science, found Vitkovic a thoughtful and likeable person. The diligent and conscientious Vitkovic had high ideals and would study for hours at home or in the library. Paul never noticed Vitkovic ever get mad or express emotions. 'He was just a likeable guy.'

During that year the Vitkovic diary entries became less frequent, but what he did write indicated a fairly happy youth, studying hard and playing plenty of competitive tennis. Then in October 1984, while jogging, Frank Vitkovic felt a pain behind his right kneecap. Although only a minor injury, the knee would require surgery, but to Frank Vitkovic it was serious and became the catalyst for his ultimate fall.

Paul was one of the few people to notice his friend's slide into depression. Something was clearly troubling Vitkovic and it was around that time he began to express his preoccupation with ethics and his views on society. 'He had an interest in the penal system and social ethics,' Paul said. 'Also the problems of society. He believed crooks were treated lightly, punishment wasn't strict enough and there were deficiencies in the system that let prisoners get early release.'

THE MEDICAL AND MENTAL PROBLEMS

There is little doubt Frank Vitkovic was subjected to considerable stress, mostly self-induced. He had complained of persistent headaches from the age of 13 but these were put down to tension. Later in life he would be treated for abdominal pains which were again aggravated by stress. He was prescribed the anti-anxiety drugs Ativan and Prothiaden, as well as drugs to reduce his blood pressure.

Various doctors he consulted noted he was a very tense young man. One general practitioner described Vitkovic as an introspective, tense person who tended to keep things to himself and would only tell the doctor things he wanted known. He became overly concerned with relatively minor problems, and when treated for bronchitis demanded a chest x-ray. Once, when being consulted for an eye inflammation, he insisted on being referred to an eye specialist. It was Vitkovic's way to consult a variety of doctors; possibly he needed reassurance he was getting the right advice. Another doctor who had seen Vitkovic on and off over eight years also noted the introverted personality, and formed the opinion that Vitkovic's mother had a great influence over her son.

But it was the knee injury that was to become the focus of Vitkovic's mind. Initially he was prescribed anti-inflammatory agents but these didn't help and he sought further treatment. Eventually he saw an orthopaedic surgeon complaining of pain and swelling to the knee. The diagnosis was that the injury was not serious, and x-rays and bone scans proved normal. The last option was an arthroscopy examination. When this was carried out a portion of damaged inner cartilage was removed, along with some tissue on the outer side of the kneecap. It was a simple procedure to resolve a relatively minor problem, but post-operative complications developed, causing swelling and some bleeding inside the knee. This was repaired with another minor operation, and on his final visit to the surgeon Vitkovic was free from pain and had full movement of the knee.

But Frank Vitkovic wasn't satisfied. He believed vehemently that his knee was not healed and was holding him back. He believed he would be permanently crippled. A year later he returned to the surgeon complaining of further problems, but the specialist could find nothing abnormal. The conclusion of the surgeon was interesting.

'Frank appeared to be a very nervous and tense young man. He appeared to be under a lot of self-imposed pressure and was very anxious to be successful in his law studies and tennis. *Perhaps he couldn't come to terms with the failures we all have from time to time.*' [Emphasis added]

The specialist's view would prove to be very accurate. Still not satisfied, Vitkovic sought opinions from two other specialists, neither of whom could detect any abnormality. Such was the demeanour of Vitkovic one of the surgeons referred to him as 'having a most peculiar affect'.

Frank Vitkovic must have convinced his parents that he did indeed have a terrible injury. In fact the family contemplated moving to Canada as nothing could be done for Frank's knee in Australia. The supposed knee injury was to see Vitkovic defer from university. It led to his total withdrawal and became the catalyst for the Queen Street massacre. There had been glimpses of Vitkovic's troubled personality when he wrote of being hated as a 15-year-old. That personality problem became clearer in late 1986 when he sat a law examination on the topic of Property and Contracts. His answer to one question was not only totally irrelevant to what was asked, but also quite bizarre. Vitkovic's answer follows:

The reforms I would make to the present laws are to reintroduce capital punishment for all civil libertarians. The present criminal laws are a farce. One person has lost all his civil rights (i.e. has been murdered) whilst the son of a bitch who killed him is entitled, according to the civil libertarian philosophy to have his future considered, his reform considered, his constitutional rights considered, his state of mind considered, the stress he was under, the so-called provocation of the deceased (which by the way never occurred but is invented by the defendant and taken for granted by idiotic judges), the fact that he only meant to scare the deceased the gun just "went off". Finally the defendant is found not guilty of the murder of the man whom he shot through the head but guilty of manslaughter and given a minimum sentence of five years jail. How unfair yell the civil libertarians as they demonstrate. I feel so sorry for that man, five years in jail, it's terrible, you shouldn't punish at all you should reform, after all he only killed a man, it wasn't my father so what the hell do I care, the law is fine. The punishment fits the crime. Aren't we proud what we've done for these criminals since 1966. Five years is too harsh a sentence for his crime, maybe if we demonstrate we can get him out in two years. He's paid his debt to society. After all he's innocent the gun simply went off and it was accidentally pointed at the other fella's head. After all that's what the law's for, to ensure civil rights. Justice is not relevant, not according to us as long as I don't get harmed. I'm not apathetic about victims of crime, I just don't care. Warning - prophetic - St Paul - The bowlers society is approaching. Laws were created to ensure an order and coherent society. That is their purpose. When laws are made impotent by groups in society who call themselves civil libertarians society regresses to an almost bowlers prehistoric age. It is not a civilised society as the morons prefer to call it. It is an ever-growing violent society where no one feels safe. It is clear that violence results from a chaotic society.

In the sub-dean's report to the university progress committee it was suggested, by virtue of the bizarre exam answer, that Frank Vitkovic had some severe psychological problems. Vitkovic's file demonstrated earlier problems of depression in the first two years of university life. In August 1985 he sought leave of absence, using his knee injury as an excuse, saying that the whole situation had left him depressed. Vitkovic was becoming disenchanted with law, believing there was too much injustice in the world.

Almost exactly a year before the Queen Street killings the sub-dean referred Vitkovic for counselling with the university psychologist. A record of those visits to the psychologist was given in evidence at the inquest following Vitkovic's death.

From the outset Frank presented as a young man with many problems, although he seemed quite willing to speak about them. Principally, he was distressed by violent fantasies that focused on damage to himself and others. He saw the world as a terrible and dangerous place, and believed that it probably deserved the nuclear destruction it was headed for.

The immediate focus that he identified as explaining his disillusionment and frustration was his injured right knee. He explained that he had been a keen sportsman, particularly at tennis, and he had had reconstructive surgery on his right knee. He expected that the operation would fix what had been wrong, and had been angry and disappointed when the knee seemed worse than before the operation. He was now reduced to watching the tennis at home on television. He felt that since he could no longer play any sport his life was virtually meaningless.

Much of the session was spent complaining about his family, particularly his father, whom he described as being a bit crazy and violent. He shared his father's disgust at the corruption in society, as evidenced by the prevalence of burglaries. He was adamant that he would kill anyone who tried to burgle his family's home, and stated that there were plenty of guns at home that he could use.

He claimed that since he had not recovered from his knee operation and had become so angry with the world his friends had begun to desert him. He felt bitter and angry about this, and wanted to confront them with their disloyalty.

He said that he often felt like dying, and that when he was contemplating suicide he usually thought of crashing his car into a tree.

The session ended with an agreement that he could return to see me, following the weekend, on 9 December.

I discussed this disturbed young man at a counsellor's case

conference, and it was agreed that I should attempt to make a referral for a psychiatric assessment as soon as possible. It was agreed that effective treatment of Frank's condition would most likely require appropriate medication, and possible access to hospitalisation.

Frank attended his appointment on 9 December and spent much of the time guiltily recanting many of the complaints he had made about his family. He was at pains to tell me of the great respect that he had for his father, and of his own unworthiness in the face of all that his family had done for him.

He seemed to regret his openness during our previous session and was much more guarded on this occasion. He appeared suspicious when I attempted to explain that sometimes when people were experiencing the sorts of problems he was, that it could be helpful to spend some time talking to a psychiatrist. I explained that I was willing to continue seeing him, but that ultimately it would probably be best for him if he were to see a psychiatrist. He expressed little faith in this proposal, and claimed that his sister had been seeing a psychiatrist for a considerable time, and that it didn't seem to be helping her. He agreed to meet with me again, and we made a time for 16 December.

On the morning of 16 December Frank rang and cancelled his appointment. I had no further contact with him.

Unfortunately there was no follow-up, and judging by what Vitkovic wrote in his diary, from that time on his reasoning deteriorated markedly. The day after Vitkovic's rampage his name was released to the media, and within an hour the university psychologist had contacted the associate registrar to tell him of Vitkovic's earlier counselling sessions and how he had needed psychiatric counselling. But by then it was too late. Vitkovic was dead and so too were eight innocent victims.

Exactly two months before the Queen Street killings, Frank Vitkovic called into the Church of Scientology and undertook a free personality test. The questionnaire of 200 questions is devised to assess personality traits and is examined by an evaluator after the tests are complete. Vitkovic answered the 200 questions with 'yes', 'no', or 'maybe' responses. He began by heading up the front page with personal details and for occupation put 'hopefully anything'. Some of the responses elicited from the troubled Vitkovic included saying yes to the question: 'Is it hard on you when you fail?' and no to: 'Are you considered warm-hearted by your friends?' In reality, those who considered Vitkovic to be a friend did find him to be warm and caring.

Clearly, Vitkovic believed life wasn't worthwhile, and exhibited particular hates and fears. To the questions: 'Do you often sit and think about death, sickness, pain and sorrow?' and 'Do you remain upset for some time following an accident or disturbing incident?' he answered yes.

With the questionnaire complete the evaluator assessed the score, concluding Frank Vitkovic was in a very bad shape mentally. He was confused and upset and referred to troubles he had in getting along with his parents. The test results were obvious. Vitkovic had had a lot of losses, he was not achieving his goals, and he was suffering from a kind of suppression.

Realising that Vitkovic was 'at rock bottom' the assessor suggested he undergo a course conducted by the church called 'Ups and downs of life'. Vitkovic, not surprisingly, never took up the offer of the course. Instead he went to the police and applied for, and received, a shooter's licence.

Though he had referred to himself as a 'gun freak', Frank Vitkovic knew little about firearms. The university rifle club had held an introductory night in March 1987 when Vitkovic and Paul went to the club and fired a .22 rifle at targets. 'He didn't like it,' Paul said. 'He displayed an amusing naivety about firearms.'

Yet Vitkovic, despite this lack of knowledge and the fact he displayed some disturbing thought processes, was able to legally purchase his M1 carbine and hundreds of rounds of ammunition.

One of Vitkovic's infrequent outings was to a school friend's 21st birthday party. Although he seemed to enjoy seeing all the old faces again, he became more depressed as the evening wore on, and made the comment, 'You know, sometimes I could get a gun and end it!' He said he had nothing to live for, was a failure in his dad's eyes and that the crime ridden violent world meant it wasn't safe for anyone to live.

Days later a party guest saw Vitkovic walking down the road in a funny bobbing motion, talking to himself.

Where Vitkovic had earlier had a few short-term labouring type jobs, he was now left to his own devices. He had no job, had deferred from university and was keeping more and more to himself.

Frank Vitkovic was on an emotional roller coaster during the time leading up to the tragic finale. Three weeks before the killings, Vitkovic's university friend Paul invited him out for drinks with a few of his uni friends. 'He seemed cheerful and in good spirits,' Paul recalled.

During the evening Vitkovic said he was keeping busy and would be returning to university. 'He looked as if he was getting his drive back.' That outing was in stark contrast to the venomous and depressing attacks on people made in the Vitkovic diaries.

THE DIARIES OF DESPAIR

Vitkovic's regular diary entries had stopped for a period of two-and-half years, but when they resumed they were long-winded, hugely depressing in tone and venomous in their hatred of people. The following edited excerpts from the Vitkovic diaries, which he now called Sally, show not only his thinking but his acceleration towards infamy:

Wednesday, 16 September 1987

Dear Sally,

I don't know why I began to write again, but I have no friends now not one. No one to talk to. I'm completely alone. All my life friends have deserted me or treated me so badly that I deserted them. Con was my good friend for about a year. Then I saw the other side of him. He began insulting me almost every time I saw him. What made it worse was that I have a bad knee and yet I was still treated so cruelly by him. He is the lowest scum on this earth . . .

I feel the end is near for me now. Sometimes I just wish it would all end. Sometimes I feel such rage it even scares me. The problem is that I have no outlet for my anger. I feel doomed. I've just had a knee operation and it hasn't worked as well as I would hope. I still limp and probably will for the rest of my life. Because of my bad knee I'm stuck at home for most of the day. When I do go out the people just don't seem real. I don't feel part of it. I never had really.

My life is such a failure. Since my HSC success it's been all downhill. I hate the loneliness but I'm too scared to reach out because people have hurt me so much. My mind is so tortured. It's horrible. I'm in hell and there seems to be no escape . . . That's the worst part of it that I'm so scared of myself.

Sometimes I feel I cannot live in this world, I'm losing it . . . Since I have no friends and my family just laughs at me I talk to this diary which I call Sally. I always wanted a girlfriend called Sally. I wish I had a girlfriend. How I wish I had a lovely Sally sleeping next to me, someone who would love me for me, what I have to offer, love. It hurts so much when love is returned with hate. When kindness is returned with hostility. The funny thing is that I cannot understand why this sudden hostility comes over me. Maybe it could be repressed sexuality I guess . . .

Previously I released my tension by playing snooker and bashing billiard balls or going to heavy metal gigs and headbanging. Now because of my bad knees I'm stuck more and more at home. How I hate the sight of these fucking walls in this fucking house. They're plain, empty, just like my life . . . Violent thoughts sometimes wrangle my mind . . . During the day I stay home alone. Mum, Dad, and Lily all go to work. I should be working. I wish I could work. These damn knees have destroyed me. My ego has gone completely. I can't walk with my head up . . . I've only just turned 22 but I feel about 80 . . . Goodnight Sally.

21 September 1987

Today was just like all my other days. Boring as hell. I walked up to McDonald's where I ate my lunch . . . Frustration, rejection, humiliation are emotions I know very well. Happiness, friendship and a sense of belonging have never been part of my life. This fact has always distressed me. The fact that I have never belonged to any group. I have always been a loner. The worst loneliness is when you are alone in a large group of people. They know you don't fit in and you know. You can sense the contempt in their eyes for you. It saddens one . . . I never go out and socialise any more. I did a few years ago and had a girlfriend or two but soon my old shy timid self returned and it was back home and reading books on Saturday nights while everyone else had a good time . . . Sometimes I worry about my sexual problems. These have been with me since eight years of age or so.

Sgd. Frank Vitkovic
ps - what a hopeless life.

Thursday, 24 September

Today was quite warm again. Lily was home and we had a few laughs. I love Lily very much. She is such a nice girl. She is a great sister and a fine person. I wish I was as good as Lily. I love Mum and Dad too. This makes my problems all the worse because I'm hurting them. I am a failure and I know it. I'm 22, no job, no money, no friends, no social life and my health isn't too good . . . I guess it's largely due to a lot of the psychological scars that I carry from my childhood. There are some events that I simply cannot forget. They linger in my mind. They recur like nightmares in situations where I should be confident . . . they turn me into a frightened schoolboy. The humiliated schoolboy that I often was.

Frank Vitkovic
I hate this guy.

Saturday, 26 September

Today was grand final day. Carlton beat Hawthorn. It was 31 degrees hot. Hawthorn fell in a heap in the final quarter. Carlton's 15th premiership. I was happy for Carlton. I was also sad because I get the feeling it was my last grand final . . . If I was dead my torture would be over. It's mainly mental torture that I feel . . . Eight years ago I watched Carlton beat Collingwood by 5 points. I had it all then. Intelligence, a good healthy body and happiness . . . I watched the grand final alone for first time since 1984. No friends, nothing . . . My spirit has just about been broken. I feel so inferior. I feel so small.

11 October 1987

It's October now. I am on downer drugs because my headaches are so bad. They make me feel drowsy. Today I heard they are going to ordain women priests. What's the fucking world coming to? Haven't they gone far enough in reversing the sex roles? That's what fucked up the world in the first place . . . I've got these downers to last me the next 50 days or so. That'll take me to about December. I've got things planned for early next year. Maybe January. But for certain by February. By February everything should be ok.

13 October

Today there is a change. The power I need is slowly but surely all coming together. I had another run in today with a car load of people. I was just walking along and as usual for no reason they heaped some crap at me. It seems everybody hates me. Society hates me. I feel I cannot cope much longer but I try to be as strong as I can. I am on sedatives at the moment. One downer tablet per day. They make me feel good. But I'm scared I will get hooked to them. What the fuck I want to die anyway. I can't live in this world. There's just no place for me.

Frank Vitkovic was now on his steady progress to destruction. He had received his shooter's licence but had made no mention of it in the diaries, just veiled references to the power that was returning to him. Having never previously been interested in firearms he must have had a clear idea about what he was planning.

Friday, 16 October

Con rang yesterday for the first time in two months. He needs someone to play snooker with. Just as I thought. He used me for snooker and treated me like a piece of shit. He was never a friend. I found out too late. I longed so much just for one good friend but none were there. Something should be done about him and others like him. The world is simply full of bastards. You be kind to people and they use you. They return love with hate, kindness with cruelty, care with apathy. I long for the end now. I know the end is near. But I'm not afraid really. It's inevitable . . . I feel depressed for my parents and my sister for having a son like me. Such a big failure. On the dole, and unlikely to get a job because of a lousy knee . . . I don't even watch TV with my family anymore. I just stay in my room. I just stay there, lie back and look at the empty walls. Empty like my life . . .

I go out occasionally. It makes me sad when I see all the young pretty girls out there and I'm stuck at home without a hope in hell of picking one up. I don't have the guts to even ask one the time. I'm very shy with girls and always get tongue tied. I just don't feel confident. I want to make love badly sometimes. This feeling occurs when I'm at home alone during the day. I'm so lonely I just want to hug someone. To love someone. To have someone love me. To make me feel human again. But I know it won't happen . . .

The old Frank died years ago and has been dead for a long time. The result is a walking time bomb which must go off. As everyone knows when the bomb goes off the time bomb itself is destroyed. However that is necessary because the time bomb is a symbol of destruction and must be destroyed itself. It does not belong within the community. It is anti community. The strangest thing is that society manufactures these human time bombs yet is so shocked when they go off. Today, somewhere, a future human time bomb is being manufactured by society.

On 21 October 1987 Vitkovic purchased his M1 carbine but did not refer to his purchase in the diary. Instead he made an innocuous reference to buying a pair of socks:

21 October 1987

I feel as though things are getting out of control. The drugs don't help me get through the day. I get so angry I just want to destroy. The world is full of vicious cruel people. The world is full of cunts. They drive me nuts. Why do they hate me? Why does the world hate me? I went to the shops today. I bought a new pair of socks. I said to the girl politely that the weather was a bit better today, she looked at me like I was diarrhoea. People think I'm worth nothing. OK that's the way they want to play. I'll treat them as nothing. I try to be nice and they're never nice to me. I don't know what's wrong with me. I'm not bad looking. But it's not just girls. It's mainly no mates. They all think I'm too wimpy to be with them. I felt like the odd man out whenever I was in that group. It's a horrible feeling when you want to be part of the group and yet you know you never will . . . I have been insulted all my life . . . The last few years especially I feel like doing something about it. They deserve it. They're all heartless cold monsters who need to be taught a lesson . . . If there is a God I think he made a mistake in bothering to make humans. They are just so bad to each other. No wonder there is so much violence in this world. I firmly believe that a man should pay what he owes . . . Sometimes I get angry but I'm trying to keep myself under control. My equilibrium has been restored. My balance and calm will come with it. I have a purpose. My life has purpose. Only I can see the purpose. It is deep in my sub conscience [sic].

Friday, 23 October

Today was a horror day. A living hell. Headaches so severe I felt like my head's gonna blow up. Palpitations, stomach churns, you name it I got it. I want to die. Life's not worth living not for me. These pains, these fears, it feels like the pains in my head are pushing me crazy. I'm sick. I'm real sick. I need help . . . I want to regain my composure. I want to be stable, composed and normal. But most of the day I feel like a raving maniac . . . I have more rage and disappointment in me now than most people have. Today I hopped on the train. I felt so alone and strange amongst those people. I'm just not like them. I know it and they sense it. I just get so cut up. Almost hysterical. I get so sad I could cry. I feel so sorry for Mum and Dad for having such a failed son and a crazy one. They have very little to do with it. It just slowly developed from my early childhood until now. With each humiliation another nail was hammered into my coffin . . .

At times I feel almost like an animal. Just uncontrollable. Being unemployed does not help because it gives you too much time to brood. Brooding leads to sick fantasies. I have had these erratic emotions since the start of this year . . . These violent rages have led to our garage furniture being smashed. It's a good feeling for me to destroy things. I like it. It gets rid of tension. One night I uprooted a small tree and walked down May Street with it at 2.00 am. I was angry after a party when an old acquaintance told me straight to my face that he hated my guts. I would have killed the guy but it was a party with people everywhere. Otherwise I'd have ripped him apart with my hands. He hates me, they all hate me. I hate them each and every fucking one of them. Every dog has his day and mine is soon.

Monday, 26 October

The headaches are still there. They are getting worse in fact. The reason is I'm more nervous and it's taking its toll: I'm close to the end. I'm crying now. I can hardly hold this pen. I just can't believe my life is so bad . . . When you're young there's so much to live for. Now I long for death . . . I've got no one. I hate myself. I'm such a piece of trash. I'm not deserving of life. I feel so down . . .

Standards have dropped. People are just so cruel to each other it just astounds me. It unravels me. Like Con for example. This last February I had to go to hospital. The night before I was due to go in we were playing snooker and I was beating him. He gets angry and says you won't be able to play snooker in hospital. What a dog. A friend huh. He always made fun of my bad leg. He is the scum of the earth. He must pay. He will die. I realised that he was the person who has destroyed me. For that he must pay. There should not be people like that in this world. They have no right to live.

God is on my side. Don't worry God I will punish these evil vicious cruel scum people. I will destroy the evil. My job will be done. My mission will be complete. I know I'm ready for the mission. I'm having my hair cut short. I'll be ready. I have to clean up the mess. Flush it right down the fucking toilet. These hypocritical money hungry heartless 'me' people, they will be destroyed . . .

I'm 22. I'm a man. But I feel like a boy. I feel like a scared boy. The humiliated boy that I was often in my childhood. Hiding in corners to escape people and life. I just don't feel mature mentally. I'll always be trapped. I get these nightmares still of being called names (Vic the dick) and that song 'Born to be a prick and his name is Frank Vic Vic Vic.' That is one I'll never forget. Worse because one of my best supposed friends Mark in primary school even joined in and sang along. He too had turned against me. They all have.

The whole world hates me. But don't worry fucking world, I hate you back three times as fucking much. Every dog has his day. One day when this dog has his day a thunderstorm will rain down.

Tuesday, 27 October

The headaches are still there so I guess he will order the tests. I feel like there's something in my head especially on the left side, but sometimes on the right. It's more than just tension. I'm real worried about it. I had my hair cut today. It looks ok but it could have been shorter. The girl who cut my hair was very friendly and polite with me. She makes a pleasant change from all the others. I made her laugh a few times which lifted my ego. I got there around 1.00. It only took about half an hour or so. I walked back home trundling across the railway tracks in the process. It was quite warm and I was buggered by the time I got home. As usual I saw silly graffiti on the walls, 'cosmetics suppress women', 'kill turks'. The trash that write that rubbish should be shot ten times in the head with a .308. They have no respect for the property of others. These uni dykes go around dressed like pieces of trash because that's what they are, trash and trash should always be kept in a cheap container. Ha ha ha . . .

The problem is no one wants to help others. They all want a business, a car, money, wealth, superiority over their friends, but what the hell for? They sweat for their cause, bring down anyone who gets in their way, then they die and presumably go to hell. What's wrong with just living a humble life and making your family happy? A man has to have a career, a woman has to have a career. It's all a load of shit. All a person needs is happiness. Without happiness and love you are the walking dead. There are a lot of people like that. Just walk down Collins Street in the city and you'll see them. Dressed resplendent in suits and ties, carrying briefcases but with eyes of glass and hearts of stone. That's the new person of the 1980s, the new person, the 'me' person. So wrapped up in their own trappings they can't even see the fences surrounding them. Sometimes these fences are invisible subconscious fences but they are there and they constrict as much as 10 feet of lead . . . I'm overweight too. I'm 14 stone and I should be 11 or 10. In 1984 I was 10 stone. Since I injured my knee I've steadily put on weight as my activity was reduced till now I am really fat and ashamed of my body.

Thursday, 5 November

I haven't been to a disco or a night club for over five months. I used to enjoy that quite a deal. Dancing, trying to pick up women and occasionally succeeding. I think about my old girlfriends. I only had one really and that was Lola. I was 19 she was 16. She wasn't that pretty but she was sweet and nice and I liked her a real lot. Sometimes we go in the lane and have a bit of fun. My best memory was when she laid her head in my lap. It was a sunny day. I gently caressed her hair. We were there alone, so together, so serene both of us so happy with the other. We were almost in love. That was the closest I've ever felt to loving a girl. After that I just don't know what happened. The meetings became less frequent, she called me less and less. I found out that she was talking with this other guy a lot and he was walking her home. I was shattered. I treated her like a queen, I never raised my voice to her and she dumped me for another guy. Worse he was ugly and had glasses. That was March 1985. For months I was hurt. What did I do wrong? I gave her presents, chocolates everything. I gave her kindness and a young sort of love and she jilted me. Perhaps I was too nice and she took advantage of me. Since then I've been right off girls. It's so hard to trust them.

Sunday, 8 November

I do a lot of reminiscing about my younger days before I wrecked my knee. Most of my memories are about tennis. I recall places I played at, people I played, the little things that happen each match but most of all the feeling that life is great. It's a feeling I lost a few years ago. For two years when I was playing tennis regularly and winning trophies and getting better and better they were about the happiest years of my life. Almost every day I would play and how I loved it. Little did I realise the damage it was doing to my body, especially my knees, shoulders and wrists. Then on that horrible night in October '84 my right knee finally went. I felt a part of me died that night. I had few if any real friends, only tennis friends and

I soon lost all of them. I passed uni exams and was on holidays and I spent most of that summer brooding. If anyone rang me up I wouldn't ring back. Me and Con had become good friends. He was a real funny guy then cracking jokes and always making us laugh. 1985 came and went. 1986 I started having a few problems with Con. His attitude and demeanour had changed. He was no longer the funny man, he had become unpleasant and rude, especially to me because I rarely answered people back. He had turned into an uncaring monster. Making fun of me, hurting my feelings and he really enjoyed it. But he won't enjoy what he's going to get.

Many of the mass killers profiled in *Killing for Pleasure* lived in varying degrees of chaos but there would be some part of their life that was orderly. While Vitkovic lived in a well cared-for home he wrote of his orderly plans to achieve goals, yet believed his surroundings were, to his thinking, a pigsty. In a brief glimmer of positiveness he continued:

I feel like I'm gathering my strength. Trying to get back on track. No smoking, no drinking, no coffee even. These are the rigid standards I have set myself. My willpower is stronger now. I haven't had a cigarette for nearly two months, there will be no relapses this time. You must set yourself goals. This is what I have. As each goal is achieved I am able to cross it off, delete it in my mind. The need to achieve it is no longer there. It's a good feeling to get things done. Some things I put off for too long. I waste my money on pizzas and playing pool. Now I'm trying to save my money. I'm more wise with my money. I don't waste it like before. It's a nice feeling having money, a feeling I've experienced far too little. Next week I'll sell some old uni books and get some good money from that. It's no use keeping a lot of the old junk I had, it just turned my room into a pigsty. Now I can keep it tidy. This year is nearly over about seven weeks to go. I don't know how I've got this far. I guess I may have more grit and courage than I think. I just keep chugging along.

Another trait common to mass killers is strongly held grudges. Frank Vitkovic not only held grudges, his writings show he held them for a very long time:

11 November 1987

Today I've been thinking back a lot. There's nothing else to do when you've got no future. I remember in grade 3 when I was 8 we were in mass. I was dying to go to the toilet. And the bitch teacher I had said no. I just couldn't hold it in any longer and I urinated during the mass in front of all those people. Then when we got back to class I was forced to sit on the ground as an example to the others. They all laughed. I smelt of piss. It was the most humiliating experience I've ever had. She was the one who had done wrong and then she punishes me, the fucking slut, I should have cut her throat. I hate fucking molls. Makes me piss in the church, what a bitch. But my earliest memory was when I was about four. These two boys about 10 or 11 who were sons of my mother's friend were playing with me. They came up to me and said hold this which I did. It was a bee and it stung me. I was in a lot of pain. Mum got a key and drained the poison out of my hand. I never forgot that one. Then when the carpenter came to do our lounge room walls when I was about 8 or 9 his son, a young bastard apprentice, jabs a nail into my arm. Not to cut, just enough to hurt. I was so small I said nothing, I just copped it sweet. But even by that age I had a feeling that people were against me. I began to hate then. I'd walk down the streets and girls would call me ugly or wog or make fun of my hair calling me a soup bowl. People have just been such cunts to me. So cruel at times they made me cry. From 4 years of age that's all we had from them shit, shit and more shit heaped on me. Secondary school was ok the first two years even though I was not very popular. Then it started again, 'Vic the dic', 'Born to be a prick and his name is Frank Vic Vic Vic oh what a prick Frank Vic Vic Vic'. I just stood there humiliated and copped it all. I couldn't fight them, I was outnumbered. Me against all those bastards. I have always fought it out alone and I always will. I don't need to hide behind a group like those deadshits. I am my own man: I could kill all those guys even now without blinking an eye.

A lot has been made of the so-called 'Rambo theory' in mass killings. While it holds credence with many people it certainly didn't with Sylvester Stallone. Immediately after the massacre by Michael Ryan the media made a lot of 'the Hungerford Rambo'. Stallone was quick to defend his alter ego.

'Don't blame me for Hungerford,' Stallone was reported as saying in *The Sun* of 18 August 1987. 'I carry the can for every lunatic in the world who goes crazy with a gun. But it wasn't Rambo who sent Michael Ryan mad.'

While Stallone and others mightn't believe in the Rambo connection, Frank Vitkovic clearly did. Amongst a collection of things found in his wardrobe was a newspaper cutting of Sylvester Stallone portraying Rambo. Written on the cutting were the words 'Rambo Rules' and 'Rambo Power'. In the diary entry of 16 November 1987 Vitkovic wrote:

I've spent the last four months coping with the fact that my legs will never be normal again. It hurts my pride because I was always proud of my fitness and now most everyone is much fitter than me. As Rambo said in *First Blood,* once you accept a problem it's no longer there. *Rambo 3* is coming out soon, I'll probably go and see it. I wish I was as fit as he is.

Numerous specialists had told Vitkovic his knee problem was minor and had been repaired. His obsession with the knee gives credence to the belief he was using it as an excuse to avoid failure. He gave a hint of this in his writing:

I wish I was a kid again and stay that way forever. As a kid you are protected but as an adult you have to make the grade and fit the image - be socially adept and economically secure.

19 November

When I was 8 years old some boys looked at my penis in the change room. Look at Frank's, his is different. It hurt my feelings a lot. It was a turning point in my childhood. Up till then I felt normal but after that I felt like the odd man out. Even in the toilet line they'd look at my penis as if to say what the hell is that . . . I knew from about 12 that normal sex was not possible for me. I avoided girls completely till I was 19 . . . I was ashamed of my penis. If the boys thought it was strange imagine what the girls would think. Even when I had girlfriends like Lola at 19 we'd go through passionate kissing and fondling but I'd never go further . . . I was slighted a lot at high school too which didn't help the problem of my feeling of inadequacy. I really wanted to be part of the group. It hurts when you go to a school camp and no one wants you in their room. You're the last pick. You are an alien among your own. An outcast. That was how I grew up. The kids sometimes baited me. They knew I was a loner, that I was unpopular.

From this point on Vitkovic wrote screeds about how he was hated, had heard the whispers of others and how some of them would love to have killed him. The few friends Vitkovic had would be amazed to learn of his deep hatred of them. He now hated everyone as indicated in the 19 November entry in the all-revealing diary:

Even when I go to the shop for a newspaper the lady doesn't look at me or say thank you. No manners at all. These people need to be taught a fucking lesson and I'd be welcome to be the teacher. Sometimes you must learn your lesson the hard way. A bullet in the right place seems to do the trick.

Just days before the killing Vitkovic wrote about how he battled along, not complaining about his knees and feeling proud of himself. And how he had more guts than a lot of people.

Friday, 27 November

More guts than scum like Con who laughs at my bad knee. He won't laugh forever. I hate him completely. I hate him more than the devil hates God. Hate is a horrible emotion but sometimes that's all I feel. Just hate especially for some people. They should be cross-bowed through the head. They think they're so good and I'm such a piece of garbage. They need someone to take them down a peg and I'm just that person. My life seems worthless to them. One day I'll show them how cheap and worthless their lives can be made.

Vitkovic then talked of his sister's engagement party, taking place the next night and how, despite being nervy in crowds, he would try and be sociable. His sister and her fiancé remarked later how Frank enjoyed himself. He acknowledged he had a good time, the next day writing, 'Overall it was a great night.' Though he admitted, 'I keep my depression to myself.'

The euphoria didn't last long and soon he was again writing about 'the enemy'. The comedies he had enjoyed in earlier years, especially Jerry Lewis films, were now replaced by more violent movies. He 'couldn't stand seeing people happy' in comedies whereas violent films 'really pump me up'. He especially liked the sound of a gun going pow! He confessed 'it's the only fun I know'.

December came and Vitkovic surprisingly showed positive signs: 'I don't feel as angry as I did in previous months.' Then in the next sentence talked about his perceived betrayal by Con:

I don't see Con any more and he always stirred me, baited me, insulted me and made me angry, he even hit me on the face because he knew I wouldn't fight back. I had bad knees and he's such a dirty cunt he would have kicked me in the knees without any worries at all. That's why I didn't fight back. Otherwise I would have strangled him and eaten his eyes and ripped his guts out. That's what he needs. He will keep for the time being. He's the dirtiest dog on all earth. It's him and others like him that produce guys like me. Rare birds one in a million. People make them, they mould them, but they don't want to accept the consequences.

Frank Vitkovic had a deep-seated hatred of homosexuals, as was evidenced in his writings just before the rampage:

The world is headed for doom. There's too many gays in this world, especially those bull dyke lesbians you get at university. Now they should all be lined up and shot. They go to Anzac Day to spoil it, with their ugly faces and their ugly demonstrations. Those men fought to keep this country ours and those sluts come along and show appreciation that way. It's only because the majority of the soldiers were men and they hate men, they're lesbians. It's got nothing to do with rape in war. It's just an excuse to protest against men, which to their sick minds are the enemy. Gay guys shit me too. All gays are disgusting, male or female. They'll all rot in hell or at least I hope they do. They go around screaming for society to accept them when if you look at the graffiti they think of us as trash. There is so much garbage in this world I'd like to have a 400-foot truck to pick them all up in and dump them in a big hole and bury them.

Vitkovic had his gun and plenty of ammunition but needed a suitable bag to carry it in. On 1 December he went shopping for it and although he referred to its purchase in the diary he made no hint of the purpose he intended it for. He was now prepared for his 'mission' and he felt powerful.

Tuesday, 1 December 1987

The weather was really cold today. A lot of rain. I went out and got myself a new bag. My old one has broken. It's a really nice bag. Just what I wanted. I got very wet. It's a nice feeling. Walking in the rain with a rain jacket over your head, a bag over your shoulder and alone. Independent, a feeling of power grew over me as the wind pushed back my hair. I wasn't scared anymore. I felt all conquering. I felt strong. I could sense that people in cars feared me. I looked mysterious, rain jacket pulled over my head you couldn't see much of my face. I like being the mystery man. Sometimes I am a mystery even to myself and they are the worst mysteries believe me.

The course of destruction was now firmly implanted into the mind of Frank Vitkovic and there was no going back. The image he had of himself was at an all time low. He knew his 'mission' was close but still made no reference to the impending tragedy in his writings:

Wednesday, 2 December

I hate myself even more today. My hatred for myself continues to grow each day. I am a worthless piece of shit. I feel like an uncontrollable maniac, I just hate my guts. Even my hairstyle shits me. My clothes shit me. My appearance I hate. I'm overweight. But most of all, my mind shits me. It drives me nuts. Why do I think and feel this way? I went out today for a little trip around town on my loyal tram and bought two spare magazines of the militia kind. I need them for extra zap.

On Saturday, 5 December 1987 Vitkovic wrote many pages in his diary. He rambled on in the same vein as before, often contradicting himself by saying he still had friends who cared, and how he would often go out with them. In the next sentence he would reject them as traitors. The veiled references to what he might do were now becoming less transparent. He said of Con:

I wonder if he will enjoy what he's going to get! He'll get what he richly deserves. A box of chocolates? Ha ha. You didn't expect that.

Vitkovic began to philosophise and pondered the difference of heaven and hell:

I've always wondered what death is like. I go to the Coburg cemetery every now and then and sit by a grave, any grave, and think to myself what it's like down there, what the person buried there was like as a person. Did he/she go to heaven or hell? Is there a heaven or hell? I think of all these things as I sit by the graveside . . . What about people who are insane, where do they go? That one always puzzles me. Some people are good and bad all in the same one. What happens to them? Some people are good and eventually other people force them to be bad. What happens to them?

The justification and planning for the attack at the post office building was now clear in Vitkovic's mind:

I was supposed to go to Steven's 21st birthday party. Con said he'd ring me up to go. "Don't worry I'll ring you." I bought a champagne bottle but no call, nothing. He just goes to the party with his sister and leaves me alone at home. Next day he rings as if nothing has happened. I was sb angry I could have killed him that night. For that he must be punished. He must receive severe punishment for that. People like him are what's wrong with the world today. Too many selfish dogs who care about no one except their precious little shit self. Someone ought to kill all the bastards. That's what they are, worthless bastards and bitches with no hearts. However there is the enemy of all that trash and that enemy is me. I'll fight them tooth and nail. They are not ready for the battle, I am. What a mighty battle it will be. Me versus the cunts of the earth. Should be quite an interesting battle. I intend to come out on top. Beforehand you must gear yourself up for the battle. I'm geared up. Once the adrenaline flows it will be really interesting, that's when I'll be right on top. The battle will be fought and I will win the war. Give 100% and you can make it. You've got to be tough mentally. Now I'm tough as nails mentally. I'm fearful of nothing. I've reached a stage where nothing will get in my way. I'm a steam train coming through and everyone better get out of the way.

On the evening of Sunday 6 December Frank Vitkovic retired to his room. He sat alone, writing to 'Sally', telling her about being in a mental prison with no way out. He knew what was ahead and had cleaned his ammunition in preparation but confessed he 'didn't like to think about it'.

> It terrifies me. I guess the worst fear is when you fear yourself. I'm scared of myself right now, I know what I could do. Tomorrow I've got a few things to do. I've got to tidy up my room and take care of a few other things.

On 8 December 1987 Vitkovic made his final and most chilling entry in the diaries:

> Today I feel funny. Jitters up my bones all over the place. Palpitations, anger all that's there. I got too much inside me. Today it must all come out. I can't understand my violent impulses. I don't know what's wrong with me. *Today I must do it. There is no other way out.* I've got to see it through. My head really pounds. I'm all shaky. It's time to die. I don't mind if the contents of these diaries are made public, what difference will it make anyway? So you have my permission to read them, do what you want with them. I only wrote them to ease my mind, let it all out what I felt. Maybe they'll do some good, I haven't done much good in my life. I've left a letter for my family. To Gino my brother-in-law sorry for all the pain I'll cause but I can't stop myself it's come too far. We had some really great times and I won't forget you. You were one of the few friends I had. You are one of the few people I will miss in this world. Goodbye Gino and his family too. Goodbye all.

Before he packed his bag and headed on 'his mission' he wrote heartfelt letters to his parents and sister:

> To my dear family,
> I'm sorry for all the trouble and heartache I've caused you. I've

been such a failure. I went down the wrong path. I should have listened to Pop and not played so much tennis instead sticking to my law studies and things might be different today. How I wish I could change the last few years and make things right and make you happy and proud of me. But the seeds of doom were planted very early as early as eight years of age several incidents hurt and changed me so much there was no hope of being the same. I carried that with me all these past fourteen years or so. To my dear Mum I love you with all my heart. When I think of how hard you worked for me and Lily and the love you gave us it made me cry. It always makes me cry. When I'm at home I think of you there at work and cry. I've let you down very badly Mama and I'm so sorry. You know how much anguish I felt over the knee injury. We all felt the same anguish. I knew I was never going to be successful and it hurt me a lot. Things looked so bright a few years ago but it faded fast. I hope Mum you can remember me when I was a boy on your shoulders and you carried me to kindergarten. Remember me when I was a bright young boy of 12 who was so gentle and kind. Then I changed slowly but surely. I didn't want it to happen but it did. I tried to fight it but the impulse has grown too strong. It has destroyed me. I just hope someday you can forgive me and remember me once in a while because I'll never forget you Mama. I'll love you always.

To Dear Papa or Pops. You deserved a better son than me. I was never good enough I admit that. I never pushed myself to the limit. I was lazy, I took the easy way out, I played too much tennis and wrecked my knee and eventually my whole life was wrecked. I know how disappointed you were. I saw the sadness in your eyes. You worked so hard to make a good life for me and I messed it all up because I thought I knew it all. How little I knew. But you don't know Pops that I felt very bad about my situation too. It was the reason I was seeing the doctors all the time, all the anxiety, stress and depression hurt my health. It didn't do you too much good either. We had some great times

Pop like our fishing trips when I almost dropped the rod in the sea. Or our trips to the expresso bar to play billiards. When I was young I just loved billiards hey dad. I always loved you too. You are just about the best father a boy could have. You gave me everything, you were so kind and loving. You're a great person. There are not enough in the world like you Pops. You were always good to me. I will miss you so much I just can't describe it. To my dear sister Lily what can I say? I wish I was never born might be the closest to the truth. But you could understand. You saw the stresses building up inside me. Only you saw why I've had the rages. I felt as though I'd had a raw deal. I was so frustrated. But you helped me through the bad times. Your optimism and sense of living kept me going at a time when I thought I was going to die. I wish I could be a better brother but I can't change the way I am. We had so many fun times together it was just unreal. We had happy childhoods it was great. Things went sour for me but you kept me laughing. We had our fights, we called each other names but we always kept loving each other. I hope you can forgive me for what I've done but even if you don't I'll understand it. It's hard to understand these things. That's been the problem. At times even I don't understand why I feel such violent impulses run through my whole body. I've had them at least since the start of this year. I've kept them reasonably under control until now though you've seen flashes of it in my rages. But now it's just reached the point of no return. These rages have been so bad the last month, they've caused me terrible headaches. I just can't go on. I just can't live in this world. I am ready to die. It's time for me to die. Life is just not worth living.

Frank Vitkovic 8-12-1987

Frank Vitkovic then left for his planned suicide. Regrettably, no one close to him was remotely aware that his suicide would not only be spectacular, but that he would take eight people with him. And one time friend Con was meant to be the first.

TERROR ON QUEEN STREET

In December 1987 Vitkovic visited the university union receptionist's office. Over the years he had confided in the managing receptionist, but on this occasion she was on the phone and her assistant dealt with Vitkovic. She became annoyed at his lack of politeness, and when she made a curt comment Vitkovic's face became very angry. Such was his look the managing receptionist became concerned. 'I didn't like it,' she recalled later.

She had always liked the polite, shy 'Vicko' but the look on his face was quite frightening.

On 8 December 1987 Vitkovic returned to the office. The managing receptionist greeted the sad-looking man, asking him what was wrong. He referred to having failed exams and being deferred. He wasn't as tidy as usual and looked as though he hadn't bothered to shave. Vitkovic said he was going to see 'the bureaucrats' and that he had a job to do at the post office. As he spoke he kept looking down at a bag he had with him. 'You're always a lovely lady to me,' Vitkovic said to the managing receptionist as he grabbed her hand, 'but I hate your assistant!'

As he turned to leave someone else came into the office. Vitkovic glanced back and had the same terrible look on his face, a look that would soon be translated into terrible actions.

After leaving the university receptionist, Vitkovic headed for the Australian Post building at 191 Queen Street. In his carry bag was a cut-down semi-automatic .30 M1 carbine, several loaded magazines capable of holding 30 rounds, a knife, spectacles, binoculars and a change of clothing. Whether he was anticipating a siege or expecting to change clothing and escape is unknown. Vitkovic hid his bag on the eleventh floor of the Post building before going to the fifth floor.

When Vitkovic arrived he asked the teller to get his one-time friend, Con, who worked for the Telecom Credit Union located there. As Con approached the counter he was totally unaware of the reception he was about to get. Frank Vitkovic mumbled an indistinguishable word as a smile crossed his face. Without another sound he drew the rifle from inside his jacket, aimed at Con and pulled the trigger.

Vitkovic was unfamiliar with firearms, especially one with a defective trigger, and had failed to cock it properly. Con ran from the office shouting to other staff to take cover.

Climbing the teller's counter Vitkovic began firing indiscriminately. As the bullets began to fly, someone pushed a panic alarm which activated a video camera. The time was exactly 4.17 pm when Vitkovic began hunting his quarry.

Judith Morris was in the teller's office located between Con and Vitkovic. She became the first victim of the rampage. Witnesses heard Vitkovic laugh before and after the first killing. Not the sort of laugh a sane human would make, more a maniacal sound. The gunman's eyes were glazed and vacant but also large, frightening and abnormal. Witnesses said Vitkovic looked and sounded drugged or insane, 'like a madman'.

The security camera captured images of the deranged man frantically working the cocking mechanism as he searched in vain for Con. As he moved about, the video camera graphically displayed the deliberate actions of the gunman moving from office to office firing his weapon.

Leaving the fifth floor, Vitkovic went to the philatelic bureau situated on Level 12. It would seem that the area was chosen at random as he could have gone to any floor in the 18-storied building unhindered. The only floor with a security system in place was the philatelic bureau. However, the system proved ineffective. When Vitkovic approached the bureau the door was opened by an employee who was instantly shot, falling to the floor seriously wounded. As frightened people began to flee or hide from view, Vitkovic walked up and down the office, firing at will. Before he left the 12th floor, Vitkovic shot dead Julie McBean, Nancy Avignone and Warren Spencer, who were hiding in vain under desks.

Moving down a floor, Vitkovic came upon Michael McGuire at the doorway to a data processing room. Moments earlier, Mr McGuire had been talking to his wife on the phone when he heard shots being fired on the floor above. After hanging up he left the office to come face-to-face with Vitkovic. The gunman shot Michael McGuire and left the room, but not satisfied he returned and shot the wounded man twice more. A familiar trademark of mass killers is the practice of execution-type murders; Vitkovic displayed this trait.

Staff were now well-aware of the danger and took refuge under or behind any furniture that might offer protection. There was no way they could escape. They were trapped, and could only hope Vitkovic would miss them. He kept moving methodically up and down the aisles shooting as he went. Vitkovic left the office briefly, but any thoughts staff had of being spared were quickly dashed. He walked back into the office and shot dead Marianne Van Ewyk and Catherine Dowling. Both women were hiding under desks, desperately trying to escape the gunman's gaze.

Others hiding behind the sparse cover the furniture provided suffered little better. Several were seriously wounded, including Rodney Brown, who later died while being treated by ambulance officers.

During the rampage Vitkovic had appeared calm and deliberate. Though he had the appearance of a madman his speech was clear and coherent. 'You all give me the shits,' he said to those he hunted. 'You're all bastards. There isn't any love in the world and nobody cares about me.'

The terrified people trapped in their offices needed little reminder of the peril they were in and took no comfort from his warnings. 'Nobody's going to leave here alive,' he told them. 'What's the point of life when nobody loves you?'

Vitkovic spat out the venom he had for people, 'Well, who's laughing now, I'll take you all with me.'

Clearly Vitkovic had expected a confrontation with police. 'Why aren't the police here, why don't they kill me?' he called out. The words Vitkovic said which most clearly indicated his thinking during the rampage related to the gun. 'How the hell do they expect me to kill people with this thing?' he said as he worked the mechanism.

Immediately after Rodney Brown was shot, a member of staff who had taken cover decided he and the others had no chance of surviving unless Vitkovic was stopped. Tony Gioia leapt at Vitkovic, pinning his arms to his sides as they fell struggling to the floor. The rifle fell out of reach and a quick-thinking staff member grabbed it and ran from the office, hiding the gun in a fridge. Disarmed but not overpowered, Vitkovic struggled free and lunged at a window He went head first through the partially broken pane and clawed his way out to the balcony. Despite being cut with shards of glass, he kicked free of the people trying to pull him back. Vitkovic scrambled out over the balcony and plunged eleven floors to the concrete below.

'That will teach you,' Vitkovic yelled as he fell to the ground. He bounced a metre high before crashing back down, lying still in a pool of blood. Seventeen terrifying minutes after the ordeal began Frank Vitkovic lay dead.

After Vitkovic fell to his death and the wounded were evacuated, police searched the three floors. Lying amongst the 41 fired cartridges were 184 live rounds. Vitkovic had plenty of ammunition but ejected four bullets for each one he fired. He had ten magazines of different capacity capable of holding a total of 255 rounds. The carbine, with its cut-down barrel and stock, was easy to conceal and was a lethal weapon at close range. Almost 1,000 people worked in the post office building so he had no shortage of victims. Had Vitkovic been more knowledgeable about firearms, the death toll could have been enormous.

PSYCHOLOGICAL PROFILE

During the inquiry and at the inquest into the killings on Queen Street various psychologists and psychiatrists offered opinions. Because Vitkovic's mental state was being looked at in a retrospective way, opinions differed. Despite the mental health professionals having a lot of written information on which to base their findings they were unable to conclusively agree on a diagnosis.

One psychiatrist believed Vitkovic was suffering from a reactive depression, with features of paranoid thinking. However, Dr Allen Bartholomew differed somewhat in his diagnosis. An internationally-recognised psychiatrist, Dr Bartholomew had previously been invited to speak in London, The Hague and at the Clarke Institute in Canada as well as at conferences in France and America. He was well-qualified in his field and was closely involved in the examination of

Julian Knight a few months earlier. In his evidence to the coroner Dr Bartholomew presented his report, part of which follows:

To attempt to fully analyse this present case would take a considerable amount of time that is not immediately available. However, it may be said that the early life of Vitkovic was essentially uneventful and little emerges of interest until about 1979. The entries in his diaries read a little oddly and perhaps suggest some mental disturbance that goes beyond adolescent rumination and dreaming. I note particularly his infatuation with his teacher, Ms McLeod. It is stated that Vitkovic 'was an above-average student who was very shy'. He was described as nonaggressive and would turn to run away rather than fight.

It seemed that he showed an ability at tennis and also a desire to achieve perfection - a somewhat obsessional personality. His main problem was that his tennis career was cut short by some knee damage and subsequent surgery- surgery that was not wholly successful.

There is some evidence that Vitkovic did not get on particularly well with his parents, not 100 per cent.

The entries in his small black diary read a little oddly and suggest some mental problems in the time period 1979/1980. This period, when he was aged some 15 years, is difficult to truly assess as adolescence may produce many features that in an adult might well be termed near, or even clearly, psychotic. I would tend to say that, with hindsight, the lad was 'disturbed'. However, not to the extent of terming his state a psychiatric illness.

By the time Vitkovic was some 18 years of age we might well have considered the diagnosis of Personality Disorder and this, I believe, became more severe or gross, so that by the time of the shootings the condition had become a psychosis, what I would term a schizophrenic illness. I do not see the matter as a depressive state but I would not unduly cavil with the diagnosis of a 'schizo-affective disorder'.

The evidence of Simpson (who described herself as a

volunteer employee at the Church of Scientology) is much more relevant as it is based upon the events of 8.10.87. At this time the client is described as 'in very bad shape mentally . . . very confused and upset'. Vitkovic was tested that day and the findings would appear to reflect the clinical picture - that he had a lot of losses, particularly as he saw the matter. His possible earlier disturbed state relating to some family conflict, his diary entries, his damaged knee, his giving up tennis, his increase in weight, his less-than-successful surgery, his deferring at university and his possible confused state regarding interpersonal relationships with his peers - of both sexes.

Simpson notes that the graph is 'low' and asks about drug taking. She cannot recall his response to her questioning. However, I note the drugs handed to the senior toxicologist were anti-depressants, a beta blocker and two types of minor tranquillisers. One of the minor tranquillisers was prescribed prior to the testing by Simpson. The others were prescribed at a later date - October, November.

Simpson stated that Vitkovic was 'at rock bottom' and 'had some troubles'. Those hardly go together. We all have some troubles, but this does not produce a rock bottom state.

The test results are difficult to assess but some answers suggest depression and also paranoid attitudes. The real problem with this aspect of the matter is that a person may be identified as grossly disturbed and nothing meaningful is done about it except to suggest the client does 'ups and downs in life's course'.

On 5 December 1986 the deceased man Vitkovic, saw a Mr Morgan of the University of Melbourne Counselling Service. This was after Vitkovic had written a 'disturbing and bizarre essay during a law exam'. A reading of the answer written in response to a question in 'contract' is only to be seen as the writings of a schizophrenic or a person suffering from a schizophreniform illness. This latter may be seen in response to a drug-induced state. For example, amphetamines or LSD or similar maybe in a Ganser

Syndrome - a *possible* hysterical state. In this case I say with conviction that the answer is schizophrenic.

In explanation of his findings, Dr Bartholomew told the court that a psychotic state was one where a person is out of touch with reality due to a disease of the mind. A schizoid state is one that is essentially a personality disorder where features of a schizophrenic illness may be seen. There is withdrawal, loneliness - a man who ruminates on his own in a room with a closed door, has few friends and does not participate in general social activity. He also explained paranoia as a sense of persecution. He concluded that Frank Vitkovic exhibited all of these things in some way, and that the paranoid part of Vitkovic's writing was connected directly with schizophrenia.

Frank Vitkovic exhibited other classic symptoms of the disease such as being secretive, even to himself. Nowhere in his diaries did he mention the purchase of a gun though it was important to him. Instead he wrote about buying a pair of socks on that particular day.

Dr Bartholomew continued:

Schizophrenics can certainly be secretive. And so can depressive people. They have got in their heads a whole variety of ideas, weird and wonderful as they may be, some they choose to publish and others not to publish. A person who is, among other things, grossly psychotic as Vitkovic was, loses the capacity for judgement and the appreciation and meaningfulness of things. They may see something malignant in it and say it is all part of a plot. Equally they could be lulled into doing a lot of things they otherwise wouldn't do.

On the question of modelling behaviour, Dr Bartholomew, on the evidence found in Vitkovic's bedroom, believed the murderer could certainly have been influenced by the character Rambo as well as the events on Hoddle Street. There is little doubt that the tragedy at Hungerford also had an influence on the thinking of Frank Vitkovic.

CONCLUSION

With the benefit of hindsight, the Queen Street massacre could have been prevented. Frank Vitkovic was an enigma. His writings indicated a deeply disturbed personality full of hatred. However, he had an extraordinary ability to hide his feelings. Those who saw him in the months and weeks leading up to the end had no idea as to what was going on in his troubled mind. He hid his weapons and ammunition from his family. He may even have stored them in a secure place known only to himself. The evening before he began his murderous attack he was seen by his family coming into the house with something 'down his trousers'. In all probability it was the cut-down carbine, but no one questioned him.

The secretive Vitkovic left other clues besides the all-revealing diaries but these weren't found until it was too late. Inside the wardrobe were telescopic sights and cleaning gear for the rifle, and empty ammunition packets. Two hardback books entitled *The Boston Strangler* and *The Only Living Witness* relating to the multiple murder of women in the United States were also in the wardrobe. Vitkovic had underlined sections of the books and made his own personal comments.

On the inside of his wardrobe door, near the newspaper clipping of Sylvester Stallone, was a film poster for *Silent Madness*. That film portrayed a paranoid psychotic who committed multiple murders only to escape custody and go on to repeat his dreadful crimes.

In a cupboard police found a pair of gloves, a mask, a military-style knife in its scabbard and two pages from a Yellow Pages telephone directory. Every firearms outlet in Melbourne was detailed on the pages and on the edge of one page Vitkovic had written, 'I hate everything, myself included.' On the adjacent page he wrote, 'I hate it all.'

A feminist magazine called *Judy's Punch,* distributed through the University of Melbourne, had really upset Vitkovic, and his extreme hatred of lesbians and women in general became evident.

'Psycho rules - I am a psycho,' he scrawled across the magazine. 'Yorkshire Ripper rules' and 'I love killing dykes' was written along with 'I hate lesbian perverts, I hate women, I have to kill, killing is my hobby.'

Some part of Vitkovic's mind knew he was on a path to destruction and he penned a plea to be stopped. 'Stop me before I kill,' he wrote. Had someone found the diaries, guns or other material stored in his wardrobe, the alarm bells would have almost certainly begun to ring. Unfortunately it didn't happen. Although Vitkovic wrote in a book 'Gun freaks rule' and 'I love guns' he hardly knew how to use them.

What he did know, however, were the indicators of potential mass killers. At the end of his diary he wrote those views he hoped to share with us all:

I don't care if you make public the contents of this diary. I wrote it in part for myself and in part for society to understand how these things happen and why and how you can pick out people who might be able to do such things.

Look for people with a history of rejection, loneliness and ill-treatment who also have a fascination for guns and you won't go wrong.

Frank Vitkovic wrote the most vitriolic, hate-filled things in his diary. To everyone else he was quietly spoken, withdrawn and shy. At no time did he show any aggression towards anyone despite having aggressive fantasies. Frank Vitkovic was indeed an insular enigma.

CHAPTER SIX
DAVID GRAY

THE CLOISTERED KILLER
Aramoana, New Zealand - 13 November 1990
Victims: 13 dead, 3 injured

INTRODUCTION

A frequent visitor to Aramoana, well-known painter H V Millar summed up what Aramoana meant to him when he said, 'Every time I visit this lovely area I find those things that man cannot manufacture, peace and serenity, beauty and solitude. One doesn't have to draw or paint here, it is justification for the trip just to look, and walk and look again. No wonder that people want to keep it unpolluted for always.'

Aramoana is 20 kilometres from Dunedin, in the province of Otago, New Zealand. Midway between the city and Aramoana is the container terminal town of Port Chalmers. Like most of Otago, Port Chalmers is rich in history and it was from here that Captain Robert Falcon Scott and his team of intrepid explorers left on their ill-fated race to the South Pole. Close by is a world-famous albatross colony and the home of the endangered yellow-eyed penguin. In the cool Otago waters seals and sealions frolic, with larger and far more dangerous creatures lurking in the depths.

The only access road to Aramoana is long and winding and the water of the harbour laps right up to its edge. The further you go the more remote and tranquil it becomes. Before the final bay, flat land separates the rest of the world from the tiny seaside settlement of Aramoana. In the 1980s bitter arguments raged between locals, who treasured the tranquillity and wildlife, and a large conglomerate, which wanted to build an aluminium smelter. After years of acrimonious wrangling the locals won, allowing Aramoana to retain a peaceful existence.

Aramoana offers endless opportunities for strolling along two superb beaches, skiing down steep sandhills to the water's edge, racing along the clear unobstructed beaches in land yachts, or leaping off the cliffs on hang-gliders to float above the clear blue waters of the Pacific. Many venture into the water, some for swimming, some for scuba diving and others to ride the endless waves on surfboards. For more advanced underwater divers, the clear deep water holds many fascinations and fears.

To many, Aramoana is a spiritual home; a place of remembrances. For those who have been lucky enough to enjoy this tranquil haven, there is a real sense of belonging. The peace and tranquillity of Aramoana attracted many people "wishing to get away from it all". Among those living there permanently were a few eccentrics and recluses, including one David Malcolm Gray.

GRAY - THE MAN

Within hours of his terrible rampage in November 1990, David Gray was being portrayed in the media as a shadowy, sullen figure; a loner with a fascination for guns. When encouraged to speak he would barely grunt and could never be engaged in conversation. The reality was that, until the last few years, David Gray was outwardly little different to anyone else. Gray's parents Dave and Molly married before the end of World War II and on 20 November 1956 David was born. Of their three children David was by far the youngest. Brother Barry was ten years older - almost to the day - and sister Joan was eight when David was born. The three Gray children and their parents were regular visitors to their Aramoana cottage and were regarded as 'nice people', though quiet and reserved. David spent a lot of time playing around the cottage and occasionally with other kids in the domain. Mr Gray was a keen fisherman and often he and young David would fish in the deep waters at the entrance to Otago Harbour.

Throughout David's childhood he was never regarded as anything other than a normal boy. Friendships formed at primary school endured throughout his years at secondary school and into working life. School friends often went to the Gray house to play with the collection of comics and toys. Gray, an avid reader from early days, had a retentive memory and an interest in a wide range of topics.

School records showed he was an average student but capable of better results. Friends travelling to school by train remembered Gray as 'not being a bad kid to be with' who joined in with others. Although a fairly solitary character, he had friends and was by no means always alone. Close friends during those early years said he was never nasty but if you got into a 'rough and tumble' with him you would know about it. David Gray was always quite strong and if upset could react. Occasionally he would be taunted about his spectacles and didn't take kindly to such abuse.

During Gray's mid-teens his parents, concerned about his inadequacies in coping with life, took him to a psychiatrist. Mr and Mrs Gray were not invited into the interview and a follow-up visit for Gray was never kept. There was little information in the report and it seems there was no spontaneity on Gray's part.

From early on David Gray was keen on the outdoors. Tramping featured prominently in his life, and as an adult he regularly visited places throughout New Zealand. One passion was to wander along beaches with a metal detector picking up coins or other valuables. Although he wouldn't make a living out of it, here was an interest that suited his lifestyle - alone with the peace and tranquillity on some of New Zealand's most picturesque and solitary stretches of coastline. He often went camping with friends, hunting for possums. David had several possum babies as pets and his older brother Barry remembers him putting a baby possum into a peg bag on the washing line to sleep, letting it wander free inside at night.

Gray's first job was as a farm cadet. This was quite a demanding position where he was expected to do farm labouring chores working seven days a week, with little time off. The farm manager recalled Gray as a remote though likeable lad with a 'chip on his shoulder' about society. David Gray lived in a caravan but ate with the family, generally keeping to himself. He never went anywhere without his small dog and after work, while sitting in a chair, the dog would be curled up on his chest.

Gray believed the farm manager gave him a hard time and although he did the work he resented the frequent gibes. During one period of feeding out from the back of a trailer Gray fell off. His embarrassment was enough, but to be laughed at by his manager was more than he was prepared to take, and he walked off the farm.

In spite of being inexperienced in farming, Gray found the country life to his liking and worked regularly on other farms. One of Gray's uncles had a farm, and on occasions he would help with harvesting when extra labour was needed.

For three years in Dunedin Gray loaded railway wagons with freight and was regarded as a diligent worker. On one occasion he was given the job of stacking 300 to 400 cartons of wine destined for Christmas tables in Central Otago. The bursting cartons were a nightmare to stack but Gray managed, receiving accolades from bosses after customers phoned to say not one bottle was broken.

Co-worker Paul Mead's vivid first impression of Gray was that of a bizarre figure with an intense gaze. During lunch breaks they would go to the hotel, but while others ate heartily Gray would only have a few chips and perhaps one drink of spirits. Gray was a moody person and often went 'off in a huff' but would soon return to make it up. In contrast, he had a tremendous sense of Monty Python-type humour, and could come out with things that had colleagues in fits of laughter.

Although he could do hilarious and innovative things, David Gray had an edge to him. He was a practical joker, but the innocuous jokes played on classmates at school became more serious in later life. Gray would set up explosive trip wires to frighten his mother or put birds in kitchen cupboards. Such tricks were certain to scare the recipient, but Gray was amused and unconcerned at the result.

He had an ambivalent attitude towards people and didn't tolerate drugs, yet tried marijuana a couple of times. His cynicism and bitterness towards people was obvious, and while part of Gray wanted to be with others, another side wanted to remain aloof. While he would readily talk to relatives and friends he always seemed to keep something back. Gray once said to a cousin he hated humans. Perhaps he meant they invaded his space - only he would know the context in which this statement was made.

From about the mid-1970s Gray always wore the same hat and never took it off. He confessed to paranoia about his appearance, especially baldness. Hoping to be able to restore his hair, he even resorted to rubbing onion juice into his scalp. On one visit to a doctor Gray lay down for an examination but refused to take the hat off. On another occasion he caused embarrassment at a family wedding by refusing to remove the hat during the reception. In later years Gray was easily identified by the rolled up balaclava he constantly wore.

As far back as 1980 Gray had an interest in militaria and admired the Vietcong soldier who could last for days on little food - sleeping in trees yet still ready to fight. The 'Ninja mystique' and Rambo-like survival techniques intrigued Gray and he marvelled at such people. He was also into an Eastern type of meditation that focused the mind.

It was easy to explain Gray's interest in the military. His father had fought in World War II and was repatriated injured before hostilities ceased. Bullet wounds to the head were so severe a metal plate had been inserted, an injury that gave him headaches throughout the rest of his life. Dave Snr often spoke about the war, the places he visited and the people he met. On retirement he intended to make a trip back. Mr Gray never made the journey. Soon after retirement he died of a heart attack while cutting the hedge, leaving David at home with Molly in a rented house.

The tales told of war in North Africa and Greece had an effect, and in later years Gray made his father's pilgrimage himself, leaving New Zealand in early January 1982. Gray was a keen photographer and sent home graphic letters and photographs of the three months he was away. He spent a fortnight touring Japan and England and on the Continent met up with a young woman. The two travelled together visiting Holland, France, Italy and Germany, followed by a week in Greece. Gray spent almost a month in Spain, Egypt and Morocco before returning through France and Holland to England.

On the Continent and in North Africa, David Gray's travels and experiences were not always to his liking. He was terrified when German police singled him out for interrogation. Short on money Gray roughed it, sleeping in backpackers' hostels and railway stations and one night was locked inside the Gard du Nord railway station in Paris. Alone with people of dubious backgrounds, he found the experience frightening, and on the Continent ran foul of some gypsies who poured oil on him during the night.

On his return, David Gray took his former workmate Paul Mead and his wife to a licensed restaurant and regaled them with his adventures, but always held something back. That night he stayed with the Meads, but when they visited Gray's cottage for a weekend some time later the friendship started to fall apart. They stayed two nights with Gray but found his lifestyle too basic. The cottage was sparsely furnished, food was scarce and the couple found it dirty and uncomfortable. Gray's cynicism and bitterness towards society was too much to take. He believed Asians were going to take over the country and was scared of losing what he had. In contrast was Gray's love of Aramoana, and he talked about it as if it was the best place on earth.

A major turning point in Gray's life came when his mother became forgetful and confused. Doctors said she might have Alzheimer's disease and would get worse. Gray did not handle his mother's illness well and often became short-tempered and nasty towards her. When required he would pull his weight around the house, but usually left the care of his mother to her sister. Despite this care, Molly deteriorated and after several months was admitted to hospital diagnosed with a brain tumour. The shock was too much for David and he broke down, and on the day she died in January 1985 he was inconsolable. From the time of his mother's death his world suddenly changed. Living in a Housing Corporation property was impossible for a single man and he had to leave. The only place he could go was the family cottage at Aramoana. Taking his mother's television set, the old Austin Cambridge motor car and his other few meagre possessions, Gray began a new life in a tiny cottage he affectionately referred to as 'The Homestead'. Years later he would rename his cottage 'Hlidskjalf' (the high seat in the palace of Odin, the legendary Norse God of War). A neighbour intrigued at the name asked David what it meant and was puzzled at his reply, 'You'll find out one day'.

Gray's sister and her family were regular visitors to his cottage at Aramoana, and after a meal they would walk along the beach, collect shellfish or go swimming. David would always join them and got on well with his sister and nieces, but not so with his brother Barry. While moving house one of the few indicators of Gray's darker side emerged. For some unknown reason David Gray suddenly produced a knife and threatened his older brother. Barry got the knife off him, but was surprised at how strong David was.

Not long after settling into Aramoana Gray lost his only means of transport. The Austin Cambridge was written off in an accident and from then on a ten-speed bike became his trademark. He regularly used it on trips into the port and occasionally into Dunedin. Aramoana was some distance from any shops and there was little alternative but to cycle. He was once seen carrying two ten-litre pails of paint home on his bike.

One of Gray's few friends in his early days at Aramoana was Niki Boon. She often went to the Gray cottage and, on occasion, he would visit her. Both were interested in ethereal things such as the occult, and would sit around the fire and talk. She found him articulate, but his humour had a rather dark side. Gray identified with what Niki called a deep and passionate nature. She said he held grudges, had a potential for extreme feelings and had a 'sharp edge' and once told her 'a Scorpio never forgets'. He never spoke about his feelings and came across as having a hard shell.

Gray was attracted to heavy reading such as Carlos Castaneda's books, full of stories of power and warrior images. With titles like *Power of Silence*, *A Separate Reality* and *Tales of Power,* the books suited Gray's mode of thinking at the time.

Niki Boon sensed David was seeking a closer relationship but as she was coming out of a bad period in her life she didn't want a relationship with someone who displayed such negative aspects as David Gray did. She told Gray, who said it wasn't that important, but he did make an offhand comment about 'just another rejection'.

Possibly the closest person to David Gray was his cousin, Jim Grainger. When Grainger visited Aramoana he had admired an oil painting hanging on the wall. The painting, titled 'The Homestead', was a self-portrait of Gray standing outside his cottage. The following day Gray handed his cousin a parcel, wrapped in newspaper. During the night he had painted a replica, but this time had included two figures in the foreground and the words, The Homestead, Crowbar and Dave, 21-1-84.

Gray always called his cousin 'Crowbar' because he kept a crowbar under the seat of his car, something David Gray found amusing. As well as painting, Gray tried his hand at pottery. One piece, a Japanese house with a detachable lid used as a storage jar indicated his interest in Japanese culture. In his letters to family he would sign himself off in Japanese. In April 1987 he wrote to Jim Grainger and talked about his new form of transport:

> . . . Bought a 10-speed bike. Self castration model by the pain it inflicts. I now buy cycle magazines to read. How much fun riding a bike is - I always end up with a head wind no matter which direction I'm heading. I'm coming up to Christchurch on the 5-5-87 so I'll probably give you a ring.
> Be well and Happy.
> Konnichi Wa, Arigato
> Dave

On the back of the envelope the return address indicated his dark humour:

> Sender: Rudolph Hess
> c/- Maximum Security Bunker
> B12, Berlin

Jim Grainger's wife Christine was expecting a baby and Gray always asked after 'Fred' and the family. He felt at home when he stayed with them. He would teach their older children how to build a house out of playing cards. Three months after one visit the Graingers received a small parcel, a pack of cards, addressed to the children, no note or explanation, just the cards. For most of his life, he was liked by those who knew him and he never posed a threat. Christine found it easy to engage Gray in lengthy conversation, but when Gray got philosophical she found it was above her head.

Gray could care about people. One of Jim Grainger's closest friends had been through a marriage break up so Grainger took him to a place he knew would be therapeutic - Aramoana and the Gray cottage. David Gray looked after his cousin's friend whom he nicknamed 'Dregs'. In the four days they were together the trio walked the beaches and talked. With them was Jim's three-year-old daughter, and David Gray was as much at home with her as with the men. Every time Gray wrote to or visited Christchurch he would ask after Dregs.

At times Jim Grainger would get 'stuck into' his younger cousin, especially about his attitude to work. David Gray's philosophy was simple. Working for someone meant making the employer rich, so why bother? The two would argue about work ethics, the unemployment benefit and the need to work to live.

Despite being regarded by some as a bit of an oddity, Gray was not physically odd. He had a reasonable build, being broad-shouldered and narrow at the hips, and had told Niki Boon he believed he was attractive to women and that some had shown an interest in him.

Gray suffered from myopia (short-sightedness) and was so impaired he was eligible to register with the Royal Foundation for the Blind and Partially Sighted. He was taunted as a child, and as an adult was never seen in public wearing glasses, though he had them in his pack the day he died. Once Gray visited an optometrist for new glasses and returned later with them badly damaged. The optometrist believed the glasses were mangled by hand, an activity associated with mentally disturbed people who, frustrated at their inability to see clearly, blame the glasses.

As time moved on, Gray gradually saw less of his family. Niki Boon moved away and, when not on one of his explorations, Gray helped neighbour Garry Holden build his house. Whether cutting and nailing timber or shovelling gravel off a truck, Gray was a willing worker.

In the earlier days Gray got on well with Garry Holden and had been trusted enough to babysit his girls, but the pair fell out over a dog. Gray was known to wander Aramoana in the company of dogs, and Holden's Alsatian, Kento, was the one he was most often with, exercising on the beach. Gray had become incensed at the way he believed Holden was treating the dog and when Kento was put down Gray became angry. From then on Gray seemed to sever his connections with the Holden family.

Gray had an affinity with animals, but suddenly became less well-disposed towards dogs. He was seen to violently kick out at smaller ones that came near his property and threw a large rock at another. Then he did something else out of character. Gray had a budgie named Condor that sat on his shoulder when he was outside and never flew away although it had the opportunity. Revealing his dark humour Gray would command Condor to attack visitors who called. Condor could perch on a matchbox and stay there as Gray added boxes to the bottom of the stack. In the end the bird would be perched on a stack of twelve boxes, gently swaying to-and-fro as it kept its balance. Inexplicably, Gray killed Condor with a brick, then promptly regretted his action. He claimed the bird flew away.

From early 1990 Gray was beginning to withdraw and keep to himself. Police were alerted to a prowler incident in the Aramoana area where women had reported a man, wearing a woolly hat, looking in their windows. The prime suspect was Gray. He lived alone, was regarded as an oddity, and was never seen without his balaclava. Some locals pointed the accusing finger in his direction, and several people confronted him outright. Gray was interviewed about the incident, and also reports of women's underclothes going missing. Enquiries showed the prowler was not Gray but few apologised to him. That incident made Gray resentful and he became even more withdrawn and paranoid. After the episode with the locals Gray remained alone for a fortnight, seldom venturing outside. He believed that if he had nothing to do with others he couldn't be accused. Gray's insecurity and disillusionment with society was being reinforced.

Towards the end, Gray began to show distinct signs of paranoia over the possession of his cottage. He began locking the door even if he was only going to the outside toilet, believing his brother or sister might come when he was out and take the cottage from him.

BEYOND PARADISE

Where once Gray regularly sent letters to his cousin in Christchurch, the correspondence suddenly stopped. The Christmas card the Graingers expected never arrived. Gray's attitude to people became blunt. In January 1990 he went into a building society office where he had investments. The loans officer asked Gray if he would mind not smoking in the building. Gray looked at him and said, 'Don't you want my money?'

When the officer said he appreciated his business, but would rather he didn't smoke, Gray ripped the deposit slip up, threw it on the floor and walked out.

For years Gray had visited the Galaxy bookshop in Dunedin. The owner sold secondhand books and magazines and stocked a lot of material that appealed to Gray. *Soldier of Fortune* and other combat magazines were favourites. The manager used to get on well with Gray, but had started to feel concerned and threatened by Gray, whose appearance and general nature had deteriorated. On his last visit to the Galaxy, Gray took exception to a part-time assistant with whom he had a verbal altercation. During this argument Gray placed a cardboard box on the counter. The barrel of a gun protruded from one end of the box. The manager reported this incident with the gun to police and when they later visited Gray they were shown a slug gun he had purchased that day. He was returning home when he called into the Galaxy. Gray frankly admitted to the confrontation, but as it wasn't one-sided police had no grounds for further action. The firearm had not been presented and it was not even referred to. A search of Gray's house failed to uncover any further firearms.

Other people noticed a deterioration in Gray's dress and demeanour, but his increasingly odd behaviour was seen more as a nuisance than dangerous. Garry Holden had a friend whose young next door neighbour was unpredictable and prone to violence. While discussing the youth, Holden had remarked, 'I've got one like that next door to me but thank Christ he's not violent!'

During 1990 Gray's health fluctuated, and although he didn't consult a doctor he believed he had ME (Myalgic Encephalitis). ME is either a post-viral syndrome or a defect in the immune system following a virus. Symptoms include tiredness, muscular pain, a lack of energy and a vague feeling of weakness. Worse still, Gray believed he had caught his disease from Garry Holden, who had earlier been afflicted. One spell of sickness lasted three days and Mrs Holden prepared food for Gray, but he shunned her attempts at friendship and slammed the door. Over five weeks that winter Gray was only seen two or three times. By night the house was dark, with no lights and no fire, despite the cold. David Gray was avoiding everyone.

He began assembling an arsenal that included military style semi-automatic rifles and huge stocks of ammunition. He was reading widely about guns and killing, and books borrowed from the library included *Killer, Military Small Arms of the World, The Dispossessed Majority, The SKS Assault Rifle, Home Gunsmithing, Fighters, Modern Fighters* and *Attack Craft.* The only title not related to destruction was one on Myalgic Encephalitis. These books were a far cry from those taken out two years previously - *How to Shingle Your Roof, Living on a Little Land,* and *Alcohol Fuel Production.*

He also had a catalogue imported from the USA called *Paladin Press* and in the space on the order form Gray had written down *Bloody Iron.* A description of the book Gray intended buying reads:

Bloody Iron by Jenks & Brown: A radically different book on knife fighting, *Bloody Iron* was written by ex cons who learned their edged weapon techniques in prison and on the streets, thus providing a new perspective on knife fighting. *Bloody Iron* begins with an informal discussion of the blades and fighting methods used by history's greatest knife fighters, from King David's son Absalom to Jim Bowie and others. Proper stance, style, choice of weapons and unarmed defensive manoeuvres are all detailed.

Other books Gray had shown an interest in included *Anarchist Arsenal* which had detailed instructions, diagrams and formulas for making explosives; *Patrolling and Attacking,* a manual on experiences in jungle warfare; a book on sniping called *The Police Sniper*; and another on knife fighting techniques from the infamous Folsom Prison entitled *Put 'Em Down, Take 'Em Out!*

Another book to fascinate Gray was written by Kurt Saxon. *The Poor Man's James Bond is* described as Saxon's classic and notorious work on improvised mayhem. The book discusses practical paramilitary information used by dissident and radical groups, how to make homemade poisons, improvised firearms and explosives, arson by electronics and other dubious topics. 'A truly informative book,' the catalogue suggests, 'by one of America's most infamous authors, only $16.95.'

Gray was impressed by the writings of Kurt Saxon and wrote to him saying, 'I have decided to risk more money on your publications which I enjoy. Your writings cause much provoking thought, somewhat a rarity in this day and age and you actually appeared on my television screen in a documentary on survival.'

Gray asked Saxon's opinion of a .22 as a defensive weapon. Saxon wrote back on the same paper Gray had used saying, 'Most any .22 rifle is good. In a pistol you can't do better than a Ruger, loaded with stingers or Magnum hollow points.'

Cloistered in his small lonely existence, disillusioned with society and believing the only way to survive was to do it alone, he penned an article entitled *Hard Line Survival Tactics -*

If you, like many, are becoming concerned with worldwide climatic changes, rising crime, inflation, recession and depression on a worse scale than eventuated in the 1930s, that our parents lived through at such cost, and if you are realistic enough to understand and realise the problems facing us are too big and too expensive for any government to handle then you must prepare. Even a small food cache will improve your ability to survive, anything you can do now will live up to the old adage, 'an ounce of prevention is worth a pound of cure'.

Protection of life and property by force of arms now that the police have been cut and re-cut in numbers and power, must be your first concern. Without the means of enforcing your safety, you are powerless. Guns are expensive and ammunition even more so. No matter the fire power or lethality of your firearm the first priority is bullet placement. Accuracy is found only in practice. For this an air rifle is the best and cheapest aid. A .177 calibre spring type is best. CO_2 arms lack power in respect that climate and temperature conditions can affect accuracy as well as amount of propellant.

For defence purposes a semi automatic is best. This is due to the stress factors in life threatening situations: The less you have to worry about the better. Panic and confusion can and will cause even the most experienced shot to miss. If you already own a .22 this will in all probability be adequate for your needs. The most accurate is the bolt action single shot, it is also the best for silencer use. Any closed breech type action cuts down noise caused by the movement of reloading an automatic. Pump and lever action are twice as fast to operate than bolt actions. Semi automatics in silencer mode are made more effective with subsonic ammunition. This will not operate the bolt fully resulting in single shot rather than repeat fire power. Noise from the bolt opening at firing will cancel the noise of self loading when using standard .22.

The unfinished article, found in a book of writing paper in his bedroom, included drawings of targets showing the brain, spine, heart and lungs. Drawings of knives, shooting positions and a variety of bombs, including one made from chemicals, were included. In a writing pad Gray had written lists which indicated his frame of mind:

Bike
New Zealand
Bike

Car
People
Bus ex Port

Fix fireplace
Family
Loner

Washing machine
Friends
Ruthless

Mower
Hate/frightened
Cold

Drill
Ignore
People
Attack
Actor
Detached

In his last few days Gray grew intolerant. Where once he did not mind children running across his land he began to place large rocks across the boundary in an attempt to keep them away. A letter from the Department of Social Welfare addressed to D M Gray was put by mistake in a neighbour's letter box. When she knocked on Gray's door he yelled, 'What are you doing here?' He took the letter and slammed the door in her face.

A woman visiting a house opposite Gray's had a young son who regularly visited Gray and had never been turned away. Two days before the rampage the boy visited Gray but came home distressed. She asked him what was wrong and he said, 'David sent me home because his mother has just fallen over and died.'

The boy's mother dismissed his claims as Mrs Gray's death had occurred five years earlier. But the boy insisted that a death had taken place in the Gray cottage that day. It is likely Gray's mental condition had deteriorated and he was fluctuating in his mind from the present to the past.

JUDGEMENT DAY

Tuesday morning 13 November dawned fine and clear. A very unpredictable David Gray was seen cycling out of the township. He arrived at Port Chalmers and, as he had done in the past, left his bike at a local greengrocer's shop. He boarded the bus to Dunedin where he intended purchasing another rifle. First he called at a bank where the female teller asked if she could help. Gray was unresponsive and pushed a slip towards her. Without speaking he watched her as he smoked a roll-your-own cigarette. Gray wanted a cheque made out to a third party and was told a $2 charge would be made.

Gray got angry. 'No way, no way, I'm not paying two dollars,' he said indignantly. 'I've been with you for years and have never been charged before.'

The teller explained that if she made out the cheque to DM Gray there would be no charge, to which he agreed. Gray became more angry when told the cheque would have to be made out again as the machine would not align properly. The agitated Gray asked about his investments, but the teller was unable to answer as the computer was down. At this Gray demanded to know where his money was and after being told it was safe, turned and walked out of the bank.

From the bank he went to Elio's Gun Shop to pay for a Papoose rifle he had ordered. He didn't take the gun with him as he wanted a silencer thread put on the barrel. The shop owner remembered Gray as a 'strange guy, sort of sunken-eyed'. The address Gray left at Elio's was 19 Albertson Avenue, Port Chalmers, the former family home. Gray may have been intent on deceit in using the old address, but more likely he had regressed to years earlier. This was only two days after he believed his mother had just died.

Not far from the gun shop Gray went to the Continental coffee bar and bought a pie. The baker was running late and the pies had only been in the warmer for about ten minutes. Gray stormed up to the counter and complained. While the pie was being heated Gray sat down again. The proprietor and her daughter were speaking when Gray leapt to his feet and came charging back to the counter shouting, 'You were talking about me weren't you, what did you say?'

The proprietor remembered his eyes. 'I've never seen eyes like them,' she commented. 'His whole manner was very threatening, like a madman.'

The woman went out to the back of the café to get her husband to come and deal with 'this guy' who was getting heavy. The powerfully-built owner came out and ordered Gray to leave. 'Don't come any closer,' Gray said as he picked up his bag, 'I'm going.'

As he left he paused at the doorway and yelled, 'I'll be back, I'm going to get you. I'll blow you away,' then raised his fist and walked away.

That evening, worried about the threat of retribution to the shop, the owner rang the police about the person with the mad eyes and the threats made. But the call was made two hours after David Gray had murdered 13 people.

On his way back to the Port, Gray approached a group of students in the back of the bus, believing their laughter and conversation was aimed at him. By the time he arrived back at the Port his mood was more subdued and he went to pick up his bike and buy some fruit and tobacco. He seemed perfectly normal.

'Bugger this,' said a tiring David Gray to the greengrocer, 'I think I'm getting too old for the bike, might have to get myself a car.' The seemingly placid nature of Gray by this time was indicative of his unpredictable mood swings.

On arriving home on that sunny peaceful afternoon, David Gray read a magazine called *New Zealand Guns*. He sat down, wrote a letter, addressed the envelope and stamped it ready to post. The revealing letter held the key to Gray's last thoughts on society, references to mass killings, and his views on how to stop people like himself owning guns. The letter read:

Sir, what a bugger, found your magazine on 13 November and so have missed your rifle draw. I have not read all gun magazines published but this seems excellent. In fact yours is the first I have ever subscribed to. So you must have made an impression.

The general public is an ass, high on drugs (legal antidepressants such as Valium), alcohol and sleeping pills, (100,000 sleeping pills taken per night), alcoholics, 55,000 in a population of 3.3M. They have as much right to decide anything as Genghis Khan's barbaric hordes did.

Liberty and freedom cannot be compromised. You either have full democracy or none. There is no, I repeat no halfway between them, only the slow slide to dictatorship.

A law has been passed requiring most owners of semi automatic weapons to give them up. Hoddle Street massacre causes: all .223 calibre weapons were summarily collected by police in the States of Victoria and New South Wales. All semi automatics were banned. UK, Hungerford, firearm certificates by police cut to one third. Many gunshops have gone out of business as a result.

As there are at least 750,000 guns in New Zealand, if outlawed the government could only pay a pittance for them. We are talking in millions of dollars. As gun owners in the majority are law-abiding citizens would they give up their weapons? The economic loss would be personal. An easy way to stop people owning guns is this:

Price increases on ammunition, e.g. firearms costing in the thousands of dollars, assault rifles nearly tripling in value in a year, so only the rich can afford it.

There is more, all of it bad. You only have to watch the TV news or read a newspaper. If you want mercy, ask it from God for you shall find none at the hands of man.

D M Gray

Within hours of writing that letter, David Malcolm Gray was to show no mercy.

TERROR UNLEASHED

No one knows what finally triggered the events of 13 November 1990 but when David Gray reacted, he was swift and merciless. One of his victims, nine-year-old Chiquita Holden, heard Gray arguing with her father Garry, then a door slammed. Moments later she heard a shot and saw her father lying face down on the grass. Chiquita, with her older sister Jasmine and friend Rewa Bryson, all ran inside to hide. Gray came through the door with a Norinco semi-automatic and shot Chiquita through the arm. She fled the house, leaving the other two girls hiding under a table. Gray killed them then set the house on fire.

Over the next few minutes Gray shot at anything that moved. Locals, attracted to the fire, became easy targets. A utility van with three adults inside the cab and three small children on the back pulled up outside the burning house. Ross and Vanessa Percy with their friend Aleki Tali quickly alighted from the ute but were cut down by Gray's bullets as they tried to take cover. The Percys' son Dion and his friend Leo Wilson hadn't had time to get off the ute before they were fatally shot, and three-year-old Stacey Percy suffered extensive injuries to her abdomen.

From there Gray fired at moving vehicles and pedestrians, one of whom was Jimmy Dickson who never had a chance to escape Gray's powerful weaponry. Moments later Gray went inside the cottage opposite his and shot two elderly men. One was Tim Jamieson, who had often given David Gray rides into Port Chalmers and the other was Vic Crimp who was retired. Both men died instantly.

Not content with having shot so many people, Gray went back over most of them and made sure they were dead by shooting again at point-blank range. Although people in the street would have been only a blur to the short-sighted Gray, he fired at figures in the distance. He hit Christopher Cole from 150 metres away and narrowly missed Jimmy Dickson's mother Helen who was crossing the road. One bullet went so close to Helen's neck she could feel the heat of it.

Within minutes Gray had killed 11 people and wounded three others - one of them, Chris Cole, died later that night. Gray's victims ranged in age from three years to 70 and six of his victims were children. Despite having ample ammunition, and potential victims close by, Gray chose to return to his cottage. He packed a bag with maps and basic equipment for a siege, blackened his face, and gathered up a lot more ammunition. Heavily armed he set off from his cottage, but not before making up a collection of molotov cocktails and smashing all of his windows.

By the time he left the cottage six police officers had arrived. New Zealand police are unarmed and had to collect firearms on the way to the scene. In a normal situation, they would have contained the scene and waited for a specialist armed offenders squad, but on this occasion Gray was on the move. The local police sergeant, Stewart Guthrie, tried to stop Gray. But he was only armed with a .38 revolver and was no match for Gray's fire power. When Gray appeared from behind a sandhill he fired at Sergeant Guthrie, killing him instantly.

David Gray knew the dense undergrowth and tracks around Aramoana intimately. He went into hiding and, apart from a series of shots fired at random throughout the night, he would not be seen again for 22 hours.

With two critically wounded people needing urgent medical help, police mounted rescues. Outside Gray's cottage Detective Paul Knox waited with three-year-old Stacey, keeping her calm as Constable Nick Harvey went for help. Silhouetted against the fiercely burning Holden house Knox was in peril, expecting Gray to attack at any time. However, Gray had set up a barricade near where Sergeant Guthrie's body lay, no doubt expecting other police to attempt a recovery. Any such attempt would have had the rescuers in Gray's direct line of fire.

Not knowing where the gunman was made the evacuation of the injured perilous, and actions to effect rescues earned some police officers well-deserved awards for bravery. After the injured victims were taken from the scene, it was a matter of blocking off any escape routes and waiting for daylight to be able to conduct a methodical search. To do this, police used their elite special tactics group (STG) who were heavily armed and expert at breaking into a room and clearing it. This was a particularly hazardous undertaking as many locals were 'holed up' in their cottages, unable to be safely evacuated.

One such resident was Helen Dickson who, despite being almost killed and having no idea where her son was, had to remain hidden inside all night as the gunman roamed about. Gray's probable location was eventually narrowed down to a few properties. Twenty-two hours after Gray had rampaged he was found in a house and surrounded by the STG. Not knowing if Gray held hostages, the STG could only return his fire by shooting high to keep him down. For a full two minutes Gray fired at the men crouched outside, hitting one policeman in the lower leg. Stun grenades fired at the windows of the house bounced off mattresses Gray had put up, and finally it was tear gas that forced him out. Suddenly and without warning Gray burst from the cottage's french doors, the freshly loaded Norinco at his hip. 'Kill me, fucking kill me', he screamed as he moved towards the police, firing as he went.

Three policemen returned his fire with machine guns and Gray fell to the ground. One bullet hit the Norinco sending it spinning from Gray's hand. Five other bullets hit the gunman, one going through his right eye and one touching his heart. Other bullets smacked into his arm and leg, yet police had to struggle to subdue him. He kept screaming hysterically, 'kill me, kill me'. Despite the serious injuries he showed amazing strength and the four policemen holding him down could not prevent him tearing free of the handcuffs several times. Only when he was finally secured did he give up the struggle. Moments later he died.

PSYCHOLOGICAL PROFILE

Dr Julia Aranui-Faed is an experienced forensic psychiatrist who provided a profile on Gray. Although she never met Gray, she gave a professional opinion based on evidence gathered about him. Her edited conclusions following a comprehensive clinical summary were as follows:

In my opinion there is a high probability Mr Gray was suffering from a disorder of the mind at the time he died. From being a normal, average, if sensitive, person he changed gradually over the years following his mother's death to becoming solitary, suspicious, irritable and convinced other people were harming him. In making a diagnosis I have considered the following disorders:

1. Organic Brain Disorder: I wondered if Mr Gray's slow personality and behavioural change with persecutory ideas might have been caused by some lesion which was damaging his brain, eg. brain cancer. But there were no abnormalities in any bodily system including his brain at post mortem. His intellectual functioning in the last 24 hours of life, where he planned and executed complex movements, tends to make an organic brain disorder unlikely. For the record his karyotype was 46XY

2. Schizophrenia: The pattern of a slow deterioration over some five years of Mr Gray's functioning as a worker, in his social relationships and his self care, coupled with this deterioration accelerating over the last year of Mr Gray's life, is of great clinical importance in diagnosing schizophrenia. So too is the duration of those signs of deterioration. Apart from the persecutory ideas, which may well have been delusions, that Mr Gray may have believed in unshakeably, we do not have any definite record of other first rank symptoms of schizophrenia. But it is highly likely that Mr Gray was experiencing auditory hallucinations, either hearing his own thoughts echoed out loud, or two or more people discussing or arguing about him in the third person, or voices that formed a running commentary on his behaviour. Mr Gray is known to have responded as if he had auditory hallucinations, at least twice, on the day of the shootings. Then there is his increasing social isolation and withdrawal. Unfortunately this occurred among a community that did not

know the younger Mr Gray. In addition, over the latter period of his life he displayed some peculiar behaviour, eg, repetitively and deliberately avoiding ordinary social contact by crossing a road sharply without looking up at the oncoming person: this is quite bizarre social behaviour in a person living in a small community.

For at least five years Mr Gray displayed the kind and degree of social, emotional and intellectual abnormalities which are commonly seen in the prodromal and residual stages of schizophrenia. He probably suffered from active symptoms of schizophrenia, eg persecutory delusions and auditory hallucinations at the time of his death. We do not know what other unusual perceptual experiences he had but we do know that he exhibited sudden and unpredictable changes in mood, often associated with inexplicable outbursts of anger. These changes are also often associated with schizophrenia.

While there was a definite reduction in his self-directed and goal-directed activity in terms of volume over the years, Mr Gray's writing, reading and his methodical buying of guns and equipment does not seem to equate with the empty, unmotivated, repetitive life seen in many people with schizophrenia. But then, schizophrenia affects each person in a different way, although the pattern of symptoms is recognisable enough for diagnosis to be internally consistent, if sufficient time has elapsed after their onset.

When we look at Mr Gray's relationships with the external world, we see that he withdrew from involvement, became emotionally detached and preoccupied with persecutory ideas, and possibly had hypochondriacal concerns. There were no descriptions of Mr Gray being confused, disorientated or suffering from memory impairment.

3. Schizophreniform Disorder: Mr Gray's illness had been gradually coming on for over six months, therefore this diagnosis is not appropriate.

4. Delusional Disorder: This diagnosis is a possibility but Mr Gray did not display the usual symptoms common in this disorder. He was neither litigious, grandiose or persistently angry. He was impaired in daily functioning over time and in occupational functioning; it is rare in delusional disorder to see such impairments to such a degree as is described in Mr Gray's case.

5. Major Depressive Episode: Chronic, untreated, moderately severe. Many features of Mr Gray's presentation over the last 18 months could fit with an ongoing depressive disorder including his persecutory ideas. Depression is characterised by a loss of pleasure and interest in all or most of the person's usual activities, and instead we see Mr Gray apparently actively pursuing some hobbies and interests, although increasingly unable to care for himself and his appearance. This unevenness of occupation and preoccupation is more usually seen in schizophrenia, rather than depression. In addition others did not react to Mr Gray as though he were depressed; he was seen as more explosive and irritable, than sad. We do not know how he ate or slept. He was not observed to be slowed up, or unduly restless but he did complain of considerable loss of energy and fatigue from 1989.

6. Personality Disorder: Whatever mental illness Mr Gray had, it developed when in his mid-20s. His abnormal social behaviours were not life-long in the way one sees in a person with a personality disorder, nor did he display antisocial behaviours; Mr Gray is not known to have lied, been reckless, assaulted or deceived people.

Diagnosis: I think the most likely diagnosis for Mr David Gray is that he suffered from an ongoing schizophrenic illness which began in his early to mid-20s, which slowly progressed and which caused his increasing social withdrawal and isolation and his uncertain temper and persecutory ideas.

He had experienced several grievous losses; his father, his mother, and his trust in his neighbours. But a normal adult man would have been able to psychologically survive those griefs. Mr Gray, already compromised by his oncoming illness, instead withdrew and alienated himself from his friends, family and neighbours. He clearly excited pity, but also elicited enough irritation by his self-centredness and emotional constriction, that people could not stay in sympathy with him, and keep on enquiring of him how they could help.

What caused Mr Gray to decompensate into the Aramoana gunman when he did? From the longitudinal evidence it is my opinion that he experienced a series of anniversary reactions around November (to his father's death, and family birthdays) without knowing it. He undoubtedly felt beleaguered and distressed and he blamed his feelings on others' actions and words, whether real or delusional. I think consciously or unconsciously he knew he might repeat the Hungerford and Hoddle Street massacres with his weapons (he probably had experienced surges of hate and/or murderous fantasies); but clearly in his last letter he did not directly apply that to himself; instead he talked of prevention through removing people's rights to have access to such weapons. It is probable that Mr Gray had had repetitive intrusive thoughts about shooting people, but that he had resisted acting upon those thoughts up until that day.

Something that happened in Mr Gray's world tipped the balance from thinking into action and he went out of control. Once Mr Gray had killed, I think he went into a "commando fantasy": probably it all seemed to him like a dream or a book coming to life, but with recurrent reminders that it was all in fact very real. This recurrent intrusion of reality probably ensured that Mr Gray presented himself finally to the police in such an uncontrolled manner that he was himself killed. I do not think that Mr Gray would have approved or agreed with what he had done at Aramoana.

CONCLUSION

Aramoana, despite its peaceful tranquillity, was probably the worst place for David Gray to live. While he could enjoy the solitary lifestyle he chose he was also easily able to step across the fine line from being a solitary figure to a total recluse. His access to a plethora of mayhem literature and weapons, coupled with the intrusive thoughts flooding his mind, was a recipe for disaster.

Cloistered in his small cottage, alienated from neighbours, there was no one to either notice his downhill slide or to confide in had he wished. When Gray wrote the letter to a gun magazine that fateful afternoon, he must have known that another Hungerford or Hoddle Street would take place outside his door.

The final thing he wrote was, 'If you want mercy, ask it of God, for you shall not find it at the hands of man.'

In David Malcolm Gray's case he was tragically right.

CHAPTER SEVEN

GEORGE HENNARD

THE LANDLOCKED MARINER
Killeen, Texas – 16 October 1991
Victims: 23 dead, 33 injured

INTRODUCTION

When the first *Santa Fe* train rumbled through Killeen in 1882 only 40 people lived in the town. Like much of the United States at that time, vast areas were being opened up with the advent of the railroad. Killeen soon became an important centre for cotton, wool and grain, but remained a relatively small farm trade town. That changed abruptly in 1942 when a military base was established at Camp Hood (later renamed Fort Hood) just west of Killeen. Thousands of construction workers and soldiers flooded into the area and Killeen was destined to expand or contract depending on the military presence. The city was all but depleted at the end of World War II, but boomed again when a permanent military base was established in 1950.

Fort Hood is today the largest military installation in the United States, sprawling across 868 square kilometres of the beautiful hill and lake country of central Texas. The Fort employs over 50,000 personnel and provides a projected economic input to the Killeen district of US$3.7 billion.

Killeen, with a population of 82,000 residents, is one of the fastest growing cities in Texas, due largely to the military base. In an attempt to entice tourists with the popular military image, Killeen adopted the slogan 'Tanks for the memories'. Visitors to the open fort can drive along Motor Pool Road and marvel at the hundreds of tanks and fighting vehicles of every description on display.

Twenty-five kilometres outside Killeen is the town of Belton, and one of its 14,000 residents was to leave an imprint on Killeen that no one would be thankful for. He would rip away the 'security blanket' that covered the people of the central Texas city, leaving them vulnerable.

A month after the massacre at Luby's Cafeteria in Killeen, an emotional Oprah Winfrey spoke with survivors on her award-winning television show. One of her guests summed up his feelings and reaction to the disaster:

> My emotions have run the gambit from feeling sorry for everybody who was left behind to being angry at the senselessness of it, to the apprehension I feel now about taking my family to a public place. If you can't be safe eating lunch in Luby's restaurant in Killeen, Texas where in the world can you be safe?

GEORGE 'JOJO' HENNARD

George Pierre Hennard was born in Sayre, Bradford County, Pennsylvania, on 15 October 1956. He was the first child of Swiss-born Dr George Hennard and his wife Jeanna. When the couple married in the mid-1950s Jeanna already had two children, Carla and Craig, from an earlier marriage. The recently-widowed Jeanna and her new husband were to have another son, Roby, in 1961 and daughter Desiree a further two years on. George Junior became known as JoJo, an easy way to distinguish him from a father with the same name. He was to be referred to by both names.

Dr Hennard had worked as an orthopaedic surgeon in public hospitals, but when he joined the army he and his family moved frequently. The Hennards lived on army bases throughout the United States as well as overseas in France, Germany and Thailand.

The Hennard couple had different, sometimes conflicting, styles of parenting. Jeanna tended to dote on the children whereas Dr

Hennard was a somewhat stricter disciplinarian. Desiree's memories of her childhood were notable for the strict atmosphere in the Hennard house. If their father said the children were to be off the phone in three minutes, he meant three minutes; if not he would take the receiver and hang up. Desiree didn't believe she or her siblings were physically abused but did recall them being hit with a belt, though in her words not unreasonably.

However, it seems that some punishments meted out to the Hennard children were somewhat unusual. Two of JoJo's classmates at Junior High School remembered an occasion when Hennard turned up to school with his hair grossly cut off. Desiree also remembered the incident well. JoJo had got into trouble for riding a dirt bike he was not meant to be on. His father had his son's hair hacked short as punishment, an embarrassing episode for an adolescent boy. The boy's reaction was to run away, but when he was found in Ohio and returned home, his hair was cut even shorter. As a youngster Hennard was regarded as a good-looking, outgoing boy, but as time went on he became quieter with a more introverted personality and few friends.

Hennard graduated from Mayfield High School in Las Cruces, New Mexico in 1974. His time there had been somewhat lonely. The White Sands missile base, where his father worked in the hospital, was a 35-kilometre bus journey from the school. Taking the daily trip alone, Hennard never had a chance to make many friends, and being rather introverted would have found forming friendships difficult anyway.

For a while he tried to join a band as a drummer, but the other members of the group soon found him unsuitable - not because he couldn't play the drums, but rather because of his selfish habit of wanting to do his own thing. Halfway through a piece he would suddenly change tempo and play as he wanted.

On leaving high school Hennard joined the navy and on 31 October 1974 went to sea. His first voyage on a naval support ship took the young Hennard to places that would feature largely in his later life - Pearl Harbour, the Philippines, Guam, Japan and Hong Kong. However, Hennard and the navy were not entirely compatible. Twice he had to front up to the captain for disciplinary matters and his overall performance fell short of what was expected. On 27 February 1977, at age 20, he was honourably discharged from the navy, but the recommendation on his file was that he was not suitable for re-enlistment. During the time Hennard was in the navy his father was transferred to a new post, taking the position of Commanding Officer of the army hospital at Fort Hood, Texas. The Hennard family moved to Bell County and bought a large house in Belton, which became known by locals as 'the mansion'.

Following his stint in the navy, George Hennard felt the sea in his blood and enlisted in the merchant marine. So began the only stable and happy time in his life.

FROM SEA TO SHORE

Hennard's time in the merchant marine was punctuated by a series of incidents. Walter Prasciunas was a seaman who worked with Hennard aboard the *Keystone Canyon* and viewed his colleague as a 'temperamental screwball'. The men had once got into a shouting match and, for Hennard, it wasn't an isolated occurrence. On other occasions he had yelled, screamed and threatened fellow seamen and in May 1982, soon after joining the service, he was briefly suspended for assault and battery while on the SS *John Lykes*. The incident had racial overtones, and, to make matters worse, Hennard disobeyed a command from the captain. He had not got off to a particularly auspicious start.

Sailing mostly out of San Diego and San Pedro, Hennard made 32 voyages on a variety of ships. Many of his trips were along the western seaboard of the United States as far north as Alaska or south to Panama. The journeys further afield, to the Orient and the Philippines, were Hennard's favourite ports of call. He found he could communicate more easily with girls in foreign ports and confided to relatives that he regularly saw prostitutes in the East. He considered they were more 'genuine', not 'stuck up' like the girls in the States. Hennard's brother-in-law Jimmy Shellenbarger felt it was those frequent visits to foreign ports that made it difficult for the naturally-shy Hennard to get along with females at home.

Although Hennard was very much a loner and one who got into trouble easily, he was nevertheless a good worker. He could be assertive but would back down when his challenges were met head on. He could socialise but wouldn't let people close to him, and always kept his feelings and thoughts at a distance from co-workers.

There is no doubt Hennard enjoyed his life at sea. The pay was good and he was comfortable in his rather solitary world. However, events took a drastic turn in 1989 and this led to his ultimate downfall.

Hennard was promoted to bosun, but on his first voyage aboard the *Green Wave* he did something blatantly stupid. As the ship returned to the States Hennard, with no thought of the consequences, took out a stash of marijuana, rolled a joint, and smoked it on the deck. Drugs and seamanship do not mix and Hennard was sent up to see the captain. The marijuana found in his shoe was sufficient evidence and Hennard was dismissed. His merchant marine senior mariner's licence was revoked, and the only life Hennard had enjoyed was taken away from him. Hennard was bitter, believing that other seamen did far worse things than he had yet retained their licences. However he was clearly the author of his own misfortune.

Following the massacre at Luby's cafeteria, police searched Hennard's home and found, amongst other documents, a radiogram advising Hennard that a seaman had been lost overboard from the *SS Aquarius*. Hennard had previously sailed on the *Aquarius* but was not aboard the day a seaman who worked in the engine room leapt overboard. The *Aquarius* was sailing off Acapulco when the man, under stress from a pending divorce, took his belongings, went up to the railing, and threw himself into the ocean. It is possible Hennard knew the sailor from earlier voyages together, and the man's suicide must have had some significance to him. It became evident that Hennard contemplated suicide during his time ashore, and the radiogram may have been a permanent reminder of the alternative way out.

Hennard was finding it increasingly difficult to handle life on land and was desperate to get back to sea. But no matter what he did, he couldn't convince maritime boards and the coastguard he was not a drug addict. He went to Longbeach, California, in January 1991 to plead with the coastguard to get the licence reinstated. Finally, in March, an application for clemency was sent to Washington, D.C. but it was to no avail.

In the week leading up to the massacre Hennard made his final attempt to gain reinstatement when he went to the Texan port of Corpus Christi. His appeal for clemency fell on deaf ears yet again, and Hennard's despair became all-consuming. Desiree had noticed the change in her brother from the time he was suspended: 'George got mad at the world over losing his job with the merchant marine. He was bitter others held their licences after doing worse things.'

While waiting for the reinstatement of his maritime licence, Hennard tried a variety of jobs, but was dismally unsuccessful. Following his interest in playing the drums, he found a job with the *Missing Link* heavy metal band playing out of Austin. Alexandria was a member of the band and, although not in any sort of relationship with Hennard, got to know him quite well. As far as she was concerned, Hennard had a bad attitude towards women and often referred to them as 'gold diggers'. It was his overall negative attitude that saw him fall from favour with the band, and when his involvement was terminated after five months, Hennard sold his drums and returned to Belton. A male member of the group, however, had a more positive view of Hennard - while admitting his former drummer was 'a little strange', he said he never thought Hennard would later commit such a terrible crime.

Hennard often went off alone into the desert where he set up the drums on a mat for a true 'solo' performance and once posted home a photograph of himself playing. On the back he wrote: 'June '91, Nevada Desert, grand final - solo. Love you mother, George.'

Band members from another group Hennard joined also felt their drummer was 'strange'. Nick Konovalski and Scott Wilson remembered Hennard well and recalled he had an obsession with serial killers. They also recollected that Hennard's favourite tune was Steely Dan's *Don't Take Me Alive*. It was not simply a favourite; Hennard became fixated with it. How that song might have influenced Hennard is unknown but he clearly identified with it closely.

Hennard knew he was ill-equipped to live a life ashore and found the prospect of being away from the sea untenable. In an attempt to get 'straightened-out' he booked himself into a drug rehabilitation clinic in Houston. He was hospitalised in the St Joseph Hospital between 14 and 31 July 1989, where he was given psychotherapy. When Hennard's father spoke to the psychologist who treated George, he was told his son had periods of extreme highs and lows and that at times could be very violent. That wasn't particularly surprising, as members of Hennard's heavy metal band had reported similar things about him, claiming he was a very intense person who used marijuana to calm himself down.

The psychotherapy went on long after Hennard was discharged from hospital and when the psychologist wrote to the US Coastguard he said he last saw Hennard in February 1991 and that he was 'doing well'. The psychologist's recommendation was for the licence to be reinstated.

THE LONER

George JoJo Hennard was very much a loner and got on reasonably well with only two men. One was his brother-in-law Jimmy Shellenbarger, and the other was his stepsister's fiancé Martin Flores. Both men initially found it hard to get to know Hennard but as time went on he began to thaw.

Shellenbarger's first dealings with Hennard came about seven years before the massacre. Hennard's voyages would keep him at sea for three-to-six months at a time. He would return home for perhaps six weeks and then was off to sea again. Whilst at home Hennard did a lot of maintenance around his mother's mansion and often spoke to Shellenbarger about his travels.

'He especially liked Thailand, Taiwan and the Philippines,' Shellenbarger said. Occasionally the two men would go fishing at Falcon Lake and it was on those trips Shellenbarger found Hennard to be 'a mild mannered type of guy, not at all aggressive'.

Martin Flores was engaged to Carla Hennard and his first meeting with George was about five years before the Luby's tragedy. However, an icy relationship existed between them for the first two years. Carla and her mother were more like sisters and when Martin and Carla socialised or went on vacations Jeanna often joined them.

'He didn't like me at first,' Flores confessed, 'and kept giving me these looks like "what are you doing here with my mother and sister?"'. The possessive and suspicious Hennard said very little to Flores in the first 12 months and such were the looks Hennard kept firing, Flores tended to stay away as much as possible. Martin Flores was a hairdresser and often fixed Jeanna's hair which angered Hennard. 'You're not 21 any more,' Hennard would say to his mother.

Only after Hennard realised Flores was serious and would be around long-term did he soften. Martin Flores found Hennard to be a 'nice guy' but that he had a bossy attitude. 'If he needed to get something done, he wouldn't ask you,' Flores remembered. 'He would just get you to help him.'

As his attitude softened, Hennard allowed Flores to cut his hair, though he was very particular about how it was to be done. While he was having his hair cut Hennard would relax and talk about the problems he was having around Belton and Killeen. He told Flores how the local girls were all stuck up and had no personalities, unlike the Asian girls he met abroad. The thing that worried Flores most was Hennard's paranoia about being followed. If someone stopped outside the house Hennard would insist they were spying on him, causing Flores to shake his head in disbelief.

'Then he would go into some sort of daze,' Martin Flores recalled. 'I don't know where his mind would be at times. I thought to myself there's something really wrong with Jo.'

One statement Hennard made while having his hair cut stuck in Martin's memory. 'If people don't stop fooling around with me someone will get hurt,' Hennard said.

Flores felt that, although Hennard was a nice guy, he still had an edge to him. 'He had an attitude of, it was his way or no way at all and he was the kind of person who wouldn't let you get too close.'

Hennard's time on the drug rehabilitation programme left him bitter. 'His personality totally changed between him, his mom, sister and me when he got suspended,' Martin Flores said. 'I was cutting his hair in Houston at a motel when he told me, "Marty, I'm trying so hard, there are people with real problems here. The guy next to me is the biggest cocaine dealer in Houston and does an ounce a day. But I'm working real hard because I know I don't have a drug problem like the others do."' Hennard was clear about why he was on the programme and said to Flores, 'I'm gonna make it though, because I'm gonna go back to sea where I belong.'

However, despite his beliefs about not being addicted to drugs, he was unable to convince the authorities and his licence remained suspended. George Hennard could rely on Shellenbarger and Flores as well as his mother and sister, Desiree, but lost contact with his father. Not long after Hennard joined the merchant marine, his father left the army and his wife of 25 years. With George at sea and her older children married, Jeanna was left in the Belton mansion with her two younger children while her estranged husband moved into private practice in Houston.

During 1990 Hennard tried his hand at a couple of jobs, but the work and the pay were not to his liking. He wasn't qualified for anything ashore and most of his efforts to find employment were in the labouring field. Jimmy Shellenbarger had a concrete business and took a crew, including Hennard, to work on constructing a missile range at a South Dakota military base. Shellenbarger realised Hennard was struggling to cope with life ashore and was starting to get on his mother's nerves so thought taking him to South Dakota was a good option, but soon after arriving Hennard had a major falling-out with his brother-in-law.

Pat Loth was one of a group of men working for Shellenbarger. At first Loth got on all right with Hennard but the more he got to know the moody JoJo the less he liked him. Others in the work gang didn't particularly like Hennard either, mostly because of his attitude. Occasionally Shellenbarger wasn't on the site, leaving Pat Loth in charge. When Loth told Hennard to do something he usually would, but at other times would whine about it and pout. Hennard had a strange relationship with the other men, always feeling they were out to get him, and constantly whined about people on the job. He didn't trust the other men and worried about what they might think about his being on the site. 'It doesn't matter what they think,' Shellenbarger told Hennard. 'I'm the boss and I'll hire or fire who I want.'

But Hennard was still suspicious, believing the other men were spying on him, and he even asked Jimmy if the contractor had talked about him behind his back.

Despite his age, at 34 Hennard was immature and temperamental. He would bottle up his feelings and when he got angry it was usually with Shellenbarger. Things came to an abrupt end when Hennard started 'smarting off' and talking back to Shellenbarger. The construction crew were staying in a motel and Shellenbarger challenged Hennard for 'slobbing out and not cleaning up after himself'. Hennard was proud of his custom-made Ford Ranger pick-up truck and washed it every day, but was found wanting when it came to other domestic chores. The confrontation took place on the work site in front of the workmen, and as the argument developed Pat Loth heard Hennard yell out, 'Fuck you Jimmy.'

The workers stopped and watched. Shellenbarger had had enough of Hennard's insolence and a fight broke out between the brothers-in-law. Shellenbarger picked up a piece of 2x4 wood and hit Hennard on the shoulder and the two ended up wrestling on the ground. When Shellenbarger held Hennard in a headlock and said, 'Watch out or I'll break your neck,' workmates stepped in and broke up the fight.

Hennard left the site and disappeared. Up until the fight Loth and the others regarded Hennard as a bit of a wimp, but with a quick temper. Loth always thought 'that little brat might lose it someday and really hurt someone'. However he didn't imagine that Hennard would ever go to the extremes that he later did. Shellenbarger wouldn't see JoJo again until July 1991. 'I whopped his ass and he left for Henderson, Nevada where his mother lived,' Shellenbarger said. Hennard didn't like the humiliation of his defeat and it took him a long time to again face his adversary.

Hennard had lived in his mother's house on Belton's 14th Street from the time Jeanna shifted to Nevada in 1990. The five-bedroom mansion was on the market and it was Hennard's job to keep maintenance up-to-date. Over the previous few years he had done numerous odd jobs on the property. Not only did he keep the grounds immaculate, he kept the interior spotless. The real estate agent acting for Jeanna Hennard had been told George was 'somewhat strange', a fact the salesman was to discover. Hennard was prepared to let prospective buyers through the house, but refused to allow them into his bedroom. Firearms he kept 'for self-protection' were stored in the bedroom so it was out of bounds. When he wasn't in Belton he would drive to Nevada where Jeanna had an upmarket apartment. With neither settled employment nor accommodation Hennard drifted back and forth between the two states.

It is clear from statements made by Hennard prior to and during his rampage that he disliked women. Whenever he visited bars he became bristly and nervous, especially around women. In a lot of ways Hennard was attractive to women, but once they looked into his penetrating eyes their instinct was to move away from him. However, there were occasions he dated women, though none of his relationships were either meaningful or long-lasting.

His longest relationship began on 16 October 1990 and ended abruptly two months later on 23 December. Judy knew of Hennard through his mother and the relationship began even before their first meeting. While at sea he wrote a couple of lengthy letters to Judy, but the content was very much about himself. When they finally began dating Judy found Hennard to be shy and 'kinda hard to talk to' but after a couple of weeks he became more comfortable with her. Although generally sensitive with good manners and a caring attitude, his demeanour changed after a couple of beers when he would become obnoxious. Whereas on one hand he had admirable qualities, Judy also found he could be very insecure and pushy. He seemed almost spoiled and seemed to believe the world owed him something, had no confidence in himself and constantly expressed paranoid beliefs. Hennard voiced strong views about life and death, and though against the death penalty was pro-abortion. When confiding in Judy he also talked about the jealousy he felt towards his brothers and sisters.

Judy recalled some of the events she and Hennard shared and in particular recalled a movie they saw, *Misery*, which obviously impressed him. Also impressing Hennard was his favourite song, *Don't Take Me Alive* by Steely Dan and he insisted Judy listen to the track time after time. During a week-long trip to California together Hennard asked Judy how many times she had been married. 'Twice,' she said, to which Hennard responded by saying he intended marrying a girl in Belton who lived down the road from him but then confessed he had never met her.

Hennard told Judy his inability to find work was all because the police in Texas were constantly following him. She told him the police weren't following him at all, but this angered Hennard and he accused Judy of just being like his mother who, he claimed, never believed him. She wasn't satisfied with Hennard's response and questioned him further. She wanted to know why he believed police wanted to follow him. Hennard claimed he once rented a house by a lake and local kids came around to listen to him play the drums. He said some of the kids would stay for two or three days and Hennard believed the police might think he was sexually abusing the kids.

Judy also felt uncomfortable with Jeanna Hennard who she thought was paranoid - 'always going on about how bad her marriage had been'. Jeanna constantly put Hennard down in front of Judy, causing friction between mother and son. Once Jeanna's Cadillac broke down and when Hennard suggested what the problem might be, Jeanna told him he was wrong. Hennard had helped finance the car and studied the manual closely. He called his mother a bitch and stormed out, slamming the door behind him. After that incident, Hennard confided in Judy that his mother was always telling him he was wrong about everything.

The moody Hennard could become obnoxious for no apparent reason. While waiting in line at a movie theatre, Hennard began giving a man in front of him a hard time, calling the stranger 'the suit man'. Judy felt uncomfortable with Hennard's totally unjustified verbal attack on the man. During their brief relationship the couple engaged in sex together, but it was not entirely satisfactory and Judy was sure that on every occasion Hennard failed to ejaculate. The end of the relationship came just before Christmas 1990 following a Christmas party. Hennard had become angry and abusive because one of his sisters had not bought a present he wanted. By now, Judy had begun to tire of his treatment of others and broke off the relationship.

One of Hennard's main interests was a study of military aircraft as weapons of war, and as well as an avid interest in air shows he collected model jet fighter aircraft. He built the large kit-set models with intricate care and put the date of completion on each one. At the time of the Persian Gulf conflict Hennard was confined to shore and watched every detail on television. He wanted desperately to get back into the merchant marine so he could become part of the 'Desert Storm' action. His failure to get reinstated only caused his frustrations to increase.

There is a popular misconception that mass murderers of the type profiled in *Killing for Pleasure* have a lifelong interest in guns. While they all have a close emotional contact with their weapons, many of them only take an interest in firearms in the months leading up to their rampages. Hennard was very much in this category.

The brief stint he had with the navy prior to joining the merchant marine would have introduced him to firearms, but he didn't enjoy guns and confessed to an acquaintance that he hated them. Why, early in 1991, he should purchase two semi-automatic pistols is unknown, but his ability to acquire the guns he would use at Luby's Cafeteria was patently obvious.

On 18 February, just eight months before the murders, Hennard purchased his first gun, a 9 mm Glock semi-automatic pistol. Responding to a newspaper advertisement, Hennard phoned Michael O'Donoghue at *Mike's Gun House* saying he wanted a pistol but was unsure as to what sort he should buy. O'Donoghue said the Glock was a good quality combat handgun and could sell Hennard one for $420. Hennard, using his driver's licence as ID, bought it with cash. As Nevada State required no waiting period, the weapon was transferred straight to Hennard, but O'Donoghue had a 'bad feeling' that something about Hennard was 'not right' - but he couldn't describe what it was. The bad feeling must have been significant, because O'Donoghue mentioned it to the receptionist when he took the registration form to the Las Vegas Metropolitan Police Department. She told him a red flag would be placed on the registration form.

Despite having a 'feeling' about Hennard, O'Donoghue sold him a second gun a little over a month later. The stainless steel 9 mm Ruger was in stark contrast to the jet black Glock, but every bit as lethal. Hennard had been suspended from the merchant marine for possession of marijuana but on the firearms transaction record Hennard answered 'No' to the question, 'Are you an unlawful user of marijuana?' If there was a follow-up check on Hennard's background it made no difference to him possessing the pistols.

It wasn't long after buying his guns that Hennard came to police notice. On 1 June 1991 Ranger Chuck Luttrell, travelling along an access road in the Lake Mead national recreation area, saw a lone man sitting in a Ford pick-up truck drinking from a can. When the ranger returned 45 minutes later the man was still there. The ranger approached the elusive and nervous driver and instantly smelt alcohol on his breath.

'Have you been drinking alcohol?' Ranger Luttrell asked the driver, who stared back through heavily bloodshot eyes.

'I can't say,' he replied.

Convinced the driver was under the influence, Ranger Luttrell ordered him from the truck and conducted a series of field sobriety tests. Hennard had gone to the recreation area to fire his guns and decided to have a drink from a six pack of Miller High Life 12-oz beer cans. Hennard had almost finished his fifth can and the sobriety tests confirmed Hennard was under the influence and he was arrested.

Only then did Hennard tell the ranger he had two loaded pistols in the cab. A fully-loaded Ruger was hidden behind the driver's seat and the Glock, loaded and with a round in the chamber was tucked away behind the passenger seat. On the way to the Las Vegas City Detention Centre Hennard was co-operative but displayed odd and bizarre behaviour. He was talkative, but it was mostly incoherent mumbling with vague statements about being kicked out of the merchant marine for drug problems. Hennard told Ranger Luttrell about his suspicions of women and how 'they' were out to get him and the guns in the truck were for his 'protection'. Hennard was charged with driving under the influence of alcohol and having loaded firearms in a motor vehicle. After being held briefly in detention and issued with a fine, his weapons were returned to him.

Hennard's only other scrapes with the law were for one speeding incident and, in 1981, for possession of a marijuana joint. The charge came about quite by accident. Hennard was driving around El Paso, Texas and before he realised, found himself approaching the US Customs international boundary with Mexico. By suddenly turning his vehicle around he raised the suspicions of border guards who stopped him and found he had a single marijuana joint. The case was turned over to the County and George Hennard gained a misdemeanour conviction for possession of a drug.

In early July 1991 Hennard decided it was time for a vacation and Panama beckoned. He tried to book a one-way ticket but was told by the travel agent it was a round-trip ticket or nothing. Hennard agreed and on 10 July was due to depart Austin, Texas bound for Panama via Dallas and Miami. However he delayed his departure by two days and when he left Austin on 12 July said he was going to visit some old 'army buddies' - though he had never been in the army and had no buddies.

The day before he left he visited Jimmy Shellenbarger. This was the first time the two had met since their fight in South Dakota. After the lengthy absence, Hennard had suddenly turned up at Shellenbarger's home around 9 pm and the two talked till 2 am. Hennard spoke about what he had been doing in Nevada, how his negotiations with the Coastguard were going and how he was looking forward to the Panama trip. Before he left he gave one of his pistols to his brother-in-law for safekeeping, and put the other in his bedroom closet with about $2,500 in cash. Shellenbarger told him it wasn't a very bright move but Hennard took no notice. He had tried to sell his Glock and Ruger to Shellenbarger who didn't want them, and as a compromise said he would try and sell the Ruger on Hennard's behalf but had no success.

What Hennard did or who he saw in Panama is unknown, but he was a different person when he arrived home a month later. He was even more paranoid, insisting that while on vacation he was constantly being followed by someone, but wouldn't say who it was. His strange behaviour was noticed by a number of people.

While Hennard's killing spree at Luby's was brought about by his paranoid belief that people were against him, the catalyst may have been linked to a wall he built at the Belton property. During widening of the street, dirt was pushed up against the deteriorating boundary wall, causing it to collapse. Hennard set about rebuilding the wall with bricks, but engineering mistakes caused it to collapse again. Undaunted, Hennard withdrew funds from his dwindling savings to buy materials and built the wall for a second time. He was proud of his achievement and was photographed while working on it. On 17 September 1991 the job was completed but according to Desiree, her brother's accomplishment violated a city code and the wall would have to be torn down. But the building inspector for the City of Belton had never had contact with George Hennard. Given Hennard's paranoia, he may have anticipated the authorities would object to the wall, giving rise to his belief that the people of Belton were against him.

Purchasing materials for building the wall had cost around $1,000, an amount which heavily ate into Hennard's reserves of $2,500. While working in the merchant marine, Hennard saved a lot of money that he invested in bonds or on the sharemarket, but he was forced to live off these investments while he was suspended. In October 1991 he was down to his final $1,500 and told his brother-in-law he did not know what would happen when that was gone.

Although he was 34, Hennard had become attracted to a couple of schoolgirls living nearby in Belton. Shellenbarger had heard Hennard call out to the girls, who were aged between 13 and 16 years. The remarks were of a flirtatious nature - never obscene - but they were directed at girls too young to warrant the attention of a man of Hennard's age. Shellenbarger teased him, suggesting perhaps he was some kind of pervert, and from then on Hennard never mentioned the girls again.

His attention then turned to two young women, but this time his actions had more sinister connotations. Nineteen-year-old Jana lived with her divorced mother in a cul-de-sac close to the Hennard mansion. Jana's 23-year-old married sister Jill often visited her family home, and the pair became the target of Hennard's obsession.

The women hardly knew Hennard. Jana had noticed him working around the mansion grounds stripped to the waist, his tall, muscular and tanned frame catching her attention. But when Hennard looked up and fixed her with a piercing stare she felt uncomfortable. Hennard wrote the women a five-page rambling letter suggesting they were 'groupies' of his. He didn't even know their names and put the letter, by mistake, in the letter box of Jana's neighbour. The occupant of the house took no notice of the strange letter and put it away in a drawer. Two weeks later, having received no reply, Hennard phoned Jana from Nevada. Having never seen the letter she couldn't make out what the strange man on the phone was talking about. It all began to make sinister sense when the next-door neighbour retrieved the letter.

Enclosed with the letter, dated 6 June 1991, was a photograph of Hennard playing the drums in the desert and Jana recognised the drummer as the man at the mansion with the frightening eyes. The letter spoke mostly of Hennard wanting to get together with the girls and contained a lot of inaccuracies. In part of it he wrote of his hatred of women:

. . . Do you think the three of us can get together someday? Please give me the satisfaction of someday laughing in the face of those mostly white, treacherous female vipers from those two towns that tried to destroy me and my family. It is very ironic about Belton, Texas. I found the best and worst in women there. You and your sister on the one side, then the abundance of evil women that make up the worst on the other side. I would like to personally remind all those 'vipers' that I have civil rights too, just because I did hire an attorney to enforce my civil rights, does not mean they have carte blanche to do what they want in violation of these rights. I will no matter what, prevail over the female vipers in those two rinky-dink towns in Texas. I will prevail in the bitter end.

Hennard finished the letter off:

> Now it is your turn to respond! Remember from the day on . . . no more talk of rejection, slander, deceit etc, the truth is now in writing.
> Peace sisters
> Love you both
> George - your fan
> P.S. How about sending me your nice 'piktures' ha ha ha ha ha.

The girls and their mother were frightened at the letter and very disturbed at the phone call. Over coming weeks they became increasingly fearful to even pass by the mansion. Hennard began to pop up in front of the young women - on the road, in the street and in the supermarket. His smirk and piercing eyes unsettled them.

The letter was shown to the Belton police, but as it contained no actual threats no action was taken. The women believed they were being stalked. A pet dog they owned was poisoned and there was clear evidence that someone had been prowling around the house. Jane, the mother of the young women, had tried to warn Hennard off, and she worried that something dreadful might happen.

The letter and stalking of the women was bizarre, but so too was some of Hennard's other behaviour. He began to throw rocks at boys riding their bikes past his home and chased a youngster who was retrieving a ball from the mansion's lawn. He fell out of favour with a former musician friend from his high school days. Hennard left his friend stranded at a supermarket after giving the man a lift there in the Ford pick-up. So irate was his friend that he phoned Hennard leaving a very blunt message on the answerphone. George Hennard interpreted the message as a threat, reinforcing his notion that everyone was out to get him.

Hennard regularly travelled to Nevada to visit his mother or sister Carla, though Carla became annoyed after he broke into her home when she was out. Shortly before the tragedy at Luby's unfolded, something happened between Hennard and either Jeanna or Carla and on returning from the visit Hennard told Shellenbarger he 'never wanted to go back to Nevada ever again'.

Only ten days before the shooting at Luby's, Hennard joined the Sportsman's Centre at the Fort Hood civilian range, but his ability with firearms was questionable. A visitor to the range left early after becoming concerned at George Hennard's unsafe practices.

THE PRIMED TIME BOMB

A few days before the shooting, Desiree had seen her brother, who seemed fine. He was still hopeful of getting back to sea and had been to Corpus Christi to check up on his status with maritime licensing authorities.

The day before the murders was Hennard's 35th birthday, and the only card he had received he discarded in his trash can. An elderly woman who lived opposite Hennard thought he was a lovely, caring, thoughtful young man. He would voluntarily help her around the house, cranking the lawnmower, killing her fire ants, changing light bulbs or doing other small jobs. Often Hennard would wave to her or call out but when she saw him on the morning of his birthday he did neither.

Hennard's birthday treat was to go for a meal at the Nomad Turnaround Café on the outskirts of Belton. As he sat alone eating his burger and fries he watched a news item on the television set about the Anita Hill/Clarence Thomas sexual harassment hearings. Anita Hill was shown talking to the US Senate when Hennard threw his half-eaten burger at the screen.

'You dumb bitch,' he shouted, before storming out. The following day he would again refer to women as 'bitches', but instead of a burger in his hand he would be holding a gun.

That evening Hennard had a long telephone conversation with his mother and talked over a problem he had. Hennard's visit to Corpus Christi had been fruitless and his application for clemency had been turned down. In his mind, Hennard firmly believed it was the people of Bell County who had prevented him from getting his licence back. His paranoia was rampant and the thought of never going back to sea became too much.

After an unhappy day, Hennard went to bed and rose early the next morning. He dressed in a blue short-sleeved shirt with orange patterns and blue flower designs on each shoulder, blue jeans and red socks. Under his shirt he wore a T shirt with the words, 'Ford - The Heartbreak of Today's Chevrolet'.

Between 5.30 and 6.00 am he rode his bicycle to Mrs Mead's *Leon Heights* grocery store where he bought sausage biscuits, a couple of candy bars, sugar doughnuts, orange juice and a Temple newspaper. Hennard was a regular customer and called most mornings to purchase something to eat. Mrs Mead always thought him to be a strange person, which was reinforced once when he told her, 'If you don't get the people of Belton to quit looking at me there will be some problems!'

She thought her strange customer was very paranoid and edgy and was always glad when he left the shop. On the morning of the killings he was different. 'He seemed almost calm, almost friendly, for the first time I can remember,' Mrs Mead said.

Hennard had no cash on him to pay for the groceries and asked Mrs Mead for credit. If she would let him have the items he promised to return later that afternoon to pay her in full. Hennard wouldn't return that afternoon but instead would lie dead along with 23 other people in Luby's Cafeteria.

After leaving the grocery Hennard returned home and ate his breakfast and, as was his custom, read the paper from cover to cover. Although he seemed calm to Mrs Mead, Hennard had found the previous weeks difficult. He had been heading into a downward psychological and financial spiral. He was rapidly eating into his savings, could not hold down a long-term job and had little chance of going back to sea.

A couple of weeks before the Luby's massacre he began to talk of suicide. He had become so paranoid he didn't trust anyone, even his family, and the only person he would confide in was Jimmy Shellenbarger. 'He said there were times he felt like putting a gun to his head and pulling the trigger,' Shellenbarger recalled.

Dr Hennard had spoken to his son only once in the previous three months, and on that occasion believed his son to be depressed with a distinct possibility he might attempt suicide.

Instead of simply carrying out his threats Hennard chose to commit a spectacular suicide, taking with him those he believed had tormented him over the past two years. When he first decided to embark on a killing spree is unclear, but it is obvious he did some planning. A couple of weeks prior to the tragedy he bought some new clips for his pistols 'that held more bullets than the ones I already had'. As he was not fond of crowds, Hennard was not in the habit of visiting large restaurants - preferring to cook his meals at home - so the choice of Luby's was deliberate. On the morning of the massacre he loaded his magazines and wrote a note to Desiree before taking the 20-minute drive from Belton to Killeen. His rampage was not a case of suddenly snapping, grabbing a gun and shooting. His actions were premeditated and planned.

After loading his bike on the back of the pick-up, he left Belton heading for Killeen, and just after 12.30 pm he approached the car-park outside Luby's Cafeteria. Inside, the 24 staff were busy attending to the needs of 150 diners.

THE MIDDAY MURDERS

At 12.35 pm on Wednesday, 16 October 1991, Judy Pfau and her husband Jim pulled into the crowded car-park of Luby's Cafeteria in Killeen, Texas. Inside, customers lined up in serving queues while others sat at tables enjoying their lunch. Staff busied themselves, waiting on the customers, or preparing meals in the kitchen area. Judy didn't see Hennard's truck at first. She heard it. The sound of the engine accelerating hard caused her to look up and then she saw it. Hennard's Ford Ranger fourwheel drive pick-up truck came powering into the parking lot. The driver suddenly turned hard left and pushed his foot to the floor sending his truck careening straight through the floor-to-ceiling plate glass window scattering tables, chairs and diners before him.

When the vehicle came to rest completely inside the dining area, several screaming people were trapped underneath the truck.

Hennard didn't wait to get out of the cab before he began firing. His semi-automatic pistols and rapid rate of fire were lethal. For a few seconds shocked diners thought it was a truck going out of control but their worst nightmares began to unfold.

Hennard climbed down from the truck, his face cold and expressionless, his eyes very large and frightening. 'Tell me people, was it worth it?' he asked the shocked patrons.

Hennard wasn't shouting but his voice was loud and forceful as if in full control. As he fired he continued his rhetorical tirade. 'Look what Belton did to me,' he said. 'Was it worth it?'

There was no swearing or cursing from Hennard, nor were there angry outbursts - just his controlled, forceful fury. The defenceless people had nowhere to hide and could only dive to the floor to avoid his bullets. As he emptied each gun he would quickly eject the magazine, slam a new clip into the butt and continue shooting, almost without a pause.

Roxanne and Connie had ridden their motorcycles to Killeen intent on buying bags from the local bike shop. The two women left their leather jackets and helmets at their table and were in the serving line when the plate glass window exploded. As the shooting began the two threw themselves to the floor and could hear the shots getting closer and closer, louder and louder. Hennard's hatred of women was made clear. 'All women in Killeen and Belton are vipers,' he called out.

Also huddled on the floor beside the women was Lee Whitney. Connie's head was a mere 25 centimetres from his and Whitney sensed Hennard was standing right above him. Connie lifted her head to look at Hennard and only had time to call out, 'Oh my God,' before Hennard fired.

'Take that, bitch,' Hennard said, then moved away. For a second Whitney thought he had been shot, but apart from the incredible ringing in his ears he felt no pain. When he opened his eyes he could see Connie had been shot in the head.

Roxanne also heard the gunman's footsteps and the explosion, then felt the vibration from her companion's body. Blood began running down Roxanne's arm. It was not hers but Connie's.

Roxanne couldn't, wouldn't, look up but heard Hennard's footsteps as he casually walked away firing at selected targets. Roxanne was shocked at the callousness of the savage attack and Hennard's voice - coherent, purposeful, loud, and strange.

Hennard specifically selected his victims, took aim and fired, mostly with shots to the head. He wasn't hurried, just walking deliberately and taking accurate aim before firing. 'Tell me people . . . was it worth it?' Hennard continued to taunt his victims.

A kneeling man raised his hands in a sign of surrender but Hennard's response was to shoot him then move on. Luby's was in pandemonium. Some people near the exit fled outside, while others followed the manager to escape out the rear service door. Dozens of people were trapped with no hope of escape. Some tried to feign death while others resorted to prayer hoping they would be spared by the hunter.

Twenty-eight-year-old Tommy Vaughn at two metres tall and weighing 137 kg is a big man by anyone's standards. He was dining with friends in the northeast corner of Luby's when they became trapped. The group could only lie helplessly near a window. As the shooting came closer they began to panic. Some kicked at the windows while others swung chairs against the plate glass. It was to no avail, and no amount of effort would break the window. When someone yelled, 'He's coming over our way,' Vaughn leapt to his feet. In desperation he ran full force at the window past a startled Lonnie Sims. 'This big, huge guy, like a bulldozer rammed himself through the window,' she recalled.

Tommy Vaughn's actions saved countless people who streamed out after him, fleeing from death at the hands of Hennard. Scars from the broken glass will be with Tommy Vaughn for life, but thanks to him, many survived who would otherwise have died.

Hennard was not just controlled during his rampage, he was also able to rationalise things as he went about his hideous task. Two women who fell to the floor as the truck crashed through the window were able to crawl to the bathroom, forcing the door shut. Soon after they heard Hennard's voice outside and a woman pleading with him. 'I'm sorry, I'm sorry,' she said. Immediately after, shots rang out shattering ceramic tiles in the bathroom. The pleading woman on the other side of the door died instantly.

As Hennard walked around he would kick at people's feet. If they moved he shot them. In one case he walked up to a Luby's employee and asked, 'Was it worth it?' As the employee was about to speak Hennard killed him at close range.

Anica McNeil had gone to Luby's with her mother and four-year-old daughter. The women sheltered on the floor, protecting the toddler as Hennard walked past, firing as he went. He turned and looked at Anica who hugged her daughter tightly while staying close by her mother's side. Hennard fired one shot at them then turned and walked towards the kitchen. Trying to escape was all but impossible. Anica had the four-year-old to carry and her mother had been shot through the thigh. Before they could even contemplate escaping Hennard came back, pointed the gun directly towards Anica's mother and fired again. The bullet found its mark and the older woman died instantly from a head wound above the right eye. The terrified Anica was at Hennard's mercy and she tried to shelter her young daughter. In an extraordinary moment, amongst all the carnage he was creating, Hennard let her go. 'You with the baby,' he ordered, 'get out and tell them Bell County was bad.'

Anica, cradling her daughter in her arms, walked through the gaping hole in the window to safety. Hennard turned away as the young woman left and continued his killing spree. In the few minutes he was at large Hennard made several laps of the restaurant, passing some people three times.

Those who could escape made their frenetic dash through exit doors or the window broken by Tommy Vaughn. Others still trapped or injured were in peril as Hennard made his third and final lap. Lieutenant Colonel Steven Dody, injured earlier and unable to move, watched helplessly as Hennard came back and straddled him. The colonel looked at Hennard and said, 'Why don't you get out of here and leave us alone?' Hennard responded by shooting him in the mouth. Some who were trapped weren't going to give up without resistance.

When Hennard approached another family with a baby, a sudden movement distracted him and he veered away. The distraction gave 71-year-old Al Gratia a split second to react and he lunged at the gunman, desperate to stop the massacre, but Hennard saw Mr Gratia coming and felled him with a fatal wound to the chest. Al's wife also died in the rampage, with only their daughter Suzanna surviving the onslaught.

With his Ruger out of ammunition Hennard placed it down on a plate amongst the remnants of a violently disrupted meal.

The Rescuers

Had Hennard arrived at Luby's minutes earlier he might have faced armed resistance from a uniformed police officer who had just left the restaurant. But other police were close by and reacted immediately.

A group of Killeen police officers were finishing their lunch-break in the nearby Sheraton Hotel. The men were attending an auto-theft seminar run by Sergeant Jody Fore of the Texas Department of Public Safety, and when Sergeant Fore glanced down towards Luby's he saw people fleeing in panic. The officers ran outside and, realising immediately that something terrible was happening, joined other police responding to the flood of emergency calls for help.

Sergeant Bill Cooper was one of the first police officers on the scene. Fleeing patrons yelled to him that a man with a machine gun was killing people inside. Taking shelter behind a car the sergeant looked into the restaurant and saw Hennard casually shoot a woman in the head. At that moment, Sergeant Fore and Investigator Olsen fired at Hennard, who returned their fire, narrowly missing the officers. Chuck Longwell and Ken Olsen were both organised crime investigators with the Killeen Police Department. The two men and another KPD officer, Al Morris, didn't hesitate, and walked through the broken plate glass window. As they moved forward the men fired, forcing Hennard towards the rest room area. Al Morris called on Hennard to drop his weapon only to get the response he expected.

'Fuck you,' Hennard yelled back. 'I'm going to kill more people.' Each time they called on Hennard to surrender they got a similar response, along with a volley of shots.

Sergeant Cooper and Ranger Clayton Smith went through another broken window and joined the other men cutting off Hennard's escape. Bill Cooper had to go around tables in front of Hennard but before he could take cover had to move across bodies. Some were dead, others were screaming for help as the sergeant, down on all fours, clambered over them just eight metres from Hennard. Luckily Hennard's pistol jammed, giving Sergeant Cooper and the others time to take cover closer to him. 'I saw his weapon had a spent round sticking up like a stove pipe,' Bill Cooper said. 'I hollered, "Police Officer, drop the gun."'

Hennard ignored the challenge and was not about to give up. Hennard cleared the jammed round and backed himself into a corner near the bathrooms. Chuck Longwell was behind a wooden counter while Al Morris crept to an alcove near the bathroom, then dashed to a serving cabinet getting even closer to Hennard. Longwell and Olsen attracted Hennard's attention while Al Morris took slow, deliberate aim and fired. The bullet hit Hennard forcing him back, but he remained on his feet. He flinched as another three bullets hit him and then fell to the floor.

Sergeant Cooper was only three metres away and watched Hennard push a fresh clip into his Glock, cock the weapon, roll onto his back and put the gun to his temple. Hennard pulled the trigger and blood instantly flowed from his nose and mouth. The fiend of Luby's gasped once and died.

Such had been the terror inside Luby's that one young employee, desperate to escape Hennard, squeezed his 90 kg-frame deep inside a commercial dishwasher. Too frightened to call out he lay still and was found 19 hours later, alive but shocked. He believed he had only been hiding for a couple of hours.

For others it seemed like the ordeal took hours but it was

over in minutes. From the first call for assistance until Hennard fired on the police only three-and-a-half minutes had elapsed. Within one minute of police arriving at the scene, Hennard was cornered, unable to take any other victims. The entire ordeal, from the first call until Hennard's suicide, took 11 minutes.

In three-and-a-half minutes Hennard fired over 100 rounds and exacted his terrible vengeance for whatever he perceived Bell County had done to him. Before George JoJo Hennard died he had managed to kill 23 innocent people who had simply been at Luby's having lunch.

PSYCHOLOGICAL PROFILE

Hennard believed he had a lot of enemies, particularly women. While he had been regarded as strange for some time, his paranoid behaviour increased from the time he was suspended from the merchant marine, accelerating in the final couple of months. Hennard genuinely believed he was being followed and could not understand why people would not believe him.

He once told Martin Flores that a vehicle was following them but when Flores turned to look behind them the roadway was clear.

'He even thought his phone was tapped,' brother-in-law Jimmy Shellenbarger recalled. 'He thought police tapped it but when I asked him why would they do that he said "they" were after him.'

Another time Hennard believed an oncoming vehicle with one headlight out was some kind of 'sign'. Hennard's paranoia became so intense towards the end that his sister did most of his shopping.

George Hennard had a habit of recording his voice on cassette tapes. Some of the more revealing comments he recorded were about a visit he made to the FBI in Las Vegas on 5 June 1991, when he complained about unknown women who had formed a nationwide conspiracy against him. He told the FBI agent that women followed him around the country, spied on him, tapped his phone, stood in front of his car and warned employers not to take him on. The 'conspiracy' theory, Hennard told the agent, was a recent phenomenon.

Hennard may have been a schizophrenic. His paranoia and appearance suggest this was a possibility, one reinforced by Dr Hennard.

'His father once told me his son was a schizophrenic and had a split personality,' Jimmy Shellenbarger said. 'For instance, there were times I would see him and he would be clean-shaven and tidy. At other times he was scruffy, unshaven and hyped-up.'

Hennard's unpredictable behaviour became apparent in those final weeks. 'Once JoJo asked me what would happen if he went outside and pulled a gun on somebody,' Shellenbarger said. Other people had also heard Hennard talk of shooting people.

Investigator Greg Holloway found hundreds of photographs amongst Hennard's personal effects and was intrigued at the subjects. Most were of ships or ports of call but only a few showed people, a sign of Hennard's solitude. Videotapes and notes written by Hennard gave an insight into his thinking. Police found a video Hennard had labelled 'Murder in the USA/Murder and Mayhem', detailing serial killers in the States. Another video was about James Huberty, who became infamous for his terrible deeds at the McDonald's family restaurant in San Diego.

Hennard was secretive in his writings, sometimes using the makes and models of vehicles to code notes that only he could follow. In trying to crack the code, police believe one of his notes may have referred to Pizza Hut, perhaps an alternative target to Luby's. In a blue notebook found in his lounge, Hennard had written:

And they shall live with what they have created. They shall find no redemption in laying guilt at an innocent man's door - curse on Belton.

On another page Hennard wrote: 'I am not an animal, nor am I a number. I am a human being with feelings and emotions.' On the October 16 square of a calendar he wrote: 'Life has become a stalemate, there is simply no hope and not a prayer.'

The phrase 'I am not an animal' is used a lot in the film *The Elephant Man*, which Hennard watched with Desiree. The film that impressed Frank Vitkovic, apart from *King Kong*, was *The Elephant Man*. That film portrayed a pathetic, lonely man, despised and ridiculed by others, something both Vitkovic and Hennard could identify with.

Placed between the pages of a Maritime Union dues book was the radiogram about the man lost overboard from the SS *Aquarius*. On the reverse side of the radiogram Hennard had written: 'The fatal mistake that the "hicks" and "whores" of Belton, Texas made!'

Hennard *always* called his sister Desi, but before setting off on his murderous rampage wrote her a final note:

> Desiree, enclosed is $100 to cover the water and electric bills. Do not pay the phone bill! I am responsible for it. Southwestern Bell violated my privacy rights therefore they don't get paid. Don't let the people in this rotten town get to you like they done to me! Take care of yourself and be strong. Love you. Brother JoJo.

CONCLUSION

During the gun battle with the police, Hennard suffered a number of wounds but none of them were fatal. One bullet went through his right forearm into his chest and a second passed through his left thigh. Another bullet hit him in the left heel and a fourth grazed his back. The fatal shot came from his own hands when he fired a bullet which went into his right temple and out the left. Post-mortem tests for alcohol, drugs or amphetamines all proved negative. Hennard, despite being a drinker and occasional drug user, was completely sober when he went on his rampage. Police did find a marijuana joint in a shirt pocket hanging in his closet but he had not taken drugs for some time before the killings. There was nothing in the medical examination of Hennard's body that could give cause for his actions at Luby's.

Hennard perceived a lot of 'enemies' were out to 'get' him, not least the police. On a small notebook found in his room he had penned: 'The Belton police department is the most worthless bunch of bastards I ever saw.'

However, minutes after starting his rampage, Hennard was to find out the Texan police were not 'worthless' but were prepared to disregard the danger to stop his killing orgy. Had police been able to take Jana and Jill's complaint further, Hennard's view of them might have been even more venomous.

It was the wish of Hennard that he be cremated and his ashes scattered on the ocean off San Diego, California. Perhaps it is prophetic that the man who longed for the security and solitude of the sea should choose San Diego as his final resting place. It was there that James Huberty, like Hennard, chose a crowded family restaurant to exact terrible vengeance on the 'enemy'.

CHAPTER EIGHT

THOMAS HAMILTON

ARCHITECT OF EVIL
Dunblane, Scotland - 13 March 1996
Victims: 17 dead, 17 injured

INTRODUCTION

The savagery and randomness of mass killings are all shocking in the extreme. If anything sets them apart from other crimes, it is the extent of the carnage. But on 13 March 1996 Thomas Hamilton perpetrated what must be one of the most despicable crimes of the late twentieth century. In a matter of three or four minutes Hamilton had killed 16 five-year-olds, along with their teacher.

If anything could be worse than the massacre of defenceless children, it is the knowledge that Thomas Hamilton planned his crime down to the last detail. He knew what he was going to do days, if not weeks, beforehand and the extent of his planning left his victims no chance.

The features of the Dunblane tragedy that make it so overwhelming were summed up by Dr John Baird, a forensic psychiatrist engaged by the Procurator Fiscal to look into Hamilton's background.

'If you were moving to Scotland and could live in Dunblane, you would probably do that. It is where families want to live. And it was mid-morning in a primary school, a safe place! When is a time more ordinary? If we are not safe in Dunblane on a Wednesday morning in the middle of March, we are not safe anywhere.'

Dunblane is a small, attractive city in the central lowlands of Scotland. An ecclesiastical centre since the 7th century, it is dominated by the magnificent gothic cathedral standing serenely amid old-world buildings. Six kilometres to the south is the city of Stirling, which historically was strategically important to Scotland. Surrounded by inhospitable terrain, Stirling is the gateway between the north and the south. Stirling Castle takes pride of place and it was there the coronation of the young Mary, Queen of Scots, took place. The streets of the city hum with people and traffic where once the surrounding areas rang out to the sounds of battle as William Wallace (immortalised by Mel Gibson in the film *Braveheart*) defeated the English in 1297. Soon after, at nearby Bannockburn, the English suffered another defeat. This time it was at the hands of Robert the Bruce in a battle that won the war of independence, uniting the Scots under Bruce. These events perhaps marked Scotland's finest hours, yet 700 years later a man living on the slopes of its most famous battlefield was to give Scotland one of its darkest hours.

HAMILTON - THE MAN

Thomas Hamilton was born in Glasgow on 10 May 1952 and was destined to suffer rejections throughout his life. The first came soon after he was born when his parents separated. By the time Hamilton was three his parents had divorced and he was left in the care of his mother, Agnes. She and the infant Thomas moved to the home of her parents, and on 26 March 1956, before Hamilton had turned four, he was adopted by his grandparents, and his name changed from Thomas Watt to Thomas Watt Hamilton.

For many years Hamilton was to believe his grandparents were his natural parents and that his mother was in fact his older sister. The family moved to Stirling in 1963 where Hamilton remained until his death on 13 March 1996. His life for the main part was uneventful.

Following the Dunblane tragedy, Dr John Baird tried to develop a profile of the life of Thomas Hamilton. There were no face-to-face interviews or contemporaneous information, but he was able to draw from the huge amount of information police investigators had put together. By listening to the accounts of family, friends and acquaintances, and studying photographs of Hamilton's flat, Dr Baird was able to come to some conclusions, but was not able to unearth much about Hamilton's early life. Most of the information available related to milestones in Hamilton's life rather than his personal development.

Baird learned little about Hamilton's early life because superficially his life was so unremarkable. He had grown up in what seemed to be a stable family, attended school with records which were unremarkable, and didn't come to attention as a delinquent or as a person with behavioural problems.

Although growing up in the belief that his mother was his sister was unusual, Dr Baird did not believe it amounted to very much as far as the stable family situation went. During Hamilton's teenage years, through fear he would find out from another source, he was told of his true parentage. Rather than responding negatively, it seems there was no particular reaction and right up until Hamilton's death his mother continued to refer to him as her brother.

After his primary education in Cranhill and Stirling, Hamilton went to Riverside Secondary School and Falkirk Technical College. He began his working life as an apprentice draughtsman in the County Architect's office in Stirling, but that lasted less than four years. He decided to open a shop in Stirling specialising in do-it-yourself goods, hardware and fitted kitchens. He continued at Woodcraft for 13 years until he sold the shop, opting for a life on the unemployment benefit. His only other employment activity while on the benefit was buying and selling cameras and undertaking some freelance photography. Later in life he became more interested in photography but for far more sinister reasons.

Things went wrong for Hamilton in July 1973 when events overtook him. It was something that he never forgot. Those events fermented in his mind, and became one of the catalysts for his infamous ending.

Comrie Deuchars was the District Commissioner of Scouts in the Stirling area and was approached by a 21-year-old venturer Scout called Thomas Hamilton. The young man had a desire to become a Scout leader and, after the normal checks as to his suitability, was appointed an assistant Scout leader of the Stirling troop. He began well and showed potential to become a good leader. Hamilton was certainly keen and for a few months presented no problems. At one time he volunteered to take boys out on to Loch Lomond, but was forbidden as his boat had neither flares nor oars and there were insufficient life jackets. Hamilton also had an inadequate knowledge of the waters.

In October 1973 a Scout troop was to be revived at nearby Bannockburn and Thomas Hamilton was appointed leader. After only four months Comrie Deuchars received a torrent of phone calls from concerned parents whose boys had returned home from a camp frozen, hungry and distressed. Thomas Hamilton had taken a group of boys in his own van to the hills above Aviemore. He had not booked accommodation and slept with the boys in the back of his van. It was so cold that February night that the van froze solid and had to be towed eight kilometres to Aviemore to be defrosted. As soon as the van could move Hamilton drove the boys home without even providing a warm drink.

Summonsed by Comrie Deuchars, the young Hamilton was left in no doubt that he had not met his responsibilities and similar episodes could not be tolerated. He was told by Deuchars to 'get a grip' and sent on his way. Rather than learn from the mistake and the chance he was given, Hamilton made matters worse. Three weeks later Comrie Deuchars received further phone calls from irate parents. Hamilton had taken a group of boys into the hills and spent the entire weekend teaching the youngsters how to build snow caves. Everything became soaking wet - clothes, sleeping bags and equipment. Had the temperatures dropped to the point they had been three weeks previously, the consequences could have been disastrous.

Clearly the irresponsible and immature Hamilton was unsuitable to be a Scout leader. The county commissioner, Brian Fairgrieve, met with Deuchars and decided Hamilton should be asked to return his warrant forthwith. On 13 May 1974 Deuchars wrote to Hamilton requesting the warrant but it was several months before it was returned.

For a number of years Thomas Hamilton would plague the Scouting movement with requests to be readmitted, claiming victimisation. On numerous occasions he met with county commissioner Brian Fairgrieve, but never again mentioned his expulsion to Comrie Deuchars. However, Hamilton and Deuchars were to meet 14 years later and, as it turned out, the association had a bizarre twist.

Brian Fairgrieve was, at the time, a doctor and made a telling observation of Hamilton. Soon after the warrant was returned Fairgrieve wrote a confidential letter to the Scottish Scout headquarters in Edinburgh. In it he made it clear Hamilton should not be a member of the Scouting movement.

> While unable to give concrete evidence against this man I feel that too many incidents relate to him such that I am far from happy about his having any association with Scouts. He has displayed irresponsible acts on outdoor activities by taking young 'favourite' Scouts for weekends during the winter and sleeping in his van, the excuse for these outings being hill-walking expeditions. The lack of precautions for such outdoor activities displays either irresponsibility or an ulterior motive for sleeping with the boys.

In a rider to the letter he said:

> His personality displays evidence of a persecution complex coupled with rather grandiose delusions of his own abilities. As a doctor, and with my acumen only, I am suspicious of his moral intentions towards boys.

Fairgrieve found Hamilton a very difficult young man to talk to. Hamilton would elaborate on everything - one moment being aggrieved, and the next apologetic. One of the interviews at the infirmary went on for over an hour and Hamilton became quite obnoxious and demanded his warrant back. Two days later Fairgrieve got a letter from Hamilton sincerely apologising for inconveniencing him. Fairgrieve's impressions of Hamilton were that he was ingratiating and devious and, if he wasn't getting his own way, would twist things round, saying things he thought the listener wanted to hear.

Fairgrieve regarded Hamilton's domination of boys as almost sadistic, and also believed he was unable to see the logic of the actions that had led to his forced withdrawal from Scouting. He never imagined Hamilton was violent or would resort to violence, even though he clearly held grudges.

Fairgrieve considers the length of a person's letters to be inversely proportional to the content. Hamilton's letter condemned itself and by the time Dr Fairgrieve reached the fifth foolscap page he realised much was repetition. Hamilton was a very wearying person, and over 20 years wore Fairgrieve down.

It is perhaps indicative of Thomas Hamilton's state of mind - believing that he had more worth than people gave him credit for - that he wrote to the Scout Association requesting they hold a committee of inquiry into his perceived victimisation. When his request was declined he wrote back saying he now no longer wished to hold a warrant 'as I do not want my good name to be part of the so-called organisation in this district.'

Despite deciding to give up hopes of Scouting, Hamilton continued sending letters of complaint. Early signs of his paranoid tendencies were now developing. Not only did he claim the Scouting organisation had ruined his reputation, he now linked it with the actions taken by other organisations, particularly the police.

Although continuing to complain to Scout officials, Hamilton never mentioned anything to the man who first raised the issue of Hamilton's unsuitability. Comrie Deuchars had nothing to do with Hamilton until, one day in 1987, Comrie was sitting in his lounge when a van pulled up outside. Deuchars recalled seeing Hamilton get out and start unloading furniture. Comrie turned to his wife and asked, 'What have we done to deserve this?' thinking there was bound to be tension between them.

Hamilton and his adoptive parents moved into the downstairs flat at 7 Kent Road, where the elderly Mrs Hamilton was to die later that same year. Five years later Mr Hamilton snr moved out into sheltered housing, leaving the 35-year-old Thomas alone in the flat.

Deuchars spoke to Hamilton almost every day, and while quiet, Hamilton never looked him in the eye.

A common trait of mass murderers has been a tendency to play pranks on people or deliberately scare them, seeming to get pleasure from the discomfort of others. Thomas Hamilton was no different. If Comrie Deuchars was cutting the lawn or doing the garden, Hamilton would creep up and whisper in his ear, 'Comrie your coffee's ready.'

Comrie Deuchars is a placid person but that behaviour struck a nerve and he told him, 'Tommy, shout from the bloody kitchen.' Eventually Hamilton got the message but Deuchars believes he somehow enjoyed giving him a fright.

The same behaviour was exhibited to another neighbour in Kent Road. An elderly woman, Mrs Grace Ogilvie, would be hanging out her washing at the back when she would suddenly hear a voice right behind her.

'How are you today?' She too got a fright, to which Hamilton would simply say, 'Did I give you a fright Mrs Ogilvie?' then turn and walk away.

Hamilton regularly invited Comrie Deuchars in for coffee and although he would take up the offers, Deuchars regarded Hamilton's house 'a tip'. The cooker was covered in grease and the fridge next to the cooker had grease all down the side, with unwashed dishes everywhere. Occasionally Hamilton would offer to clean the Deuchars' cars inside and out which he would do immaculately, in stark contrast to Hamilton's personal and domestic cleanliness.

In almost a decade of living close to Comrie Deuchars, and interacting with him, not once was any mention made of the scouting episode. But six days before Thomas Hamilton went on his rampage at Dunblane he wrote a letter to the Queen, patron of the Scouting Association. In the letter he complained bitterly of his treatment by the Scouting administration and blamed Comrie Deuchars for his predicament. After the killings at Dunblane, Deuchars was interviewed on the BBC *Panorama* programme. They asked him about the letter to the Queen and produced a copy. He was shocked and stunned that Thomas Hamilton had been hoarding that grudge for 20 years.

When Hamilton's life with the Scouts ended, he switched his energies to boys' clubs which, with ulterior motives, were to become his passion. One was his need to exert dominance, the other a tendency to paedophilia. There were numerous things about Hamilton's behaviour that were indicative of his personality. Firstly was his interest in young boys, especially if they were scantily clad, and his tendency to have favourites among them. Secondly was his complete change in personality when he was with children. He went from being a quiet, almost hand-wringing sycophant when with most adults, to a domineering, almost sadistic personality with children. Then there was his cavalier attitude to the needs and comfort of boys on his camps, and his strict disciplinary actions against them. Finally was the way in which he fiercely defended his actions and the belief that he was right and others were wrong - blaming others for the downfall of his clubs, and ultimately his standing in the community.

From 1981 until he died he operated 15 different clubs in and around the Stirling district for boys aged seven to 11, attracting members by leaflets sent out to homes through primary schools. The clubs were almost always held on school premises. A couple of clubs lasted a number of years but more often than not they folded after a year or sometimes two.

Hamilton had a grade five certificate from the British Amateur Gymnastic Association that allowed him to provide a limited degree of coaching but only when someone with higher qualifications supervised him. On occasions he was assisted by volunteer parent help but not often and mostly he ran the clubs entirely on his own. He even resorted to using the word 'committee' in the clubs' titles, implying there was some sort of governing body overseeing the groups, but the only person involved was Thomas Hamilton.

In the early days the clubs were popular, attracting up to 70 boys, but rumours of his domination and his behaviour would see numbers dwindle to less than a dozen. Eventually the clubs folded.

Hamilton's intentions were, on the surface, laudable. He claimed he wanted boys to do something to keep them 'off the streets', to experience discipline for later life and to become physically fit. But his style of running the clubs attracted much comment, and Hamilton was later described as a 'Jekyll and Hyde' character.

Gordon Crawford was a gun club associate of Hamilton's who had known him for ten years, and regarded him as a quiet, lonely chap who didn't talk much and socialised even less. Hamilton only ever spoke to the group's officials and never got into the spirit of the club. Women particularly distanced themselves, though no one could say why they found Hamilton to be creepy. At the club Hamilton tended to do his own thing and disregarded the normal conventions. He even made his own targets, and during free time on the range the rapid fire of his pistol was noticeable. If he ever made a minor mistake such as firing too many rounds and it was brought to his attention, he would become extremely apologetic, almost to the point of being nauseating.

Crawford described Hamilton as always being dressed the same, 'wrapped up tight, almost claustrophobic and wearing an anorak, usually with the hood up. He would carry two bags, one strapped across his shoulder, the other in his hand.'

But it was the difference between Hamilton's demeanour at the gun club and at the boys' clubs that caused Crawford to use the Jekyll and Hyde analogy. Hamilton had developed a façade to prevent bringing attention to himself. After his death, local television screened clips from videos Hamilton had made of boys doing gymnastics at his club. Gordon Crawford saw a different man in these videos, one who was outspoken, a more 'in-your-face' character. Especially with the younger boys, Hamilton was very domineering, and Gordon Crawford couldn't believe the personality change. Others noticed the change in his dealings with parents and occasional helpers, believing Hamilton was over-regimented - bordering on the militaristic. There was too much shouting and many of the exercises boys were expected to do were over-strenuous for their age.

Typically Hamilton became defensive and blamed others for his inadequacies. The mother of a boy who applied to join one of Hamilton's clubs wanted to ensure everything was 'above board', and went to the club to speak to Hamilton. He was the only adult there and she asked him how the club was run and what organisation was behind it. She found Hamilton very difficult to talk to; he wouldn't look her in the eye, was evasive about the organisation of the club, and clearly uncomfortable about the conversation generally.

The further he was probed for answers the more defensive he got. At that point the mother left it, deciding to speak to other parents. Each time she picked her son up from the club he seemed more and more troubled. Although she couldn't say why, she felt increasingly uncomfortable about Hamilton being alone around children. Following her maternal instincts she declined to allow her son to go on one of Hamilton's summer camps. One would have thought that would be the end of the matter, but soon after she received an irate and paranoid letter from Hamilton accusing her of being a bad parent for not allowing her son to have this 'wonderful experience'. Another mother recalled a similar meeting with Hamilton, and came away with identical feelings and misgivings.

Summer camps were a significant part of Thomas Hamilton's clubs. Hamilton was known to have 'favourite' boys, and put pressure on them to attend his summer camps even after only one appearance at the club. One evening he was at his door when his next door neighbour, Mrs Ogilvie, went past. He asked her inside and, despite reservations, she went in and was ushered to a seat. Hamilton showed her a video of small boys, all bare-chested and wearing swimming trunks, doing gymnastics. He was obviously proud of what he called 'his boys' and took from a chest on the floor a picture of a six-year-old.

'This one's my favourite,' Thomas Hamilton said to her. Half-an-hour passed, then Mrs Ogilvie made an excuse to leave as she felt uncomfortable while viewing the video, sensing Hamilton was watching her.

Hamilton always insisted the boys wore black swimming trunks, which he provided, and made them change in front of him rather than in the changing rooms. He claimed the boys wore unsuitable clothes so he would provide a uniform, all in black. While this insistence of Hamilton's made parents suspicious and wary, he seemed nevertheless to be a plausible individual who always had an answer to their questions.

In July of 1988 Thomas Hamilton fell foul of the law He claimed to have run over 50 one- and two-week summer camps, and with access to boats, he held a camp on Inchmoan Island on Loch Lomond. Following a complaint to the Strathclyde police, two constables paid Hamilton an unannounced visit. They found the campsite messy, with dirty dishes strewn about. Food was far from wholesome, being only tinned and powdered, and there was no sign of any fresh food. Accommodation was in tents with damp sleeping bags. Children were unsupervised in and around the water and those not swimming were inadequately dressed for the weather conditions. Boys were not allowed to wear trousers, Hamilton's excuse being legs dried quicker than trousers, and their legs bore scratches from bracken around the island. Although a few boys were enjoying their stay, others were homesick - they were not allowed any contact with their families - and complaints about the food were numerous. Hamilton did not deny he punished cheeky boys by slapping them. The camp was not considered dangerous, but nevertheless was badly run and very basic. Soon after, parents picked some of the boys up and took them home, but no one made an official complaint. Further enquiries revealed most of the boys had been struck by Hamilton or had witnessed assaults, but because of discrepancies in the stories no action was taken - another instance of Hamilton feeling unjustly accused.

Doreen Hagger was one mother who had occasion to take Hamilton to task. Her son had only been to a club for a few weeks when he came home with an invitation to a summer camp. She had doubts about Hamilton's overbearing attitude towards the boys right from the start. Her son got a bruise when Hamilton hit him for not running after a ball fast enough, but she assumed this must have been more accidental than deliberate. The application form for the camp said accommodation would be in chalets, but that parents would not be welcome at the camp, 'as boys might get upset'. Hamilton seemed plausible enough, so she relented and let her son attend the camp. He didn't enjoy the experience for a variety of reasons. He had a fear of water, but Hamilton nevertheless took him out with other boys in the boat and made everyone swim back to the shore. He was too frightened to go in the water so Hamilton threw him in to teach him survival skills. The only food on offer was curried potatoes, and if the boys refused to eat they were hit with a wooden spoon.

When confronted by Doreen Hagger, Hamilton claimed the police had it in for him and that there was nothing wrong with the camp. She insisted she would join him and help with the cooking, but only if she could take her closest friend. She was still uneasy about being alone with Hamilton. Mrs Hagger remembered Hamilton as someone who always tried to be polite, but she found him creepy. She got firsthand evidence of what an expert later believed were Hamilton's sadistic tendencies of getting pleasure from the boys' discomfort. Hamilton was sitting outside his tent on a chair when a boy asked if he could go to the toilet. Hamilton looked at the lad and pondered for what seemed like a minute. Then he just said, 'No!' It was that sort of domination Hamilton enjoyed having over the boys.

First aid equipment and skills were almost non-existent, children were not allowed to talk at meal times, and boys had to line up to clean their teeth from a bucket of water taken out of the loch. These recollections of Doreen Hagger epitomised some of Hamilton's tendencies towards domination and sadism. But it was Hamilton's alleged sexual behaviour that Doreen Hagger took exception to. She claims individual boys would be selected to go to Hamilton's tent at night to rub suntan oil over his naked body. Hamilton was investigated for the sexual abuse of Mrs Hagger's ten-year-old son, along with others who alleged that Hamilton had sexually assaulted them by rubbing his hand on the inside of their thighs.

Because he was never prosecuted, Doreen Hagger decided to take things into her own hands and concocted a mixture of foul-smelling liquid which she fermented for a few days. She alerted a reporter and newspaper photographer as to her actions and waited for Hamilton to emerge from a hall. As he came out she threw the putrid contents of the bucket over him shouting, 'Sorry I didn't bring any little boys to rub it in for you - you pervert.'

The next day his photograph appeared in the local newspaper.

Mrs Hagger's action was intended to bring the matter to a head. But instead of him laying a complaint of assault - thereby giving her a chance to appear in court and accuse him in her defence - Hamilton chose to ignore the incident.

Hamilton's brushes with the law were of little consequence to him. Predictably, he turned things around and claimed police, in collusion with the Scouts, were out to discredit him. From then on Hamilton's fixation of a 'brotherhood' conspiracy led to a stream of letters to police, his member of parliament, newspapers and anyone who would listen - ultimately the Queen. A distinct trait of mass killers is their paranoia, and Hamilton was no different. His correspondence became more personalised and critical of police - and was particularly vindictive against police officers who visited his camps.

Complaints about a subsequent summer camp came forward. Assaults on boys, Hamilton's photographing of them, and inadequate supervision (despite his promises of having up to four adult overseers) were of concern. Unsupervised boys were some distance from the camp, jumping in and out of a boat tied to a jetty. The water was deep, no one had life jackets and the youngest boy was just six. Hamilton didn't seem to regard this as a problem. Police investigated, but Thomas Hamilton denied assaults saying he only chastised a boy for throwing stones by slapping him on the legs. It was on this camp in 1991 that Hamilton did something unusual when he took one boy to a tent and photographed him wearing red swimming trunks. On all other occasions boys had worn tight-fitting black trunks.

During an investigation, photographs police seized showed boys in various poses, but as there was nothing explicitly indecent, no official action was taken. Despite the gathering evidence the police file was endorsed, 'No pro: no crime libelled - not in the public interest'. Police were not only unable to prosecute Hamilton, the photos had to be returned to him.

Thomas Hamilton's unusual personality was described by Chief Inspector Ferguson who investigated a complaint he had made against the police officer who tried to prosecute him. At the public inquiry into the Dunblane killings Ferguson said:

I have completed 30 years' police service, a long number of these as a CIB officer. Throughout these years I interviewed many hard criminals, many aggressive people, many reluctant witnesses, many complainants against the police, but I can honestly say that interviews with Mr Hamilton were the most exasperating of my career.

True to form, Thomas Hamilton even complained about the way the chief inspector investigated his original complaint.

By 1992 Hamilton had had enough of summer camps so opted for what he called 'residential sports training courses'. More complaints were received but again no crimes were considered to have been committed, and this reinforced Thomas Hamilton's belief he was being picked on. There can be no doubt that Hamilton's clubs were an opportunity for him to gain some perverted pleasure. After the Dunblane massacre, police searching his flat found 445 slides, 542 photographs and 4,260 negatives, almost all showing boys in black swimming trunks, along with 37 videotapes of boys doing gymnastics.

Few, if any, considered Hamilton a danger. As is so common with mass killers, at some time they threaten someone, but the threat is often not reported. Thomas Hamilton was no different, and he had a dark, hidden side to his character, a side shared by similar mass murderers. In Hamilton's case, he was investigated by police twice for taking handguns and a semi-automatic machine gun to the home of families whose sons attended his clubs.

Only a few weeks before the tragedy at Dunblane, Hamilton was talking to a Mr Gillespie, who was a frequent visitor to his Kent Road home. Hamilton had a 9 mm pistol in his hand and asked Gillespie if he had any boys, would he let them join his club? When Gillespie said no, Hamilton pointed the pistol at him and pulled the trigger. The pistol was unloaded but frightened Gillespie who called Hamilton a stupid bastard and tipped coffee over him before walking out. The incident was not reported, as Gillespie believed Hamilton would just deny it.

THE GATHERING CLOUDS

The last six months of Thomas Hamilton's life were turbulent. Three of his clubs had recently collapsed and another he proposed never got off the ground, as only one boy attended. In August 1995 he went on a vigorous recruiting campaign, delivering a large number of circulars to parents in Dunblane, hoping to change what he believed to be false and misleading information about himself.

As the clubs' activities fell into decline, Hamilton's interest in firearms gained ascendancy. This again is a common trait of mass killers - their interest in firearms manifests itself in the lead-up to their rampages. From 1987 to late 1995 Hamilton had not purchased any ammunition, yet from 22 September 1995 until 27 February 1996 he purchased 2,200 rounds of ammunition, a 9 mm Browning pistol, a .357 Smith & Wesson revolver and two holsters. He was to take both these handguns to Dunblane primary school two weeks later.

Hamilton had now become a much more active shooter at the Stirling Rifle and Pistol Club and again he was noticed for his rapid firing. Where competitors were required to fire three rounds at each of two targets in six seconds, Hamilton would fire 12 rounds at one target. A member of the club had referred to Thomas Hamilton as a 'right weirdo', commenting that he 'talks about his guns as though they were his babies'.

Hamilton spoke to people about guns and what bullets could do, including the 'spray' of bullets which disintegrate rather than pass through their target. He would shoot at books to see the spray of bullets going through the thickness of the pages. He also tested which bullets were best at avoiding jamming on his handguns.

Around this time a person who spoke to Hamilton on the phone noticed he seemed more depressed and talked increasingly of firearms with comments such as, 'I'm going back to my guns'. He had said shooting more and more took his mind off his problems. A phone conversation to someone else was perhaps more indicative of Thomas Hamilton's mood. He had said he was lonely and 'that it was not good to be alone'. A visitor to Thomas Hamilton in those last few days knew he was home, yet Hamilton never answered the repeated knocks on the door.

Adding to Hamilton's worries were serious financial difficulties. Insurance monies he had received in 1983 for a boat destroyed by fire, and the proceeds of his shop sale in 1985, had dwindled away. He made losses on his boys' clubs and summer camps over the years, and the camera equipment he bought and sold meant the end of his unemployment benefit from November 1993. By the end of 1995 there was a substantial reduction in his camera business on which he had taken out a large loan, and he also suffered a setback when the *Amateur Photographer* refused to carry his advertisements.

His day-to-day living expenses were mostly covered by credit cards. In March 1996 he had no capital in the bank and was in receipt of a housing benefit. He owed money to shops and his bank, and was in arrears with credit card companies. A loan application had been declined and he was behind in the payment of council tax. Thomas Hamilton's debt was in excess of £8,000.

Just over a month before the massacre Thomas Hamilton wrote a letter to Councillor Ball, who had supported an earlier application by Hamilton to run a boys' club by being a referee. He headed the note, 'Private and Confidential' and sent copies to a number of principals of schools, including Dunblane primary school. Hamilton complained that teachers at Bannockburn were informing parents that he was a pervert, and that letter showed his first indication of his problems with Dunblane primary school. A part of the letter said:

> At Dunblane primary school where teachers have contaminated all of the older boys with this poison, even former cleaners and dinner ladies have been told by the teachers at school that I am a pervert. There have been reports at many schools of our boys being rounded up by the staff and even warnings given to entire schools by head teachers during assembly.

Thomas Hamilton complained that he had no criminal record, had never been accused of sexual child abuse and claimed not to be a pervert. He was right in that he had no criminal record, but he certainly had been accused of sexual abuse, and the thousands of photographs of boys in tight-fitting swimming trunks was evidence of an unhealthy attitude towards children.

The effects of the so-called misinformation spread by police, scout officials and others had, in Hamilton's own words, 'been the death blow to my already difficult work in providing sports and leisure activities to local children as well as my public standing in the community.'

On 7 March Hamilton wrote a similar letter to the Queen, posting it shortly before the killings at Dunblane. His closing words to the Queen were:

I turn to you as a last resort and am appealing for some kind of intervention in the hope that I may be able to regain my self esteem in society.

Copies of this letter were sent to numerous people, including the principal of Dunblane primary school.

Thomas Hamilton was now on a suicidal course. He began organising his rampage - and it was the extent of his planning that sets him apart from other mass killers of his ilk. On the day Hamilton wrote to the Queen he approached a nine-year-old boy playing at the Dunblane boys' club. He was a pupil of Dunblane primary school and Thomas Hamilton sat the boy on a bench and asked him about the school, the gym, the way to the hall, where the stage was, what time different classes went to assembly, and where the fire exits were. Thomas Hamilton gained the information that the youngest pupils would be in the gym at 9.30 on a Wednesday morning. The next Wednesday Thomas Hamilton would strike.

In his pre-planning, Thomas Hamilton approached a retired police officer and quizzed him on police response to firearms incidents. He mentioned Hungerford, where Michael Ryan went on his killing rampage, and remarked on how police had seemed scared to go after Ryan. He wanted to know which police offices held firearms, and asked questions in such a way that it seemed he was just indulging in conversation and not seeking information.

Thomas Hamilton had also been seen coming out of the Braehead primary school in Stirling carrying a type of briefcase used to carry guns. When approached he said he had been organising another boys' club but seemed agitated - as if he had been caught out. As part of his planning he may have been looking for an alternative target for his orgy of destruction.

It is evident from a chance remark he made to an acquaintance that from as far back as the beginning of March, Thomas Hamilton was intent on his plan. Hamilton had just bought two shirts on credit and the remark he passed was, 'The beauty of it is that I will never have to pay for them, ever . . .'

Hamilton's mood on the days immediately prior to the onslaught appeared normal. Agnes, his natural mother, had met him on 11 March and then on the 12th, the day before the killings, Hamilton went to her home, had a bath, a meal, and passed the time of day with her for about four hours. The day before the killing Thomas Hamilton travelled to Dunblane, but by three o'clock in the afternoon he was back in Stirling, where he hired the white van that he was to use the following day. The receptionist at the hire company was to comment later: 'He unnerved me quite a bit, the way he spoke mainly. He spoke very slowly, very clearly, precisely, but with no emotion or expression. There was just nothing, nothing in there. You couldn't have held a conversation with him.'

That night Hamilton parked the van a short distance down the road from his flat in Kent Road and prepared for what was to be a shockingly vile crime. As a draughtsman he had been commended for neatness and detail and was later described as being methodical, thinking in advance before acting. He was about to put those skills to use.

Sitting at his dining room table, Thomas Hamilton marked his 25 magazines, each capable of holding 20 rounds of ammunition, with a yellow sticker on the front and an orange label at the back. This was to ensure he inserted the magazine into the butt of his pistol the right way round. Each magazine had been loaded in a uniform sequence, with part-metal jacket, soft nose, hollow point bullets at the bottom of the magazine, full metal jacket, semi-wadcutter types in the middle, and full metal jacket, round nose bullets at the top.

Experts consulted later had never come across such an arrangement before, but concluded it could have been done to avoid the risk of a cartridge sticking between the magazine and chamber.

The canvas bags carrying Hamilton's ammunition were tied open so they could not close accidentally, and had cardboard inserts so they would not collapse. A man preparing for such a dreadful event might be preoccupied and be at best casual, if not careless. But not Thomas Hamilton - his careful planning was significant. Dr Baird believed the way Hamilton loaded each magazine and the marking with colour-coded tape showed he was thinking clearly. Furthermore, police found a Mars bar wrapper discarded amongst other bullets on the dining room table. It was quite clear Thomas Hamilton sat at the table carefully preparing while eating a Mars bar. Dr Baird believes Hamilton was relaxed and felt very much in control.

No one knows what happened in those last hours but presumably, after loading his magazines and arranging them into the canvas bags, Thomas Hamilton went to sleep.

THE EVIL VISITOR

The following day, 13 March 1996, began with a cold morning in the central lowlands of Scotland. Comrie Deuchars rose as normal and got into his car to drive to the newsagent. He picked up the paper for his wife but when he got home Hamilton's van, which had been parked further down the road, was now in the spot he had left vacant moments before. Hamilton was scraping ice off the windscreen and as Comrie couldn't park outside his house he wound the window down and shouted, 'Tom, would you put the paper through the letter box for my wife?'

'Certainly,' Thomas Hamilton replied. He took the paper and watched Comrie Deuchars drive off.

Soon after, Hamilton drove off towards Dunblane and infamy. On arriving in Dunblane at about 9.30 am Hamilton parked his van beside a telegraph pole in the lower car-park of the Dunblane primary school. A pair of pliers he had bought in January were in a tool wrap which he took from the van. Hamilton's intention was to ensure no one at the school could use the phone to ring out, but by mistake he cut the telephone wires of adjoining houses, not the school. Carrying two semi-automatic pistols, two revolvers, and 743 rounds of ammunition, Hamilton crossed the car-park and went into the school through a door near the gymnasium.

The school day had begun half-an-hour earlier with assemblies in the hall. Dunblane primary school is one of Scotland's largest primary schools with 640 pupils and, as the assembly hall is too small to take the whole school, year groups are taken in rotation. On that day the 250 youngest children went to the hall from 9.10 am to 9.30 am along with their teachers and the school chaplain. Primary 1/13, a class of 28 pupils all aged five, except for three who had just turned six, were with their teacher Mrs Gwen Mayor. With a physical education class first thing that morning, the youngsters had already changed into their gym gear. Following assembly, the little ones went off to their classes ready to start what should have been an uneventful and normal day's schooling.

Mrs Harrild, the PE teacher, was in the gym with a supervising assistant when the 28 boys and girls bustled in. The children were marshalled into the centre of the gym as Mrs Harrild spoke with Mrs Mayor. As she was about to start the class Mrs Harrild heard a noise behind her and turned around. Entering the gym was Thomas Watt Hamilton dressed in black, with a black woolly hat and shooter's ear muffs on. In his hand he held a pistol.

Immediately Hamilton began firing indiscriminately and very rapidly. Mrs Harrild, who was facing him, took bullets in both forearms, her right hand and left breast. As she stumbled into the open-plan storeroom area a number of children followed. Mrs Mayor died instantly from a number of bullets hitting her. The supervisory assistant, Mrs Blake, was also shot but managed to reach the store, bravely ushering children ahead of her.

Within seconds Hamilton had fired 29 shots from the doorway. While the two surviving teachers tried to calm and comfort the children around them, others lay helpless in the middle of the gym surrounded by their injured classmates amid screams, cries and pools of blood. As he walked towards the huddled group of children Hamilton fired a fusillade of shots to either side of the gym. He then walked in a semi-circle firing 16 shots at the group of children lying on the floor, too injured or shocked to run away. He stood above the little ones and fired at them at point-blank range. The noise of Hamilton's gunfire was deafening and the terrified children in the storeroom began screaming. Frightened that Hamilton would be alerted to their hiding place the badly wounded teachers put their fingers to their lips and said, 'shush'. Immediately the children sensed the danger and lay down in silence. Despite the noise from the guns and their wounds the children lay still. There wasn't a sound from them, not even a whimper. The next few minutes were terrifying as they listened to Hamilton, moving about and shooting continuously.

Hamilton fired at anyone or anything that moved. A boy on an errand walked past the gym and heard loud banging and screaming. Horrified, he looked into the gym to see Hamilton shooting and was lucky to survive, with glass fragments showering him as Hamilton fired out the window. A bullet aimed at a farther member of staff struck her a glancing blow to the head.

Thanks to another teacher's presence of mind, more young lives were spared. As Hamilton left the gym the teacher saw him, and screamed at the children in her classroom to get on the floor. One of the nine bullets Hamilton fired into the classroom passed through a chair where seconds earlier a child had sat. Hamilton turned and went back into the gym, put his 9 mm pistol down and drew out his revolver. He placed the muzzle of the revolver into his mouth and pulled the trigger. Within a short time the perpetrator of such a cowardly and despicable act was dead.

Around him Mrs Mayor and 15 children lay dead with another child critically injured, who was to die on the way to hospital. Thomas Hamilton's terrible rampage had taken just three-to-four minutes. Alerted by a terrified teacher, the principal phoned for the police before running to the gym. The gunman had been seen to shoot himself and Mr Taylor burst into the gym to be met by what he described as 'a scene of unimaginable carnage, one's worst nightmare'.

Immediately people rushed to comfort those children injured and traumatised until police and ambulances arrived. Mr Taylor noticed

Hamilton who seemed to be moving. The pistol on the floor was kicked away and the revolver in Hamilton's hand was taken and thrown aside. From thereon, the day was to prove stressful for the emergency services teams, harrowing for staff at the school, and heartbreaking for the families and friends of the children and teacher killed in such a horrific way.

PSYCHOLOGICAL PROFILE

'If you accept that it takes a woman's touch to turn a house into a home, then certainly Thomas Hamilton lived very much in a house,' said Dr Baird, consultant forensic psychiatrist, who gave evidence on Hamilton's mental state at the Dunblane inquiry headed by Lord Cullen.

Hamilton's house was drab, cold and unwelcoming. He slept on a mattress in a sleeping bag with clothing strewn all over the place. Rooms had the basic fittings and necessities such as chairs, table and television, but there was virtually nothing in the way of personal effects that indicated someone had lived there for any length of time. On one wall he had pinned up home-made targets that he had used at the firing range, but apart from that there was no sign of anything personal to Hamilton.

Also giving evidence at the inquiry was David Cooke, professor of forensic psychology at Glasgow Caledonian University. Like Dr Baird, he was highly-regarded in his field of expertise and provided an insight into the thinking of Thomas Hamilton. David Cooke believed major difficulties in Thomas Hamilton's life threatened his self-esteem. He was heavily in debt, had recently been refused a loan, and was being refused access to premises for his boys' clubs. Like many mass killers he probably obtained feelings of power and mastery by fantasising his revenge on those whom he perceived as persecuting him.

Dr Baird's impression of Thomas Hamilton went back to when he was expelled from the Scouts in 1974. From that time he had a grudge and a grievance against people he believed were treating him unfairly, not seeing his point of view, and wrongly accusing him. He tirelessly campaigned to clear his name and re-establish his reputation in society. That persistence seems to have been to the exclusion of almost everything else. Dr Baird was sure that Hamilton did not simply 'flip' and go on his orgy of destruction. The pre-planning, especially on the night before when he loaded and marked his ammunition, supported his contention.

However, where Hamilton was relaxed and in control during the planning phase, he was not like that during the massacre. Once he began, he shot indiscriminately and at random. He then shot himself when there was no particular reason to do so. The police had not arrived, and nothing was happening to take control from Hamilton and make him feel he had to kill himself at that point. It seems unlikely Hamilton relished what he was doing - in contrast to his demeanour during the preparation.

The choice of gun used by Hamilton also intrigued Dr Baird. The semi-automatic used in the murders had a very light trigger. If someone used such a weapon to end their life it could possibly fire prematurely and cause injuries rather than death. Dr Baird speculated that Hamilton discarded the semi-automatic and used the revolver to end his life for that reason, another indication of Hamilton's meticulous planning.

Dr Baird is also adamant Hamilton's main intention was to commit suicide and he chose this way for a number of reasons. Firstly, there was the likelihood that Hamilton used children to get back at those he perceived caused him harm. Secondly, schools, and in particular gymnasiums, were well-known and familiar to him. Thirdly, if Thomas Hamilton had just shot himself in his flat his death would have gone almost unnoticed. That would not be in keeping with his beliefs of being the one who was wronged. By doing what he did he would be remembered.

Dr Baird also speculated whether Thomas Hamilton, in some sort of perverse way, wanted to put himself into a corner where suicide was inevitable. It is possible Hamilton didn't have the courage to simply kill himself but engineered it - by committing such a heinous crime that he would be forced to make the final act himself. Dr Baird believes this hypothesis has some validity.

Both Dr Baird and Professor Cooke ruled out any form of mental illness. There were no changes that one would expect with the onset of mental illness. Not only was there nothing to suggest mental illness but any illness at all. Apart from a sprained ankle in 1993 Thomas Hamilton had not attended a doctor since January 1974. He neither smoked nor drank, and a post mortem examination showed that he was clear of alcohol, drugs or physical defect.

Both experts detected signs of an abnormal personality in Hamilton. Personality disorders are not conditions, like hypertension or diabetes, but are merely descriptions of particular personality features that all people have. They start early in one's life and continue as a pervasive feature affecting all aspects of life. Mental disorder, however, is normally episodic - it comes and lasts for a period then goes away again. When the person is not unwell they function quite normally.

Dr Baird believes the personality traits of Thomas Hamilton showed a paranoid personality. Such people are sensitive to rebuffs and difficulties in their lives, they bear grudges and see malignant intent in the innocent actions of the people with whom they come into contact. Generally they have an over-inflated view of their own importance - an egocentric view - and are suspicious and sensitive. Hamilton's paranoid personality never allowed him to take responsibility for any of the failures in his life. He blamed parents for not sending their children to his clubs, blamed the children for not having the stamina or persistence to continue, blamed the locals for suggesting he was a pervert, blamed the police for alleging he was mishandling his summer camps, and blamed the Scout Association for not allowing him into their organisation. He did everything but blame himself.

Professor Cooke's analysis tended more towards a personality disorder characterised by a lack of empathy and a sadistic nature which sought to have control over others. Hamilton possibly fantasised about this, and as pressures built his fantasies about control and revenge grew. A sadistic personality involves a disorder in which the subject uses violence or cruelty as a way of establishing dominance. These people commonly humiliate and demean others, use harsh discipline, take pleasure in the suffering of others and are fascinated by violence, weapons, martial arts, injury and torture.

In Thomas Hamilton's case his strict control and dominance of boys at his clubs was evidence enough. Some people could hardly believe the changes in his personality when they viewed videos of his gymnastic classes. This personality change was noticeable in other ways. Hamilton was variously described as a quiet man who would not look a person in the eye, would not engage in conversation, did not laugh at anything, and could not engage in small talk. Yet he never seemed remotely intimidated by senior figures he met - be they politicians, police, local authority officials or others. The pleasure from others' suffering was evidenced in the way Thomas Hamilton treated his family. On one occasion he phoned his natural mother, Agnes, to say an ambulance was coming to pick her up for an operation in Inverness, some three hours drive away. This was completely without foundation and caused Agnes acute distress.

Hamilton often locked his adoptive father out of the house for up to 20 minutes, and would not allow the old man to watch television. He seemed to enjoy his power and control and it wasn't just family he frightened. His habit of creeping up on his neighbours, Mrs Ogilvie and Comrie Deuchars, caused them alarm, and he had terrified Mr Gillespie by firing an empty gun at him for no perceptible reason. His ill treatment of boys on his camps - the way he made them wait to go the toilet, or forced them to lie in cold water for long periods of time - are other signs of a sadistic personality. He only gained control over the boys by shouting and disciplining in a harsh, insensitive way, not through strength of personality or character. Thomas Hamilton was certainly not alone in his tendencies and more than a few mass murderers have shown these very same characteristics.

Hamilton's interest in violent videos such as *Alien* and *Terminator* and the way he referred to his guns 'almost as if they were babies' are classic features of his personality type. Hamilton had few friends and apart from one very short liaison with a girlfriend had no apparent interest in adult sexual contact. While Lord Cullen held reservations about some of the indicators Professor Cooke used to reach his conclusions, Hamilton's treatment of people closely resembled other mass killers who performed sadistic tricks or caused shocks from which they gained some pleasure. In the context of comparing mass killers throughout the world, the conclusions of Professor Cooke might be closer to the mark than he was given credit for.

Dr Baird's observations, suggesting Hamilton had a paranoid personality, have as much worth. The callous unconcern for the feelings of others and an incapacity to maintain enduring relationships are indicative of paranoia. These people are over-sensitive to setbacks and difficulties, bear grudges and are habitually suspicious and mistrustful. They have a tenacious sense of their own personal rights - often totally unrealistic - and are self-important, showing tendencies to consider unrelated events as being specifically directed at them. Neither expert consulted had the opportunity to examine Thomas Hamilton, so their conclusions can only be speculative. However there was sufficient evidence to conclude that, without doubt, Thomas Hamilton did have a personality disorder - be it sadistic or paranoid.

Thomas Hamilton also demonstrated paedophilic tendencies. The videotapes he had were typical of what paedophiles collect. They showed in tedious detail young boys, semi-naked, in stereotypical poses with long, lingering shots of the boys' torsos, usually with hands held above their heads, or suspended from wall bars or rings. The swimming trunks were suggestive of a fetishistic interest in boys. The nature of his sexual fantasies is a matter of speculation, but his boys' club activities were not innocent; they had sinister undercurrents and were unhealthy.

CONCLUSION

Thomas Hamilton was the epitome of the 'wronged' man. In his eyes he was a fine, upstanding individual. Society was to blame for preventing him reaching his potential. In reality he was a lonely, embittered man with a paranoid personality who took 17 innocent souls on his journey to suicide. He lived for years literally in the shadow of the Wallace monument - a tribute to the architect of Scotland's finest hour. Seven centuries later, Thomas Watt Hamilton became the architect of what is arguably Scotland's darkest moment. The architect of evil.

CHAPTER NINE
MARTIN BRYANT

ONE OF NATURE'S BAD MISTAKES
Port Arthur, Australia - 28 April 1996
Victims: 35 dead, 20 injured

INTRODUCTION

Following the Hoddle Street and Queen Street shootings in Melbourne, Australia, debate raged over introducing tougher gun laws. The politicians received violent opposition from gun owners and thousands of people demonstrated in Melbourne, making their views very clear. The New South Wales and Victorian State Governments wanted tougher laws, not only in their states but also throughout the whole country. The Australian Prime Minister convened a special Premiers' conference, but the Premiers of Victoria and New South Wales made little headway in their endeavours to convince their counterparts. Following the meeting, New South Wales Premier Barrie Unsworth was interviewed and clearly showed his disappointment and frustration.

'Unfortunately the Queenslanders and Tasmanians are not prepared to come with us,' he told waiting journalists. 'Tasmania wants to adopt their laissez-faire approach and it would take a massacre of the proportions we have seen in Hoddle Street and Queen Street to get the Tasmanians to change their minds.'

That approach was to see Tasmania with the most lax and liberal gun laws in Australia. Less than a decade later a simple man with abundant problems and a desire for people to like him was able to easily acquire weapons of mass destruction. Martin Bryant had suffered rejections all of his life. After being rejected in April 1996 he had said to a woman, 'Nobody listens to me, I'm getting fed up. I'll think of something and everybody will remember me.'

A few days later Bryant took his lethal weapons to the Port Arthur tourist resort and in minutes ensured he would be forever remembered.

ISLE OF THE DEAD

Port Arthur is Tasmania's premier tourist attraction. The beautiful picnic spot of vast lawns and sandstone ruins covers 40 hectares, surrounded by the rugged coastline of the Tasman Peninsula.

Port Arthur has not always been a peaceful location - far from it. From 1830 to 1877 it was home to 12,500 convicts from all over the British Empire. Most were transported from Britain for minor thefts and the sentence was often life imprisonment. The minimum sentence, even for children, was seven years in the cold, forbidding exile of Port Arthur.

The convict settlement, famous for its harsh conditions, floggings and leg irons became the setting for Marcus Clarke's 1874 novel, *For the Term of His Natural Life*. Escapes were rare and although those sentenced to solitary confinement were well-fed, they led a lonely and frightening existence. Their windowless cells were behind metre-thick walls deep inside the buildings. When exercising, those in solitary confinement wore masks to hide their identity, and communicating with another human being was strictly forbidden.

A few hundred metres offshore is a small island, the final resting place of nearly 2,000 convicts. The Isle of the Dead is a popular destination for tourists visiting Australia's pre-eminent symbol of its convict heritage.

THE DEVELOPMENT OF 'SILLY MARTIN'

Martin John Bryant was born on 7 May 1967. The son of Carleen and Maurice, he was to grow into a man who, before he reached the age of 30, would be etched into infamy. Right from the start there was something very wrong about Martin Bryant. His father, particularly, had high hopes that his son would be an achiever, a dream that never had a chance of being realised.

As a child Martin Bryant was never short of material possessions. If he wanted it, his indulgent parents gave it. At five years old Martin was enrolled at the Friends School and early on was given the Stanford-Binet intelligence test. Martin's IQ was assessed at 87, placing him in the 'dull-normal' range of intelligence. When not occupied, the young Martin would revert to poor behaviour and tended to giggle all day. Teachers found it difficult to communicate with him, and before long suggested he needed a specialised education and that keeping him at Friends was a waste of money.

Bryant had a tendency to show aggressive and destructive behaviour. He spat, kicked and even urinated on other children. At the time Martin started school the Bryants had a second child, Lindy, whom Martin tormented to the extent that she would eventually be sent to a boarding school only two kilometres from their home.

Following his brief time at Friends, Bryant spent two years in the diagnostic and assessment centre at Newtown Primary School in Hobart. Only with the use of medication was the youngster manageable. His behaviour improved but his ability to communicate did not. About this time Martin was put on the Feingold diet, devised especially for hyperactive children. It had no effect. To succeed, the diet needed to be followed carefully and Carleen could not keep to the strict regime. She would give in to Martin, letting him have artificially-coloured foodstuffs such as ice blocks. The boy's behaviour further deteriorated. He would call out in class, and disrupt other children, tripping and hitting them as they passed by. Classmates barely tolerated him and refused to play with 'Silly Martin'. The boy had no friends and was socially isolated, a situation he would find himself in throughout his life.

For a time he was known as 'The Shadow', a name given to him for his habit of suddenly appearing behind a group, not communicating, then just as quickly disappearing. When reprimanded by teachers he would laugh, but if he became annoyed he would fix the antagonist with a cold stare, his eyes going blank.

Finally, at the age of ten, his effect on other children's progress - not to mention the teachers' health - became too much, and he was suspended. One teacher, who described Bryant as 'not a shy or sad child, happy and carefree', said of his reliability, 'he tells lies like other people tell the truth'. Bryant's IQ had been reassessed downwards to 74.

Early on he came to the notice of a variety of medical and mental health professionals. One of the first doctors to examine Bryant concluded that 'aggravation is his principal occupation'. Following therapy and an improvement in his behaviour Bryant was allowed back to school but his return was short-lived. For reasons known only to Martin, he lit a skyrocket and put it in his pocket. Two weeks in hospital, skin grafts, and a period of convalescence kept him from the classroom for some time.

Bryant's preoccupation with fire did not end there. Often as a youngster he was seen carrying a can of petrol. Other children would tease him. 'Here comes Silly Martin with his petrol,' they taunted. Bryant had once poured petrol on his clothes and set them alight. Quick action from older children who rolled him in the sand saved him from serious injury.

Martin Bryant progressed to secondary school and was placed in a special needs unit. But while the school had a supportive learning environment, it was not set up to cope with severe behavioural problems. Bryant was capable of working, but his social adjustment was woeful. His disappointed father wrote on a school report, 'I can only hope Martin is like an oak and matures eventually'. To the relief of the school, Martin Bryant decided to leave, supposedly to get employment, just a few days after his 16th birthday.

As a teenager Bryant had very few male acquaintances. He was regarded as a dreamer, wandering around in a world of his own. During school holidays he would hang around with Danny, who made observations about Bryant's racist beliefs. Bryant seemed to be against anyone who did not look 'Australian' and could not resist making racist remarks about 'foreigners'.

In his early years Bryant was fascinated with guns and knives, and while showing Danny a flick knife accidentally cut his friend on the hand. But of all the Bryant traits that Danny remembered it was his cruelty to animals. Martin Bryant displayed his hatred of cats and had been seen trying to pull them apart. 'Once in the park he grabbed a cat by the tail and hit its head against a brick wall, then tried to flush it down the toilet,' Danny said.

Bryant's only other known male friend was Greg, a boy who went to secondary school with him. Greg, who felt sorry for the often-bullied Martin, befriended him. The two were close and Bryant once said Greg was his best friend, the boys often staying over at each other's homes. A regular activity the boys enjoyed together was scuba diving, but it was this shared interest that led to their friendship ending abruptly following a diving expedition in 1981. As Greg began to surface Bryant deliberately stabbed him in the head with a Hawaiian spear. Only his wetsuit prevented Greg from injury, and on reaching shore he punched Bryant who had treated the incident as a joke.

That incident was not the first time Bryant threatened Greg. Earlier, the two, accompanied by Maurice Bryant, had been flounder fishing at Nubeena when Bryant tried to stab his friend in the foot, again using a spear. As on the other occasion Bryant found it amusing.

Though the boys were friends, Greg found it difficult to hold conversations with Bryant, finding him vague and distant. Although the majority of mass murderers are known to be generally non-violent before they finally explode, they almost invariably have been known to offer threats. On several occasions Bryant pointed an air rifle at Greg and pulled the trigger. While Greg was frightened, Bryant's response was to laugh.

Greg found - as others would later in life - that Martin was constantly comparing material possessions. 'My house is better than yours, my parents are richer than yours, my things are better than yours,' Bryant would say.

Although the friendship with Greg ended in 1981, the two saw each other occasionally and in fact met for the final time just before the tragedy at Port Arthur unfolded. Greg saw Bryant in the street, and although they had not seen each other for some years, Martin was pleased to see his former friend and gave him a 'high five' greeting.

Greg asked after Bryant's father's health. 'I said, how's your father? And Martin replied that he had passed away. Then he giggled.'

Martin Bryant had more female acquaintances than male but no relationship lasted long. His bizarre behaviour led to break-ups and his habit of making the most inappropriate comments to women, often total strangers, would only result in rejections.

One woman, old enough to be Bryant's mother, had known him since he was ten. When Bryant was in his mid-20s he began to phone the woman, pestering her to visit him. When Bryant said she must be alone as he had seen the woman's husband drive by, she phoned the police. Bryant must have felt comfortable with older women. On New Year's Eve in 1995 he called on an 80-year-old woman to whom he had sold vegetables as a youngster. He gave her a crayfish and she invited him to lunch the next day. Over the next few months he took the elderly lady out to meals and shows. Just before the Port Arthur massacre Bryant confided in the woman that he was having trouble sleeping and some nights would lie awake until dawn.

Once when a woman 20 years older than Bryant walked her dog past his home Bryant called out, 'It's awful being lonely.' He engaged her in conversation, asking her where she lived, if she was lonely and whether she would go out with him. The woman told him not to be silly and walked on, but when she saw him again she relented and began seeing him. The couple went to dinner, the casino and out dancing, but the relationship didn't last long.

Other women had short-term relationships with Bryant but his personality was such that they were always very brief encounters. When he went out with girlfriends Bryant would confide in them. He said he hated pubs and girls who smoked, that if he met a girl and settled down he hoped she would be like his mother and that his mother had a secret code to phone him. He usually frightened girlfriends off by pestering them to move in with him.

When the direct approach didn't work, Bryant resorted to placing an advertisement in the paper for a cleaner. Janice got the job to clean his home. On her first day, while she was vacuuming, Bryant brought out a camera and began to photograph her, telling her she had a beautiful face and to take her top off. Needless to say Janice quit, taking $50 from Bryant for the inconvenience. He then advertised for a gardener and when a woman applied he asked her to go out with him. Bryant used newspaper advertisements in other ways, hoping to attract a mate. After the Port Arthur tragedy, police searched Bryant's home and found a handwritten advertisement for the newspaper:

'A lady companion is required for scuba diving, tennis, camping and wine and dining for an attractive, slim, caring, sincere 29-year-old male. Genuine replies only please.'

Some of his approaches were even more direct and sinister. Whilst visiting the Public Trustee's office to make a will he told a receptionist she should bend over so he could 'smack her bottom'. He left, but as he went he promised to return with champagne. Another woman who worked in a takeaway bar was questioned by Bryant about her boyfriend, where she lived and so on. He then asked her to roll him an ice cream saying, 'so you will lean over and I will see your tits'.

When Bryant entered a Melbourne hat shop for a sunhat, the manageress bent over to take one from a pile on the floor. He came up behind her, gently placed his hands on her shoulders and asked her if she had seen horses 'do it'. He told her horses had penises 'this big', indicating the length with his hands. He then began doing pelvic thrusts and became flushed in the face. He paid for the sunhat and left the shop. Amazingly in January 1996 he again visited Melbourne, went into the same shop and asked if the woman remembered him. He bought an $80 felt hat, paid for it from a large wad of notes then, after a brief conversation, left.

Bryant travelled widely, and long haul flights provided the ideal environment for a 'captive' audience. On a trip from London's Heathrow to Sydney he sat next to a 23-year-old woman. He told her that when he next rang his mother he would tell her he had just met the girl he would marry. When he pestered the woman to stay with him in Melbourne so he could take her shopping, and how good he was at lovemaking, she feigned sleep - all the way from Bangkok to Australia. On another flight from Los Angeles to Sydney in 1995, Bryant sat beside a woman who found him eccentrically if not oddly dressed. He wore avocado linen trousers, a white shirt, a leather hat and a long coat. He quizzed the woman on a variety of topics, and she felt reasonably comfortable until the stewardess served ice cream. Bryant patted the woman on the stomach saying, 'you shouldn't eat ice cream, you've got a bit much weight there'.

Bryant was fit and kept in shape with a strict fitness programme. He did have membership cards to a number of gyms but these were often withdrawn due to his bad behaviour. In one Hobart gym he was found sitting on equipment staring at females and getting into close proximity to them. When he began following female staff outside the gym, his membership was terminated. There were several other incidents with women relating to Bryant's inappropriate behaviour which were never reported to police, but came to light after the Port Arthur tragedy. Although some of his approaches were outrageous, Bryant was so effeminate and quiet that he was never perceived to be a real threat.

Bryant had three close relationships that were reasonably long lasting and of a sexual nature. Heidi, whom he had known most of his life, was coming out of a low period in 1985 and the two became friendly. To Heidi, Bryant had been sympathetic and helpful, and the friendship developed into a sexual one. Their relationship came to an abrupt end when they were in the attic of Bryant's parents' house. The two were talking about sex when Bryant said he got one of the chickens out of the pen and had sex with it. He told Heidi it died. Then, when he said he had sex with the farm horse several times, Heidi asked him if the horse liked it. Bryant immediately reacted, saying she had upset him with the remark, telling her to go home, and never to visit him again. They did not see each other for six or seven years then took up their relationship where it had left off. They parted again in November 1993 when Bryant announced he had found another girlfriend.

Janetta became Bryant's steady girlfriend, with their friendship lasting five months. They saw each other on a regular basis and travelled to Sydney and Surfer's Paradise for brief holidays. Janetta got to know Bryant well, and though she never saw any guns in the house she knew there was at least one, which Bryant said was for protection. He also had handcuffs with which he said he would handcuff any intruders.

One of the couple's pastimes was to watch videos, including thriller/horrors such as *Child's Play II, Nightmare on Elm Street* and *Aliens*. Their relationship ended abruptly after the pair went out in a small boat. The engine stopped and they tried rowing for shore but the tide swept them out to sea. Adrift for eight hours, the pair were finally rescued by a fishing boat. An argument arose when Janetta insisted Bryant sue the boat's owner, believing an engine part was missing. Bryant refused to confront the owner and Janetta broke off the relationship. Bryant then sold his own inflatable Zodiac boat, outboard motor, trailer and scuba gear, saying his girlfriend had left and life was no longer worth living.

Petra met Bryant in early 1996 when she applied for a gardening job at his home. Within a week a sexual relationship had developed and she stayed overnight with Bryant on a regular basis. When Carleen Bryant showed Petra photographs of Bryant with a previous girlfriend he became aggravated and was rude to Carleen, pretending to hit her. He often called his mother 'silly' and 'stupid' in front of Petra, but was never physically violent to her.

By now Bryant was living in a fantasy world, telling Petra he hoped Steven Seagal would come to Hobart and liven the place up. Two weeks before the tragedy at Port Arthur, Bryant went shopping with Petra. He bought a large sports bag, measuring its dimensions with a tape. He told Petra he wanted the bag for T'ai chi, but told the shop assistant he needed a strong bag to hold ammunition.

Though he spoke of guns, Petra was never shown the arsenal hidden in a locked cupboard under the stairs. The day before the tragedy Petra and Bryant went to Richmond to test a camera. Characteristically, Bryant engaged a German couple in conversation, offering them a lift to Hobart. They politely declined, and Bryant referred to them as silly people. He went into a takeaway shop and made a comment that only became relevant the next day: 'There are not many Japs around today,' he said. 'How busy is it on Sundays?'

That night the couple dined at Carleen's, then visited a club and went home. Before going to bed around 11 pm Petra noticed Bryant do something she had never seen before. He took the alarm clock into the bedroom and set it for 6 am saying he had something to do the next day. Normally, Bryant and Petra would go for a morning walk, but on that day he rushed her out of the house at 8 am saying he had 'somewhere' to go.

THE MAN OF MEANS

Michael Ryan, the Hungerford mass murderer, had been 'befriended' by a rich, mystery colonel who showered him with gifts and cars. In Ryan's case the character was a figment of his imagination. But the wealthy person who befriended Martin Bryant was far from imaginary.

When Bryant was aged 20 he got a job cleaning up the garden of a 50-year-old spinster living in a large two-storied house at 30 Clare Street, Newtown. Helen Harvey was without doubt an eccentric, but she was to have a profound effect on Martin Bryant's life and future. It was several months before Bryant was allowed inside the home where she lived with her elderly invalid mother, but once inside he was to become Harvey's close companion until her death.

Helen Harvey was a very rich eccentric; she was heiress to the Australian Tattersall Lottery fortune. She was so wealthy that over a short period of time she bought and sold 50 cars. Martin Bryant would accompany her to car yards and announce her arrival, as if everyone should jump to attention. Looking around the car yard Bryant need only say, 'That's nice, I'll have that one,' and Helen would buy it.

She would often sell the car back soon after, at a fraction of the purchase price. Once she drove a car for four-and-a-half hours before swapping it for another. A new Toyota car which cost $28,000 was reversed into a tree, so Helen and Martin set about repairing the car using house paint to hide the damage. Soon after, she sold the car for $7,000. After paying $16,500 for a Honda vehicle she sold it back three days later for $4,500. The car yard, however, had to spend $3,000 repairing the car's interior, extensively damaged and covered in animal excrement.

Helen hadn't used the Honda as a car but as a shelter for some of her menagerie. When council officials called police to 30 Clare Street in June 1990, they found Helen and her mother living in absolute squalor and called an ambulance to take the women to hospital. The women's beds were in the kitchen surrounded by piles of rubbish. Unwashed bedding was covered with animal hair from the 18 dogs that roamed the house. Most of the dogs slept on beds in 'their' bedrooms, while others slept in cars outside. A badly-ventilated outside shed was home to 26 cats. Clothes, linen, furniture and household goods littered the house, in places half-a-metre deep. Animal droppings were liberally sprinkled throughout.

Following the women's removal, Martin and Maurice Bryant cleaned the house, using a garden hoe to scrape the encrusted floorboards. It took a month's work before the house was deemed habitable. With her mother in hospital, Helen Harvey stayed with the Bryants. Carleen was shocked at Helen's hygiene, describing her as 'malodorous'. The clothes Helen wore were often kept on for days, then discarded on the floor never to be worn again.

Helen may have been untidy, but many found the eccentric woman likeable, and she was the only person who could keep Bryant in his place. On moving back to Clare Street, Helen was lonely and unable to cope. It was then that Martin Bryant moved in permanently. With access to almost unlimited funds, Bryant began the first of many overseas trips. His first visit was to New Zealand, arriving on 3 December 1990 accompanied by his father and Helen Harvey. It is unknown where they went in New Zealand's South Island, but they did arrive at Christchurch, just four hours' drive from Aramoana where David Gray had killed his 13 victims a few weeks earlier. Gray's rampage would have still been very much headline news though whether Bryant got to Aramoana isn't known. But he was well aware of Aramoana, Hoddle Street, Hungerford and other similar tragedies. Sergeant Terry McCarthy, a Tasmanian police officer attached to the Port Arthur enquiry, has no doubt.

'There's a lot we don't know about Martin Bryant,' he said. 'But one thing we do know is he had a very good knowledge of other mass shootings, including Aramoana. He certainly knew more than the average person would, almost a morbid interest.'

In October 1991 Helen Harvey bought another property, a farm called Taurusville in Copping. She and Bryant were often seen driving around. Bryant had never held a driver's licence and Helen's driving was so bad she was referred to as a 'traffic hazard'. The minor accidents and scrapes were testament to their driving 'ability'. The couple's time at Taurusville was no more hygienic and no less eccentric than the time spent at Clare Street. Martin had a piglet, and to keep it warm at night slept with it in his bed. Helen laughed when telling a visitor how the pig urinated on him. Carleen had seen her son's unusual bedmate and found Helen's behaviour strange, if not bizarre.

Bryant's level of intelligence was estimated to be that of an 11-year-old, and his behaviour reflected that assessment. His habit of grabbing the steering wheel to give his eccentric companion a fright once put her into a ditch and she responded by telling the 24-year-old to 'stop being a silly boy'.

One accident that dramatically changed the course of Bryant's mixed-up life occurred while Helen was driving her car on the Arthur Highway on the way home from a shopping expedition. Less than two kilometres from Taurusville, Helen's car veered into the path of a Ford Fairmont. Bryant, who was in the passenger seat, claimed to have turned to look at three dogs fighting on the back seat of the car when the accident happened. He was knocked unconscious and hospitalised with an unstable fracture of the cervical spine. Helen was less fortunate, never recovering from severe multiple internal traumas, and died soon after.

Helen's death caused intense speculation among the Copping locals. Bryant was known to have previously pulled on the steering wheel to frighten her. There was no reason why she should have veered on to the wrong side of the road. Rumours circulated that perhaps he was responsible for the spinster's death, but it was never proven.

Helen Harvey had clearly been very fond of Martin Bryant. So much so that she had made elaborate funeral plans for them both. The prepaid funeral included expensive blackwood coffins which cost several thousand dollars each. Her instructions were that

Martin was to be buried beside her in the elaborate family plot. A few months after making the arrangements, Helen signed a will leaving her fortune to Martin Bryant. This included her house at 30 Clare Street, the Taurusville property, livestock, chattels and the residue of her estate.

Martin Bryant was now a wealthy man. The properties at Clare Street and Copping were valued at many hundreds of thousands of dollars. Chattels alone were estimated in excess of $100,000 and soon after Helen's death Bryant was to sell $50,000 worth of furniture. Bryant had a substantial fortune yet had never held a real job. He may not have liked the fact he had been a beneficiary and often lied about his occupation, describing himself as a painter, a farmer or self-employed. He told others he was a carpenter and that he never had to work as he had been left a lot of money.

Where Michael Ryan received nothing from his fictional colonel, Martin Bryant had to declare income for tax purposes. Silly Martin, who never had a job in his life, declared his income for 1994 at $71,506 and the following year at $89,191.

THE BEST AND ONLY FRIEND

Despite the frictions between brother and sister, it was Lindy who spent time nursing her brother back to health following his release from hospital. Soon after, Maurice Bryant moved to Taurusville to be with his son, but another disaster was looming. Maurice had been proud at the birth of his son, but the hopes he had for a high-achieving heir never eventuated. Instead of enjoying the success of his first-born, Maurice Bryant was forced to retire from his job as a watersider to look after Martin. When Dr Eric Cunningham-Dax was asked in 1984 whether Martin's 'condition' had improved or deteriorated he said, 'It would deteriorate rapidly but for the fact his father devotes all his spare time looking after his son, working with him in the garden, etc.'

Maurice not only looked after Martin but was his companion, taking him fishing and diving or selling vegetables door-to-door around the neighbourhood.

Maurice Bryant, however, became a troubled man. He was now

living apart from Carleen, and with deteriorating health received treatment for depression and anxiety. Carleen noticed the changes, especially the loss of Maurice's normal cheerfulness. His personality altered and he became easily affected by the stresses of everyday life. As the depression increased, so too did comments about taking his life. When Carleen spoke to Maurice by phone on 13 August 1993 she had trouble holding a conversation with him. The following day a constable visited the Copping farm and found a note on the door, 'Call the police'. After two days of searching, Maurice was found face down in a four-metre deep dam with Martin's diving belt wrapped around his neck. Before his death, Maurice Bryant had changed his will, leaving a rollover account worth $250,000 to Martin. Silly Martin was now even wealthier. His mother and younger sister had been left nothing but the joint family home.

The coroner's finding of suicide by drowning was not easily accepted by some Copping locals and again speculation was rife. Martin's reaction to his father's death fuelled the speculation. He seemed unconcerned as police searched for Maurice, and unaffected when a constable took him to identify his father's body at the dam. Police were surprised when Martin returned giggling and smiling; within half-an-hour he was chatting to policewomen. Carleen believed that Maurice's death did impact on the younger Bryant, and led him to consult a doctor complaining of recurring nightmares. Bryant was also plagued by nightmares following the death of Helen Harvey. 'Martin was a very lonely person most of his life,' Carleen said of her son. 'He was so devastated, he became more withdrawn, lonely and isolated . . . because he had lost his best friend . . . best and only friend and loving father.'

THE CONFUSED TRAVELLER

Martin Bryant, with his new-found wealth, began to travel widely - usually on a whim. He mainly journeyed alone to overseas destinations. He made visits to Singapore, Bangkok, London, Sweden, Los Angeles, Frankfurt, Copenhagen, Germany, Poland and Tokyo. His destinations were as haphazard as his departures. During one trip he went to the USA but returned to Australia from Miami via

Frankfurt. On several occasions Bryant paid deposits for trips he never took. At other times he would change his mind about the destination.

On a trip to Lizard Island he left after a couple of nights incurring a $1,500 cancellation penalty. He was still entitled to a $2,500 refund but never bothered to collect it. He paid for a trip to England and France but changed it for a visit to Kuala Lumpur, telling travel agents he wanted to buy his father Christmas presents in Asia. At that time his father had been dead for two years.

During his travels Bryant often came to the notice of police and customs. Once, following a mix-up, his baggage was mishandled and arrived unaccompanied. Customs found a set of four bestiality videos that were prohibited. Another time when he was returning home from London, customs officers became suspicious about his demeanour. Suspecting that Bryant had concealed drugs they detained him, then took him to a Melbourne hospital for x-rays, after which he was released.

It was Bryant's behaviour that had attracted attention. In 1994 he took a trip to England and booked into an expensive hotel in Hereford. He paid 70 pounds in cash and went up to his room. A few minutes later he went to the reception desk saying his room was too warm. He checked out and was offered his money back, but told the receptionist to keep it as a tip. His appearance did not suggest affluence and the hotel's interest was heightened when he booked into a small guest house. Nearby was an SAS training base and with suspicions aroused, the West Mercia police contacted the Tasmanian police to find out who this strange visitor was. Bryant's only transgression with the law came about in 1994 for being an unlicensed driver. His explanation for not producing a driver's licence was simple. 'I've never held a driver's licence,' Bryant told the police officer, 'but I will have to get one.' He never did.

Bryant's few hobbies had always been connected with water sports. He enjoyed fishing and especially scuba diving, where he displayed a natural ability. He regularly surfaced with a good catch of abalone or large crayfish. The deterioration in his appearance coincided with his supposed passion for surfing. He owned two surfboards - one a 'Malibu' - and was regularly seen heading for the surf with boards atop his Volvo car. He told people he was a surfer, and looked the part with his clothing and pink zinc ointment smeared on his nose. But no one ever saw him surf. Janetta once went surfing with him but all he did was paddle around. Bryant's phantom passion earned him the name, 'The Highway Surfer'.

THE CHRISTIAN NEIGHBOURS

A person who saw Martin Bryant regularly and could comment on his behaviour was Anitra Kuiper, Bryant's next-door neighbour at Clare Street. Anitra saw enough of the strange young man to be an able judge. It was known that Martin Bryant had a habit of creeping up on people and that was how Anitra Kuiper first met him. The Kuipers' property was next to Bryant's and the washing line was near his fence.

'I was hanging washing when all of a sudden I heard a voice say, "Hi, I'm Martin". Even though the ground was overgrown I didn't hear him come. I turned around and he was inches from my face. I dropped the washing and fled inside,' said Anitra.

She believed Martin Bryant wanted to frighten her and enjoyed doing so. He succeeded. That night Anitra and her husband Harry talked about their strange new neighbour. They thought he wasn't dangerous and perhaps they should treat him as they would any other neighbour. Anitra particularly felt guilty about her first reaction to Bryant, so intended to be friendly the next time she saw him. She was, so they often used to see him, and eventually their children would go across to Bryant's to play.

It was the Kuipers' strong Christian faith that saw them befriend Bryant. Anitra believed her first reaction to Bryant had been a bad response. Bryant needed friends and they wanted to help.

'When you spoke to Martin the answer you got wouldn't fit the question you asked,' Anitra said. 'It was always childlike. I'd never leave the kids there for long. He was a male in the house alone and our children were young. I'd go over after a while and chat, then make an excuse to leave.'

The children accompanied Bryant to the local pool and once he bought himself and the Kuiper children expensive 'Super Soaker' water pistols with which they would play for hours.

This childlike young man never proved a problem, though Anitra felt uncomfortable, as if he was sometimes mentally undressing her. 'On one occasion Martin wanted to take the children to a market and called around on the Saturday morning at 8 o'clock,' Anitra recalled. 'He was dressed in a suit and had a tie on. I'd only just got out of bed and called him into the hall and said to wait while I got dressed.'

She had only got into her underwear when she saw Bryant in her bedroom, grinning, aware he'd caught her with little on and enjoying it. 'I know he did it on purpose, to catch me with nothing on,' Anitra said.

Bryant's overgrown property was affecting other neighbours. When they asked politely if they could trim trees blocking their windows he said he wanted nothing touched. If the neighbours cut the foliage back Bryant took photographs of them saying, 'My solicitor will be very interested in these photos.' He seemed vindictive and the next night a child's bike was found smashed in the neighbour's backyard.

'Martin was gentle, kind, generous and anxious to have friends,' Anitra said. 'Yet he could be outrageously inappropriate to strangers. Once we went to a cinema in Centrepoint and we saw a pregnant woman looking in a shop window. Martin went up to her, placed his hand on her stomach and said, "You've got a baby in there". He did it to spook her and embarrass us. I could tell he enjoyed the reaction from us.'

Bryant used inappropriate methods to attract adult friends and his craving for any form of friendship led to bizarre behaviour. He once wrote a letter to the Kuipers' 11-year-old daughter's teacher asking if he could go back to school to be in her class. The 27-year-old's letter was simple and childlike.

Anitra felt they never received friendship from Martin; it was more a case of what they offered him. She believed he craved relationships, but treated women as objects and was incapable of anything deep or meaningful.

The only time Anitra ever saw Martin Bryant really agitated was over his mother. He said his mother was selling her house in

Newtown and would move in with him. 'I won't be able to do what I want,' Bryant told Anitra. 'She'll always be bossing me about.'

He resented his mother's authority and believed she was trying to organise his life. When Anitra told him to talk to his mother he said, 'If she comes to live with me I will kill her.' Bryant went on about his mother for over an hour though Anitra didn't take him seriously. 'He was always saying silly things,' she said.

Despite their strong Christian beliefs, the Kuipers broke off contact with Bryant when he showed the children some pornographic cards. From then on they were forbidden to go to Bryant's house. 'You are very generous and have been good with the children but we have to protect them,' Harry Kuiper told Bryant.

Bryant's response wasn't to acknowledge his wrongdoing but to blame his mother. 'I suppose my mother has rung you and told you to stop our friendship,' Bryant replied.

Mrs Bryant had phoned Anitra on one occasion suggesting the children shouldn't go out in Martin's car. Carleen Bryant was very secretive and wouldn't say why, but Anitra assumed it was because Martin was not sensible.

Martin Bryant couldn't accept he was no longer welcomed by the Kuipers and called several times with a peace offering of flowers, wanting to take the Kuipers' 11-year-old daughter out to dinner.

In the few months before the Port Arthur incident, Anitra noticed a deterioration in Bryant's dress and grooming. 'When we first knew him he was smart, shirt and tie, well groomed, even when casual. Towards the end he changed - his hair grew long and he took on a scruffy, surfie appearance.'

'His home was chaotic,' Anitra said, emphasising that it looked like the place hadn't been touched since Helen Harvey died. 'He would do the shopping and put the bags down in the kitchen. There they stayed until he had used everything up. The floor was littered with things . . . just a shambles.'

THE ARMING OF SILLY MARTIN

The profiles of mass murderers usually reveal chaotic living conditions but there is always one part of their life that is very orderly. In Bryant's case it was a severe and quite strange exercise routine he outlined on paper.

Bryant had an enormous collection of videos, mostly bought while Helen Harvey was alive. She would give him $200 at a time to buy videos, and some would remain unopened, while others were multiple copies. Titles ranged from *My Fair Lady, Singing in the Rain* and *The Sound of Music* through to pornography and bestiality. After her death, Bryant watched more and more violent and action-type videos. Despite his having sold several hundred titles from his collection police still found 1390 videos in Bryant's house after his death.

Consistent with the activities of other mass killers, Bryant amassed martial arts and firearms magazines in the months leading up to his rampage. Titles such as *Fighting Firearms, Guns & Ammo* and *Special Weapons for Military & Police* formed part of his collection. He also had a recent copy of *Paladin Press*.

Bryant had used firearms, but not at a club or for shooting game. He just liked the feeling of 'letting off a few rounds'. As a youngster he had used air guns which were confiscated from him because of indiscriminate shooting. If he wasn't shooting at street lights he would take shots at horses, cats, birds and people. He once fired pellets at tourists who stopped to buy vegetables from a stall at the Bryant's gate. The inappropriate behaviour with firearms was sometimes accompanied by threats. Barry Featherstone lived next to Helen Harvey's Taurusville property and introduced himself to her and Bryant. For unknown reasons Bryant warned Featherstone off, threatening to shoot him.

Martin Bryant bought his first gun through a newspaper advertisement in late 1993. The black Colt AR10 semi-automatic cost him $1,700 and during the next two years he would visit gun shops inspecting sporting rifles, shotguns and military style semi-automatics. By March 1996 he had acquired a 12-gauge shotgun and another rifle.

A month before the Port Arthur tragedy Bryant took his Armalite Colt AR10 into a gun shop for repair. While there he asked if it was easy to buy a submachine gun. During the week preceding his rampage he enquired about buying a $3,800 AR15 and that same day went to another shop saying he had been shooting at balloons and needed guns with plenty of punch. The next day he purchased shotgun cartridges and on the Friday, two days before the tragedy, was seen looking at a 9 mm semi-automatic rifle. He was able to do all this despite never having held a firearms licence!

SLAUGHTER OF THE INNOCENT

When Martin Bryant hurried his girlfriend from his home early on Sunday 28 April 1996, he said he had 'somewhere' to go. That somewhere was the historical convict settlement at Port Arthur, 93 kilometres away.

On his long drive to Port Arthur, Martin Bryant had plenty of time to change his mind, but he was set on his course of destruction. His first stop was the Seascape Guest House owned by Sally and David Martin, a couple in their early 70s. The Martins had owned a farm that the Bryants had wanted to buy years earlier. A theory on the motive for the Port Arthur tragedy was that Bryant believed the Martins had treated his family badly. Holding the grudge all that time, Martin Bryant believed his father's unhappiness, illness and ultimate suicide was caused by the Martins' refusal to sell their farm. The area around Port Arthur had played a significant part in Bryant's childhood as a place where he had been shunned, and he associated the area with feelings of rejection.

Whatever the real reason for Bryant's rampage, it was the respected and sprightly Martins who were his first victims. About midday Bryant arrived at the Seascape. Soon after, an elderly couple walked up to the guest house and knocked on the door, hoping to be met by the Martins.

Instead an agitated young man with excited, rapid hand movements answered the door. He spoke in a strange voice and couldn't stand still. The couple didn't want to stay around and left, with the young man staring intently after them. They were not to know that just before their arrival Martin Bryant had killed Sally and David. Both had been stabbed and bludgeoned to death.

On leaving Seascape, Bryant called on a number of people

believed to have aggrieved him. Fortunately, they were not home and were spared the fate that had befallen the Martins. The belief that Bryant's motives were based on deeply-held grudges was reinforced by his conversation that day with Roger Larner. He had known Bryant for many years and the two met on the road within minutes of Bryant killing the Martins. During their brief conversation Bryant mentioned that the Martins would not sell their farm to the Bryant family years earlier. Although having just killed, Bryant had calmed considerably, and Larner remarked that he was, at that moment, the calmest and most lucid he had ever seen him. After the brief chat Bryant drove off towards Port Arthur.

Tourists were assembling for the afternoon tour to the Isle of the Dead when Martin Bryant arrived in his yellow Volvo car. He had with him a Colt AR15 semi-automatic assault rifle complete with 30-round .223 calibre magazines, an FN FAL semi-automatic rifle with 20-round .308 calibre magazines and a 12 gauge shotgun with 10-round box magazines.

Some tourists wandered around the extensive lawns and ruins while others were eating lunch in the Broad Arrow Café. Martin Bryant walked in to the café carrying the multi-coloured sports bag he had bought earlier that month. Casually, he unzipped the bag, took out a gun and shot a Malaysian couple at close range. The rampage had begun. Bryant calmly selected his next victim, took aim and fired. He would fire from the hip, raise the gun in the air, spin around, lower the gun to the hip and fire again. The initial attack was very quick. Some survivors said the gunman laughed as he fired. Police estimate that the first 12 to die in the Broad Arrow Café were killed within 15 seconds.

Rather than being frightened off by the noise, people outside the café thought it might have been a re-enactment of the site's violent past and were drawn to the site. With many people trapped inside and unable to defend themselves, Bryant continued unimpeded. Within two minutes, 20 people lay dead inside the Broad Arrow and many others were horrifically injured. Bryant then left the café and walked the short distance to his car from which he took a second rifle. He went into one of the many tourist buses at the car-park and killed a woman passenger, then walked around firing on people at random.

As horrific as all mass killings are, Martin Bryant then did something that is about as bad as it gets. He went back to his car and drove towards Mrs Nanette Mikac and her daughters, Alannah (6) and Madeline (3). Thinking the yellow Volvo might be a means of escape, she did not run away. Bryant got out of his car, placed his hand on Nanette's shoulder and told her to kneel. Despite her pleas for mercy Bryant shot her and three-year-old Madeline. Alannah fled in terror, hiding behind a nearby tree. Bryant fired twice at the little girl and missed, but then walked over to her, pressed the muzzle of the rifle to her neck, and fired.

Bryant was far from finished. He walked over to a BMW car. The owner and a male passenger were outside of the car and two female passengers were in the back seat. Bryant shot all four, then dragged the women's bodies from the car. Taking the BMW Bryant drove over to another couple and forced the man into the boot of the BMW, slamming the lid shut. He shot the man's female companion before driving off, heading once more for the Seascape Guest House.

Left behind were 32 bodies and many injured and traumatised people. With him, Bryant took his two rifles but left the shotgun in his Volvo. Arriving at the Seascape, Bryant forced his hostage, Glenn Pears, into the guest house where he handcuffed him to an immovable object. Police believe Mr Pears was killed soon after arriving at the Seascape, probably just before Bryant poured petrol on to the BMW and set it on fire.

It wasn't long before police surrounded the Seascape to prevent the gunman's escape. But Bryant told police negotiator Sergeant McCarthy he had three hostages, so storming the guest house was not an option. He said his name was Jamie; that he was fine and things couldn't be better. He even told Sergeant McCarthy it was just like a Hawaiian holiday.

The way in which Bryant held grudges again became evident. He said to Sergeant McCarthy that Sally Martin had prevented the Bryants from buying the farm. He said Mrs Martin was a troublemaker and was part-Jewish and that he hated Jews, two of whom had snubbed him in Miami.

Throughout the night, Bryant fired 250 rounds out of windows in the guest house, the last being fired at 7.37 am. Soon after he began throwing furniture from the windows and then smoke was seen billowing from the guest house. At 8.24 am Bryant ran from the Seascape, his clothes alight. As he tore them off he was arrested, naked and badly burned on the back. The terror perpetrated by Silly Martin was now at an end.

The Kuipers couldn't believe that Martin Bryant was the Port Arthur murderer. 'We were stunned,' Anitra said. 'It seemed so out of context. The Martin we knew was so gentle.'

PSYCHOLOGICAL PROFILE

After Martin Bryant's atrocities at Port Arthur, psychological profiles were quickly provided. He was examined at length by a variety of forensic psychiatrists who concluded that Bryant was sane at the time of the shootings and would have known that what he did was wrong. While he may have been legally sane, what he did was so abnormal people found it difficult to rationalise.

From early days Bryant had undergone examination by doctors, psychologists and psychiatrists. In the search for answers as to why mass murderers commit their atrocious deeds it is common that the perpetrators of these crimes have 'unusual' personalities, but they seldom have an extensive psychiatric history. Martin Bryant was an exception. He had been seen regularly by school psychologists and psychiatrists who knew there was something wrong, but were unable to make a clear diagnosis.

In 1984, aged 17, Bryant was provided with a certificate for neurasthenia, a nervous disability, enabling him to receive an invalid's pension. Some medical professionals felt that Martin Bryant was a paranoid schizophrenic with a personality disorder. Whatever the diagnosis, Bryant was declared unsafe without parental control, owing to his 'strange and abnormal' behaviour. In 1991, when Bryant was 24, two independent psychiatrists examined him. One determined him to be a paranoid schizophrenic with a personality disorder. Bryant's prognosis was not good, the doctor wrote of his future, 'Bad, he can only slowly worsen and will eventually be institutionalised'.

The other psychiatrist examined Bryant later in the year, and the signs were even stronger that here was a disaster waiting to happen. The doctor wrote of Bryant:

> Came with his father, did not know his age and could not work it out. Likes gardening but cannot remember the names of plants but knows what weeds are. Likes accidents, car smashes and violence, to him that is funny. *Martin tells me he would like to go round shooting people.* [Emphasis added] Totally inconsequential manner and conversation, likes the blue carpet in my office, asks me if I had blue carpet at home.
>
> Actually sat quietly but swung in the chair and gazed intently around the room. Did make the most inappropriate remarks. Watched a television programme on Hitler last night and roared uproariously at bodies being bulldozed into mass graves.

In hindsight, it might be asked why, when someone talks of wanting to go around shooting people, no action is taken. The reality is Martin Bryant, like so many mass killers, was a weak, ineffectual person who made the statement in a high pitched, giggly and effeminate way. People like Bryant are easily 'written off' as being incapable of committing such horrendous deeds. It was just Silly Martin saying silly things again. If we are to learn anything from these killers it is that while they are unarmed they are virtually powerless. Having a gun in their hands makes them feel powerful and they are consequently very, very dangerous.

Dr Ian Sale is a Crown forensic psychiatrist based in Hobart. He works regularly with the Tasmanian police and their negotiators during armed sieges. During the events following the Port Arthur massacre Dr Sale was involved with Martin Bryant - firstly during the negotiation phase at the Seascape, then later in interviews. Because he was involved in numerous phases of this tragedy the following are excerpts from a lengthy interview given by the doctor:

From a very early stage Martin Bryant was seen as an abnormal child. His parents didn't pick this up as they were probably a rather insular family and didn't have other children of like age for comparison. Once Martin began at Friends School he was quickly seen as difficult and soon after, Friends decided they couldn't cope and asked politely to find somewhere else for him. This is fairly remarkable when you consider the child is only five years old. The key thing is there was no interaction, no two-way process between him and other children.

There is something about Martin Bryant's appearance and voice that causes your initial impression to be one of a gentle and passive person yet one who can say outrageous things to women. The remarkable thing is that these women did not report this to police and I think that if most males behaved in that way they would be reported. But not Martin. It is his high-pitched voice that is most striking. His appearance is one of gentleness so even when you meet him, and know what he's done you do not get a sense of menace.

When I was called to the police negotiation team and listened to Bryant I anticipated I would hear the usual very angry, intoxicated and depressed male making all sorts of threats but I was astonished when I heard Bryant's voice. There was a lack of affect, it was casual, there was no anger, no paranoid feeling, no signs of intoxication. The voice was effeminate and playful. I must say this utterly bewildered me and threw me into an absolute spin as to what we were dealing with. It was something different to what all the training suggests should be there.

When I first went to the prison to interview Bryant it was with a sense of real apprehension. You see this childlike, fatuous, silly individual and you keep on having to remind yourself why he is here and that he is a 29-year-old male.

When I interview prisoners I find one of the most useful instruments to find out what's going on is your own emotional response to them. They may make you feel menaced, quite fearful, sometimes sad or simply revulsive. The striking thing with Bryant is that there was no sense of emotional involvement and I remained somewhat bewildered.

My impressions were that I was talking to a man of limited intellect, a man who was effeminate and gentle with a voice to match. This was absolutely against what you might expect to be the gunman of Port Arthur.

He was not sad, and showed no emotional response but occasionally would make the words indicating some emotion. But there was no accompanying expression either by his facial expression, change in the tone of his voice, or his hand gestures. The way he expresses emotions is all wrong, it doesn't tally with whatever emotion might be there.

That is consistent with some observations at the Seascape. Bryant would have inane conversations with negotiators, talking about a Hawaiian holiday and a response about helicopters. Yet in between these conversations he was trashing the house and there was no indication from his voice that he was doing that.

There were some unusual gestures with Bryant's hands. Normally people's gestures are very expressive, depending on what part of the world you come from. We use hand gestures unconsciously to emphasise what we are saying or to display emotion. With Bryant the hand gestures were all out of kilter with what he was saying. Sometimes they were frankly bizarre. He made some odd sinuous or wavy motions with his hands whilst speaking which I couldn't make anything of at all. After an interview I watched the video film of Bryant's behaviour. A few minutes after he had returned to his cell Bryant did this unusual dance, a sinuous sort of motion, a cross between T'ai chi and Oriental dancing. I've never seen an individual do this sort of thing before.

His abnormalities, emotional expression and interpersonal behaviour was so gross that he could be diagnosed as suffering from a pervasive developmental disorder. Bryant is a very unusual person but there is, I believe, a connection between different spree killers. You can't do this unless there is some barrier to your normal human response to having caused massive and terrible injuries to another person. Your own anxiety and revulsion will force you to stop. Bryant, I believe, has some fundamental disability that prevents him from having these experiences. The strong impression I gained about Bryant is that there was something very, very wrong in the way he displayed emotions and probably the way he read other people's emotions. I believe the lack of connection between emotions and behaviour tells us something about why he could continue where others could not unless they were thoroughly disorganised by reason of a mental illness or in an absolutely impossible rage and Bryant was not in a rage.

There are various patterns of developmental disorder such as autism, but his pattern of behaviour fits more with a condition known as Asperger's disorder. In Asperger's disorder the core feature is this problem with expression of emotions, reading the emotions of others and inter-personal behaviour. In Bryant the machinery for that seems to be absent. People with Asperger's disorder show other symptoms such as oddness of gaze and voice and show areas of circumscribed interest. The vast majority of people with this disorder are very reclusive and show no propensity to violence. When violence does occur it is usually callous. Bryant had an intenseness of gaze and at times would gaze past the side of you making it difficult to develop any sense of engagement with him.

Helen Harvey and Maurice Bryant's deaths were, I believe a tragedy for him but his emotional expression of being bland and unconcerned is so unusual there is no way of really knowing. I think losing them both in such a short period of time had a devastating effect on Martin Bryant.

Bryant probably wasn't physical enough in his demeanour to cause a sense of menace. But if we look at what he did it suggests he carried grudges. He occasionally displayed those grudges in a guarded way. For example he told negotiators that Mrs Martin at the Seascape was the worst thing in his life.

Although he had intellectual limitations there was nothing wrong with his memory and he would have remembered events such as being denied access to a neighbouring property to collect pine cones for a fire. I believe he did harbour grudges.

Apart from his father Martin Bryant couldn't relate to males. He tried to form relationships with women but they found his bizarre comments and behaviour odd and rejected him. He would take that hard, more than we would know and more than he could convey to us.

He had sexual fantasies and judging by what he said there was no prevailing theme, more someone who was sampling various possibilities. Bryant also tried various persona. Sometimes he was dressed as a classy young man with a panama hat and linen suit. Other times he was a surfer. He didn't have a sense of self and was shopping around for a sense of identity.

No one would want to emulate Martin Bryant. Except for Port Arthur he was a non-event, an oddity who never worked and wasn't going to. Why would anyone want to be like Martin Bryant?

People should see him as a natural disaster, rather than a man-made disaster. They should regard him as one of nature's very bad mistakes.

CONCLUSION

The man who committed the most devastating mass killing of this type is a complex individual. The expectation of a man who can coldly kill 35 people is at odds with his appearance and demeanour.

Inspector Ross Paine had the task of interviewing the Port Arthur killer in Risdon Prison. Contrary to his anticipated impression of the gunman, Paine met a pathetic, insipid young man who, throughout the first three-hour interview, seemed to enjoy being the centre of attention. Bryant, though simple, surprised Ross Paine with his excellent memory. Bryant had prepared what he would say in response to Paine's questions and his answers were consistent when a further interview took place two months later.

Martin Bryant, though pleading guilty later, denied all knowledge of the Port Arthur rampage and the Seascape arson yet made some quite amazing admissions about abducting a man at gunpoint, forcing him into the boot of his own car, then driving to the Seascape Guest House.

'It was stunning,' Inspector Paine said. 'He would admit to the abduction, but deny everything else.'

When the interviewers were packing up at the end of the second interview, the videotape, unbeknown to Bryant, was still running. Ross Paine and his colleague heard Bryant say, 'I hope you find the person who did this.' Neither policeman was looking at Bryant but when they played the videotape back later Bryant had, when he made the comment, pointed to himself and silently mouthed the word 'me'.

Another who had found Bryant strange to converse with was Sergeant Terry McCarthy, the police negotiator. When Bryant was holed up in the Seascape it was Terry McCarthy who had to talk to him. The response he got was not quite what he expected. 'Given the nature of Port Arthur I expected either a hyper-aggressive person screaming "come and get me" or someone, realising what they had done, to be depressed.'

He got neither. Throughout the negotiations Bryant remained unemotional and detached. His mood never changed, except for a couple of angry responses. 'They were almost script-like, as if it was expected or necessary.'

To McCarthy there didn't seem to be any genuine emotion. Bryant was, to the police investigators, a meek, mild, softly-spoken, almost angelic individual.

One of the forensic psychiatrists who interviewed Martin Bryant was Professor Paul Mullen. For Professor Mullen, Bryant had a simple explanation for the lead up to the atrocities: 'All I wanted was for people to like me.'

CHAPTER TEN
THE PSEUDO-COMMANDOS

GATHERING THE EVIDENCE

Developing an accurate profile of a mass murderer can be a long and frustrating exercise. The subjects are, by their very nature, solitary and secretive people, and in most cases choose death to end their terrible crimes. In some instances, as with Frank Vitkovic, clues to their behaviour are written down. On other occasions, anything that might help investigators piece together the killers' motives is destroyed by fire, such as in Hungerford. Nevertheless, it is clear from the evidence gathered that all nine men profiled possess a large number of characteristics that inextricably link them together. While some of the shared idiosyncrasies are well-established, there is a degree of speculation regarding others. It is up to the reader to decide on the credibility of the claims made in this chapter and the degree to which one may place significance on the conclusions.

Evidence from statements in police homicide files, coroners' inquest files or commissions of enquiry was used to develop the profiles. These statements were supported by interviews with family, friends, neighbours and acquaintances of the killers, along with witnesses to the tragedies.

The emergence of the significance of the behavioural patterns described in *Killing for Pleasure* arose naturally from research. Evidence that would simply provide the right answers to a set of predetermined questions was not actively pursued.

MULTIPLE MURDER

Multiple murder is a rare phenomenon, but when it occurs it causes intense and widespread alarm. According to P E. Dietz, Professor of Law and Psychiatry in Virginia, USA, multiple murders are divided into two main categories, 'Mass' and 'Serial'. He defines 'Mass Murder' as offences in which five or more victims are intentionally killed by a single offender in a single incident. This contrasts with 'Serial Murders' where five or more victims are killed in separate incidents, sometimes with long intervals between events.

Dietz defined Mass Murders under the following categories:

Mass Murder

1. Pseudo-commandos. Generally young male loners who have a preoccupation with firearms. Their prominent psychopathology is paranoia.
2. Family annihilators. These are usually highly-depressed individuals who are suicidal and kill their family and themselves.
3. Set and run killers. They set a lethal trap, such as a bomb in a car or building, allowing themselves time to escape.
4. Psychotic killers. The essential diagnosis is usually one of a florid paranoid schizophrenia and/or a depressive psychosis. In certain cases, where the illness has been in its early stages, some schizophrenics exhibit unsocialised aggression a decade before their illness manifests itself.

Serial Murder

1. Crime spree killers. Individuals involved in a crime series motivated by excitement and greed, for example, Bonnie and Clyde.
2. Functionaries of organised crime or political killings - for example, the Mafia or the IRA.
3. Custodial poisoners and asphyxiators. Professional carers such as doctors, nurses, babysitters and foster parents who kill their patients or charges.

4. The sexually sadistic psychopath. The victims may include young women or children.
5. Psychotic serial killers. Again, may be paranoid schizophrenics.
6. 'Missionaries.' An example of this type is the Yorkshire Ripper who wanted to clean up the world by ridding the streets of prostitutes.

The essential difference between the two groups is that the serial killer will kill, then hide, then kill again. The mass murderer hides for a lifetime and then on one terrible day erupts. Unlike serial killers, mass murderers do not necessarily relish their actions, nor do they care about the potential for survival. Serial killers value their survival a lot more and for them the thrill comes from dragging out the chase, often taunting police to try and find them. In many cases, victims are tortured, sometimes over days, to extend the killer's period of pleasure. With mass murder there is a burst of savagery and then it's over.

The people profiled in *Killing for Pleasure* are all mass murderers by definition and closely fit the category of 'pseudo-commandos'.

THE PSEUDO-COMMANDO

The pseudo-commando is *always* a male, generally in his 20s or early 30s. He will have a preoccupation with firearms that are almost inevitably of the military-style, semi-automatic variety. He will be essentially a significant loner and his prominent psychopathology will be paranoia. In most cases he will carry out his murderous acts in a calm, controlled manner, free of emotion, following a lengthy period of deliberation and planning. These characteristics are dominant features of the forensic criterion 'predatory aggression'. It will not be uncommon for him to have earlier revealed his homicidal tendencies to other people. Whitman, for example, who was 'oozing' with hostility, told a psychiatrist he wanted to kill. Huberty told his wife he was going to hunt humans and Hennard talked of going out on to the street to shoot people. Both Bryant and Vitkovic mentioned their predilection to kill.

They consciously choose a spectacular suicide and most of them either have periods of depression or exhibit suicidal tendencies. Almost invariably they kill themselves during the rampage or alternatively, force police to kill them - in effect, suicide by proxy. Before going out on their 'mission' they often leave suicide notes knowing full well they will not be returning.

CONCLUSIONS

Few of the nine men profiled in *Killing for Pleasure* suffered an identifiable mental illness, such as schizophrenia, though this was suspected in a minority of cases. All subjects, however, could be said to be suffering personality disorders and there has been no evidence of organic considerations accounting for their behaviour. Unpalatable as it might be, the conclusion is that all nine individuals *chose* the course of action they embarked upon. It may have been easier for people to accept that they 'snapped' and went berserk - but the stark reality, well-supported by evidence of pre-planning, is that they did not. Each man fits the pseudo-commando profile.

THE PROFILES

The following pages summarise and compare a wide range of behavioural traits each subject shares. While some are common idiosyncrasies, other traits - such as paranoia, an inability to hold long-term employment, avoidance, withdrawal, committing serious though unreported crimes, threatening others with firearms, living out fantasies and their relationships with women - are regarded as more powerful predictors.

Trait: Held conspiracy theories and paranoid beliefs

Whitman	His unhealthy obsession and intense driven belief to outdo his father turned into paranoia.
Huberty	Believed a nuclear war was imminent, so stockpiled food and weapons to survive.
Knight	He felt persecuted at Duntroon and his defence psychiatrist believes it was at a paranoid level of intensity.

Ryan   Was paranoid about his appearance and baldness, but there was no evidence of hair loss. Became territorial and paranoid about his neighbours.

Vitkovic   Was paranoid about homosexuals and lesbians and society's problems - particularly crime and punishment - even advocating capital punishment for civil libertarians.

Gray   Was consumed with the idea that Asians would invade New Zealand and he would be ready when it happened. Went to extraordinary lengths to cure or hide his baldness.

Hennard   Was paranoid about being constantly followed and talked about by people, complaining to the FBI about a nationwide conspiracy against him.

Hamilton   Believed there was a conspiracy of 'brotherhood' in the police and Scouts working against him. Even wrote to the Queen about people spreading malicious rumours and innuendoes about him.

Bryant   Little evidence of conspiracy theory, but made several statements indicating a deep mistrust of Asians and Jews.

Trait: Were known to hold grudges

Whitman   Held a deep-seated grudge against his father and an embittered hatred of the Marines.

Huberty   Blamed the working classes for causing inflation and the rich for conspiring to create the oil crisis. Became anti-America, and said he hated the president.

Knight   Had a pathological sensitivity to rejection and held a grudge against the army cadets who assaulted him. Had feelings of revenge against the cadet he stabbed and was disappointed he was unable to maim or injure the others.

Ryan	Held a grudge against the people who had 'warned him off' the barmaid he was pestering.
Vitkovic	He held long-term, intense grudges and wrote how people would pay for their actions.
Gray	An acquaintance was adamant Gray held grudges and had been angered and hurt by the accusations of being a 'peeping Tom' and at being 'sorted out' by locals. Told Niki Boon a Scorpio never forgets.
Hennard	Had an intense hatred of those who forced him from the sea and at women he thought were conspiring against him.
Hamilton	Held an intense grudge against the Scouts, Comrie Deuchars and the police for the failure of his boys' clubs and became incensed when a school principal advised parents to keep their children away from him.
Bryant	Held a deep-seated grudge against the Martins for their failure to sell his family their farm years before.

Trait: Were regarded as 'odd' or 'strange'

Whitman	No, but in reality his demeanour was a façade and he exhibited some strange behaviours.
Huberty	Regularly referred to as 'strange' and 'weird'.
Knight	Evidence of strangeness only became obvious after leaving the army. His ex-girlfriend did not want him to visit her again as 'he seemed really strange'.
Ryan	Referred to as a 'Walter Mitty' personality for the elaborate lies he told.
Vitkovic	One medical specialist referred to him as 'having a most peculiar affect'. Vitkovic's university examination answer was regarded as disturbing and bizarre.
Gray	Described as a very, very odd person who would

avoid contact with people in the street. Even the local police sergeant, on his way to the shootings, recalled Gray as 'certainly an eccentric'.

Hennard   Many people, including his mother, described him as 'strange'. The dealer who sold him guns had a 'bad feeling' about him.

Hamilton   A member of his shooting club referred to him as a 'right weirdo', while others called him 'Mr Creepy'.

Bryant   His custom of making outrageously inappropriate comments to women was regarded as very odd. Called 'Silly Martin'.

Trait: Were significantly lonely individuals

Whitman   While in the Marines wrote, 'I don't associate with very many people here now'. Although married with some friends he chose a more lonely existence than he needed to. Members of his study groups found him difficult to deal with.

Huberty   Although married, was still a loner. Etna said his dog was his best friend.

Knight   A school teacher described him as a self-contained loner. He had a small circle of friends and girlfriends but most were 'on again, off again' relationships.

Ryan   Grew up as an 'anonymous sort of lad, a rather awkward loner'. Was a very solitary individual. When having a drink at the 'local' was always seen at the bar alone.

Vitkovic   Never had a lot of friends, preferring his own company and confessed in diary entries to loneliness. 'I have no friends now, not one. No one to talk to. I'm completely alone.'

Gray   Had few friends in life and was alienated from family and neighbours. Had virtually no one to talk to and lived an almost hermit-like existence.

Hennard	Was a very solitary character. Turned workmates off with his selfish, whining attitude.
Hamilton	Told an acquaintance on the phone soon before the killings, 'It was not good to be lonely'. Had virtually no friends and lived alone.
Bryant	Tried desperately to make friends without success. Had remarked to a woman, 'It's a terrible thing to be lonely'.

Trait: Threatened, presented or otherwise used firearms inappropriately

Whitman	Aimed a pistol at a pedestrian for no reason.
Huberty	Scared an acquaintance by shooting at a rock at close range.
Knight	Took 'pot shots' at cars and trains with an air rifle and hit a friend in the back of the head with a pellet, then kept on shooting. On a trip to New South Wales said, 'I wish I had brought my firearms so I could shoot at road signs.'
Ryan	Threatened a 'stroppy' man with a pistol. Regularly carried loaded pistols with him. Took 'pot shots' at road signs with his pistols and fired an air rifle at neighbours.
Vitkovic	No record. Kept his ownership of a gun a close secret.
Gray	When he challenged someone to a fight had an air rifle with him, the barrel protruding from a box. As a schoolboy, fired a rifle at targets in a basement, hitting one boy in the back of the head with a ricochet.
Hennard	Said to Jimmy Shellenbarger, 'What would happen if I went outside and pulled a gun on someone?'
Hamilton	Pointed an unloaded gun at James Gillespie and pulled the trigger.
Bryant	Twice aimed an unloaded gun at a friend and

pulled the trigger. Fired an air gun at cars and people buying vegetables at a roadside stall.

Trait: Were involved in serious incidents that went unreported

Whitman   When a student went to collect a debt, Whitman intimidated him by throwing a hunting knife into a door.

Huberty   Threatened to 'get' the father of neighbouring children.

Knight   Was involved in two violent incidents, one in a hotel and another an assault on his girlfriend at his home.

Ryan   Fired pellets at a neighbour hanging out her washing and threatened another neighbour with a knife.

Vitkovic   None reported, but his writings indicate a strong possibility they may have occurred.

Gray   Using a knife, he threatened his brother who feared for his life. On the day of the massacre threatened the owners of a coffee bar with the comment he would 'blow them away'.

Hennard   Seriously harassed two young women in his neighbourhood.

Hamilton   Pointed an unloaded gun at Mr Gillespie and pulled the trigger.

Bryant   Threatened a friend twice with a gun and twice stabbed him with a spear. Also threatened neighbours with a gun.

Trait: Lived out their fantasies to some extent

Whitman   Fantasised he was the 'world's finest' marksman and carried out this fantasy from the tower.

Huberty   Had an 'involvement in war' fantasy. Said, 'I've killed thousands and I'll kill thousands more'.

Knight   Had a burning desire to be a mercenary, fighting in the world's trouble spots. Acted out this fantasy in the army reserve, regular army and ultimately on Hoddle Street.

Ryan   Lied that he was an ex-paratrooper and had been to Africa four times as a mercenary. Acted out his fantasies by dressing in camouflage clothing and creeping up on picnickers in a forest then disappearing without being detected.

Vitkovic   Wrote of having sick fantasies to destroy things. Smashed furniture in his garage and uprooted a small tree, carrying it down the road at 2 am. Also fantasised about being the 'teacher' of people he thought were against him. Carried out this fantasy on Queen Street.

Gray   Had an admiration for Ninja warriors and the Vietcong soldiers in Vietnam. Was seen running around undergrowth in camouflage clothing in the weeks before the killings. Held off police in a commando-style siege.

Hennard   Had a fascination with mass killers and spoke of this to people, and owned tapes on mass killing in the USA. Some were specifically about the killing of women.

Hamilton   Owned and displayed thousands of photographs of young boys in brief swimming togs which he used to satisfy his fantasies.

Bryant   Liked to act out the persona of an English gentleman in restaurants. Was also known as the 'highway surfer' and carried a surfboard on his car, dressed as a surfee, wore zinc ointment on his nose and told people he was a surfer - despite never going surfing.

Trait: Were powerless, insignificant people

Whitman   Although tall and powerfully-built, he lacked direction and achievement, making him shallow and powerless. He considered himself inadequate.

| Huberty | Regularly referred to as nondescript. |

Huberty — Regularly referred to as nondescript.

Knight — Generally withdrawn, keeping to himself. One army colleague regarded him as a 'wimp' lacking leadership skills.

Ryan — Was insignificant in stature and manner. Relatives regarded him as inadequate and a work colleague called him a 'wimp'. Was referred to by one person as more of a Bambi than a Rambo.

Vitkovic — Regarded himself as being too 'wimpy' to be with any mates.

Gray — An insignificant, lonely figure who was not regarded by anyone as a threat or dangerous.

Hennard — Although tall and well built, was referred to as being insecure and 'a bit of a wimp'.

Hamilton — A meek, mild, insignificant man some called a sycophant.

Bryant — Almost childlike and effeminate in speech and demeanour.

Trait: Planned the mass murder in some detail

Whitman — Extensively planned the murders.

Huberty — Prepared rather than planned. Used to watch McDonald's with binoculars.

Knight — Another exception to the rule, who prepared rather than planned.

Ryan — The degree of planning is unknown but from what he was able to put together in a matter of minutes it appears he had prepared to begin his campaign.

Vitkovic — Wrote in his diaries about the 'mission' he had to complete and how he was getting ready. Made specific purchases weeks before the killings and wrote suicide letters.

Gray — Collected firearms at an increased frequency prior to the shootings and cut crosses on bullets so that they would shatter on impact. Had prepared molotov cocktails to use.

Hennard	Bought new clips for his pistols that held more bullets and wrote suicide notes. He loaded his magazines before taking the 20-minute drive to Luby's.
Hamilton	Purchased a special bag and inserted cardboard partitions so he could get to his ammunition quickly. Colour-coded the clips so he could reload efficiently. His planning over several weeks was meticulous.
Bryant	Pre-purchased a special bag to carry his guns and ammunition and even measured it in the shop. Set his alarm clock the night before which he never normally did.

Trait: Had been seen by medical professionals as a result of their behaviour

Whitman	At his wife's insistence, saw a psychiatrist. He was 'oozing with hostility' and said he was 'thinking about going up the tower with a deer rifle and start shooting people'.
Huberty	Telephoned a mental health clinic for help the day before the massacre and an appointment was to be made.
Knight	Had not been referred to a doctor for 'strange' behaviour, but did receive psychological assessment before joining the army. He was assessed as 'marginal' with one member of the panel saying, 'He may be over-confident and his ability may not match his belief in himself.' Considered the need to seek help for his temper but never did.
Ryan	Not in this case, though he was treated by a specialist for a throat condition associated with stress.
Vitkovic	Visited a psychiatrist after having looked up a woman's dress, saw a university psychologist,

	and claimed he was distressed by violent fantasies.
Gray	As a result of restricting himself to his room and being disinterested in life he was referred to a psychiatrist.
Hennard	A psychologist treating him said he had periods of extreme highs and lows and at times could be very violent.
Hamilton ·	After an interview, Dr Fairgrieve wrote, 'Formed the impression that he had a persecution complex and delusions of grandeur'.
Bryant	Seen by psychologists and doctors for behavioural problems. At age 24 was seen by two psychiatrists and told one he would like to go around shooting people.

Trait: Had a calmness about them prior to and during the murders

Whitman	Whilst typing the note about his intention to kill his wife he was interrupted by friends who found him engaging, amusing and remarkably calm. Someone speaking to him as he prepared his weapons said he was very, very calm.
Huberty	Acted with 'long, slow, methodical precision'.
Knight	An uncle said, 'His mood on the day was the best he had been in for some time', and a female acquaintance said he was remarkably happy just before the offending.
Ryan	Throughout the rampage he was deliberate, calm and in control.
Vitkovic	Although sad before going to the post office building, he appeared calm.
Gray	Had been 'grumpy' earlier in the day but was very calm when speaking with the last person known to talk with him. During the shootings was calm and deliberate as he prepared for a siege.

Hennard	Early on the morning of the killings a shopkeeper said he was the calmest she had ever seen him.
Hamilton	Neighbour Comrie Deuchars spoke to Hamilton just before he left for Dunblane and he seemed 'brighter and cheerier than usual'.
Bryant	Roger Larner spoke to Bryant minutes before the massacre and said, 'He was the most normal I had ever seen him.'

Trait: Had a detailed awareness of other mass killings

Whitman	No, as he was the first of this type of offender.
Huberty	No, but probably knew of Whitman. Huberty was the second killer of this type.
Knight	Knew in detail about Whitman and Huberty and was fascinated by other killers such as David (Son of Sam) Berkowitz.
Ryan	Burnt his house down so any evidence was lost. However as the Hoddle Street massacre had occurred ten days earlier it is assumed Ryan would have at least known of Knight.
Vitkovic	Listed Ryan's weapons in his diary and had newspaper cuttings about Knight's rampage stuck to the inside of his wardrobe door.
Gray	On the day of the massacre wrote a letter referring to Hungerford and Hoddle Street in some detail.
Hennard	Had a video about Huberty's attack at McDonald's restaurant in San Diego seven years earlier. Knew of Whitman in detail.
Hamilton	Unknown if he had any in-depth knowledge of similar events.
Bryant	Sergeant McCarthy said, 'There is a lot we don't know about Bryant but one thing we do know is he knew a lot about other mass killings, almost a morbid interest.'

Trait: Used execution style of killing and lacked empathy

Whitman	Chose ammunition that would cause maximum injury, taking deliberate aim; not a 'hit-and-miss' attack.
Huberty	Shot babies and elderly victims, all through the head or chest at close range.
Knight	If people were injured he would 'finish them off'. Spoke calmly about how he killed, showing no compassion or empathy.
Ryan	Shot his mother in the back from very close range. Smiled at some people he shot and entered a house to execute the elderly occupants.
Vitkovic	Hunted down hiding victims and shot at close range. Taunted people, saying they would not get away. Returned to some injured people and shot again.
Gray	Returned to injured people and killed them at close range, usually with shots to the eye. Entered a house and killed two elderly men inside.
Hennard	Kicked people to see if they moved, shot at close range if they were still alive, and killed people begging for mercy. Let one woman escape with her child but then went on shooting.
Hamilton	Walked in a circle around the children as if herding them. Wore earmuffs to deaden the noise. Reloaded his gun and shot again and again at very close range.
Bryant	Very deliberate. Would aim, fire, pick out his next victim and fire again. Killed a woman on her knees, begging to be spared then followed her young daughter and killed her.

Trait: Gave veiled indications of what they were about to do

Whitman	Talked to a psychiatrist about shooting people and, following his parents' separation, told Larry Fuess he had 'something personal to settle'.

Huberty	When laid off said, 'I'll take everyone with me,' and told his wife, 'Society had its chance - I'm going hunting humans.'
Knight	Told Lisa, 'No one has been nice to me so I will treat them the way I've been treated.'
Ryan	A few days before the massacre talked of a neighbour as 'needing to have his head blown off'.
Vitkovic	Wrote in his diary about having a 'mission' to complete and on the day of the killings told the University Union receptionist he 'had a job to do at the post office'.
Gray	Renamed his shack 'Hlidskjalf' and when asked by a neighbour what it meant he said, 'You'll find out one day'.
Hennard	Told Mrs Mead, 'If you don't get the people of Belton to quit looking at me there will be problems', and to Martin Flores said, 'If people don't stop fooling around with me someone will get hurt'. Had told a co-worker to 'watch and see' while talking about killing.
Hamilton	Before the massacre bought two new shirts on credit and told an acquaintance, 'The beauty of it is that I will never have to pay for them, ever'.
Bryant	Shortly before the massacre said to a woman, 'Nobody listens to me. I'll think of something and everybody will remember me'. On the day of the massacre told his girlfriend he 'had somewhere to go'.

Trait: Had emotional attachment to firearms

Whitman	Grew up with guns and followed in his father's footsteps as a gun fanatic who regarded himself as the 'world's finest'.
Huberty	His only animated conversations were about guns, especially automatics.

Knight	Girlfriend said he was fanatical about guns and was fastidious about cleaning them.
Ryan	Took his guns to work to show colleagues and talked of his deep interest in guns.
Vitkovic	Very secretive about his guns but wrote in his diary, 'gun freaks rule, I love guns'.
Gray	Wrote to magazines about his views on firearms and which ones were best in combat.
Hennard	No reports of a close attachment to firearms, but joined a shooting club ten days before the murders.
Hamilton	Reported having talked of his guns as if they were 'his babies' and took them to the homes of other people to show them off. When depressed he talked about 'going home to my guns'.
Bryant	Loved the thought of owning guns and told a psychiatrist how holding a gun made him feel powerful. Told police he was attached to his AR-15. 'I wish I had the AR-15 in here (Risdon Prison) then I could probably get out . . . I could probably jump through the window and escape.'

Trait: Came from backgrounds with elements of being dysfunctional

Whitman	Father was a dominating, strict disciplinarian who beat his wife and sons. Whitman was pressured by his father to achieve perfection and excellence. Parents separated in the year of the massacre.
Huberty	His mother left home when he was nine to be a minister in Tucson. Huberty was affected by the separation.
Knight	Had a troubled upbringing. Was the illegitimate son of a young woman and adopted as a baby. When aged 12 his parents separated after years of arguments.

Ryan	Elderly father was a strict disciplinarian towards both his wife and son.
Vitkovic	A psychiatrist believed the dress incident was because of a 'minor adjustment reaction to adolescence in the setting of a dysfunctional family'.
Gray	Father was severely wounded in the war and had a metal plate inserted in his head making him a moody, temperamental man. Older siblings left home early leaving him alone with ageing parents.
Hennard	Parents separated after 25 years of marriage and two of the five children were from Mrs Hennard's previous marriage.
Hamilton	Was the only son of Agnes Hamilton who was herself adopted. He was raised by his grandparents, believing Agnes was his older sister. His natural father left Agnes soon after the birth.
Bryant	Brought up by both parents until they separated. Spent several years as the 'adopted' son/companion of eccentric Helen Harvey. His father committed suicide.

Trait: Had poor relationships with women (especially of their own age group)

Whitman	Had one steady relationship and after five months was married but immature behaviour and a violent temper almost caused the marriage to founder. Kept a typed card reminding him to be nice to his wife.
Huberty	Treated his wife as a motherly figure. Etna referred to their marriage as 'not being typical'.
Knight	Had three steady relationships but all broke up through his behaviour. He found relationship break-ups hard to handle.
Ryan	Had no girlfriends and his 'romances and

	fiancées' were all imaginary. Ryan lacked the skills to engage females as companions.
Vitkovic	Became tongue-tied and could not engage females of his age in conversation. Had two brief 'experimental' relationships with girls.
Gray	Believed women found him attractive but he never formed any relationships with females.
Hennard	Had one brief relationship but found it difficult relating to women and believed that was due to a conspiracy.
Hamilton	Was reported to have had a girlfriend in earlier years but when she got serious he 'didn't want to know'. Was nervous around adults and found female company uncomfortable.
Bryant	Had two short-term relationships with teenage girls much younger than himself. Tended to treat women like they were his mother.

Trait: Had been physically or verbally attacked or ostracised by acquaintances or neighbours

Whitman	When 'jumped' by a group of Marines was kicked in the head and face.
Huberty	Was in regular conflict with neighbours.
Knight	Assaulted by a group of soldiers, resulting in him later stabbing one of them.
Ryan	Was 'warned off' a barmaid after he pestered her. Ribbed by colleagues at a work scheme to the stage he threatened to shoot them and had numerous confrontations with neighbours.
Vitkovic	He referred in a diary entry to having another run-in with a carload of people who 'heaped crap at me' for no reason.
Gray	Falsely accused of being a 'peeping Tom' and was 'sorted out' by locals.
Hennard	Jimmy Shellenbarger 'whopped his ass' in front of workmates.

Hamilton	Accused of paedophilia and felt so persecuted complained to the Queen. Was doused with a foul-smelling concoction in front of a press photographer; photo appeared in newspaper.
Bryant	Was often ostracised by people he unsuccessfully tried to befriend.

Trait: Became territorial

Whitman	Unknown if he did.
Huberty	Sat inside his home with a shotgun on his lap.
Knight	Not established.
Ryan	Argued with a neighbour and fired an airgun at her when her children encroached on his territory.
Vitkovic	No evidence of being territorial though the house he lived in belonged to his parents.
Gray	Used large stones to mark his boundaries but previously had not minded children running across his unfenced section. Began to refuse entry to his home and became abrasive to anyone calling.
Hennard	Chased a boy retrieving a ball from the lawn and threw rocks at children encroaching on the property.
Hamilton	Towards the end refused to answer the door when an acquaintance called. He did not own a car but was possessive over the car-park in front of his house and even complained when an ambulance parked there.
Bryant	Became defensive of people coming onto his property. Pointed a gun at one neighbour telling him to get off the property.

Trait: Had older women as significant people in their lives or were possessive of 'mother' figures

Whitman	Shared a joint bank account with his mother who doted on him to the stage her other sons felt

neglected. Late on the night of her murder, she phoned him to say where she was then rushed home to meet him.

Huberty	Etna referred to 'being sick of playing the mother figure'.
Knight	The army selection psychologist noted, 'He is a bit sensitive about his family situation - may be a bit emotionally close to his mum.' His mother was close to him. He admitted she was affectionate towards him.
Ryan	Mrs Ryan doted on her son and provided anything he wanted. She resorted to coded phone calls to let Ryan know her whereabouts. He lived alone with his mother and would deny visitors a chance to see her.
Vitkovic	Wrote in his diary, 'I love my mother very much. I adore her,' believing his mother was the only type of person he liked. The family doctor believed Mrs Vitkovic had a great influence over her son.
Gray	Was very possessive of his mother when he lived alone with her. Was adored and spoilt by her, while he expected her to 'fetch and carry' for him. Became distressed when she died and spoke of her two days before the rampage as if she had only just died.
Hennard	Gave Martin Flores looks of 'what are you doing here with my mother?' Flores felt Hennard was possessive towards his mother. She was reported to have a financial and emotional hold over her son.
Hamilton	It is unknown how significant Hamilton's mother was towards him. She was in reality his grandmother.
Bryant	Physically attacked a woman visiting his mother, pushing her down some steps, and threatened people off Helen Harvey's property. Was

extremely close to Harvey who arranged for him to be eventually buried beside her.

Trait: Were reported to have a strange look in their eyes

Whitman No reports in Whitman's case.

Huberty Unreported. He was wearing sunglasses at the time.

Knight On the night of the shootings his sister described him as having a 'weird look' on his face but was not specific about the eyes.

Ryan Witnesses described him as having a crazy look on his face during the murders, with a 'terrible vacant look in his eyes'.

Vitkovic During the rampage his eyes were glazed and vacant and also 'large, frightening and abnormal'.

Gray Always had an intense stare and on the day of the killings a threatened coffee bar owner said he had a look in his eyes she 'had never seen in others before'. A gun shop owner referred to his strange sunken eyes.

Hennard Reported to have piercing brown eyes that made people afraid. At Luby's his face was cold and expressionless but his eyes were 'very large and frightening'.

Hamilton A policewoman who interviewed him over firearms registration matters was disturbed at the strange way he looked at her.

Bryant When upset would stare at people with an intense gaze. Would look 'straight through people' or just past their eyes, making it difficult to engage in conversation.

Trait: Had minor or no criminal convictions but had come to police notice

Whitman Had some traffic violations, mostly for speeding. Was investigated by police for deer poaching.

Huberty   Had minor traffic infringements and one conviction for disorderly conduct. Was regularly visited by police over disputes and was interviewed at length when he claimed to be a war criminal.

Knight   No previous convictions but had a case discharged following an assault while a schoolboy. Charges were pending for the stabbing incident.

Ryan   Had one speeding infringement. Police made several visits to his home while carrying out firearms registration enquiries.

Vitkovic   No convictions, but investigated for looking up a woman's dress.

Gray   Was visited by police twice, once for threatening a bookshop employee and once for allegations of being a 'peeping tom'. Had no criminal convictions.

Hennard   Had one speeding infringement, a conviction for possessing a single marijuana joint and a conviction for being under the influence and carrying loaded weapons in his truck. Was investigated for inappropriate correspondence to two young women.

Hamilton   Investigated several times as a paedophile, but charges were never laid.

Bryant   Came to attention of British police for suddenly leaving a hotel close to a SAS training base. Investigated for bringing pornographic videos into Australia. Had one conviction for driving without a licence.

Trait: Were in debt or had limited means at time of killings

Whitman   Complained that at age 25 he had never been financially independent and relied on his wife's job and the joint account with his mother to survive. Died with $13.87 in his bank account.

Huberty   Had money but it was tied up in Massillon or frozen in Mexico.

Knight   Was earning $200 a week of which $50 went on board and $55 towards paying off his car. Was two weeks behind with payments. His car, valued at $5,000, was for sale to help pay off a $7,000 debt.

Ryan   Had £1,000 in a building society from selling his antique sword collection. Had no income and relied on his mother for money. She had £25 in her building society but was £800 overdrawn at the bank. Ryan's 'income' was affected when she lost one of her two jobs.

Vitkovic   Had no job and lived at home with his parents. Wrote in his diary about the frustrations of having no money.

Gray   Lived on an unemployment benefit and had few possessions and no assets. He had some small investments in a building society.

Hennard   Whilst at sea he saved a lot of money but in the two years on land his resources dwindled. At the time of his death he was down to his last $1,000 and told his brother-in-law, 'I don't know what will happen when that's gone'.

Hamilton   Was in serious financial difficulty. His cash reserves were dwindling and he was making losses on his boys' clubs. He had substantial loans. His debt was in excess of £8,000.

Bryant   Was the exception. Up until he met Helen Harvey he relied on his father for money but upon Harvey's death he inherited a fortune.

Trait: Displayed a significant degree of cruelty to animals

Whitman   Known as an animal-lover, and no recorded cruelty is known. His skinning of a deer in his shower was unusual.

Huberty	Shot his dog for jumping on a car.
Knight	No references to cruelty, but reputedly had a firearm confiscated after threatening to shoot his dog.
Ryan	Offended workmates by shooting a green woodpecker for no reason. Shot his dog at the beginning of his rampage.
Gray	Had an affinity with dogs but in later life tried to kill them with large boulders. Owned a budgie he taught tricks but crushed it with a brick.
Hennard	Suspected of being responsible for poisoning a dog belonging to the family he was stalking.
Hamilton	Unrecorded if he was cruel to animals, but had a cruel, almost sadistic nature.
Bryant	Had a hatred of cats and was seen trying to pull them apart. Once killed a chicken by having sex with it.

Trait: Enjoyed playing cruel pranks, abused or taunted parents

Whitman	Gained pleasure from telling acquaintances that a friend died in a motor accident. Laughed uncontrollably when the 'dead' man walked into the room.
Huberty	Unknown.
Knight	Nothing is known about cruel pranks, but was responsible for dangerous practice of letting fireworks off in a school classroom.
Ryan	Was suspected of assaulting his mother for going into the shed where he stored his guns.
Vitkovic	Unknown if pranks were cruel but he did write in his diaries, 'I love playing jokes on people'.
Gray	Used trip wires connected to explosive charges and put birds in a cupboard to scare people. Abused his mother, at times making her sit in the corner to eat her meal.
Hennard	Was known to taunt his mother over her

appearance, for example saying, 'You're not 21 anymore'.

Hamilton	Had a habit of creeping up on people. Once told his natural mother her doctor was sending an ambulance to take her to hospital, which was completely false. Abused his grandfather (father), locking him out in the rain for up to 20 minutes.
Bryant	Had a habit of sneaking up on people and giving them a fright. Regularly pulled on Helen Harvey's steering wheel while she was driving.

Trait: Lived in a shambles with some part of their life being orderly

Whitman	Was an exception. His wife kept their home very neat and tidy.
Huberty	Another exception. His wife kept the house tidy.
Knight	Although living conditions were not a shambles they were cluttered and untidy. While his army gear was slung across an exercycle in the hall, his military books were meticulously arranged on a bookshelf.
Ryan	The house was untidy and cluttered with furniture, but his sword collection was neatly displayed on racks.
Vitkovic	Although his mother kept his room clean, he acknowledged in his diary that his room was turning into a pigsty.
Gray	His small shack was a shambles, but his books, stacked on shelves, were neat and orderly.
Hennard	An exception in that he kept 'the mansion' immaculate. However, was rebuked by his brother-in-law for 'slobbing out' and not cleaning up after himself.
Hamilton	Lived in a disorganised flat described by a neighbour as a 'tip'. It was untidy and dirty but his boys' club material was neat and orderly.

Bryant   Lived in a very disordered house. After buying groceries he would leave everything on the bench until it was used up. Bedrooms were littered with clothes, but his health and fitness regime documents were orderly and neat.

Trait: Were unemployed or had difficulty holding long-term employment

Whitman   Despite university training and a high IQ held a variety of short-term menial jobs. His career in the Marines, punctuated with a spell at university, was cut short because he could not take it any more.

Huberty   Was laid off from his last three jobs and was unemployed.

Knight   Was unemployed throughout most of 1985. Worked briefly as a kitchen-hand for McDonald's, then sold plastic weatherboards door-to-door. After his army career was cut very short he found a job as a storeman two weeks before the shooting spree.

Ryan   Had sporadic, short-term employment as a handyman/gardener. Tried to get fired from a work scheme so he could qualify for an unemployment benefit.

Vitkovic   Expressed a wish to find work but did not try hard to find any. His occasional jobs were menial and of short duration.

Gray   Had labouring jobs in earlier years but none were long-term. Had lived on an unemployment benefit for some years.

Hennard   Had long-term employment in the merchant marine, but after losing his licence, tried a variety of labouring jobs. All were inconsequential and none lasted long.

Hamilton   Was self-employed in a 'do-it-yourself' shop for

13 years but sold it and went on an unemployment benefit. Was employed on-and-off selling cameras and doing freelance photography. Had no other long-term employment apart from his involvement in running boys' clubs.

Bryant   Never employed. He was incapable of working and when he inherited Helen Harvey's fortune he never had to.

Trait: Were at some stage regarded as generous, kind or polite

Whitman   Many spoke of Whitman as 'nice' or 'charming'. This was a façade and it was easier for him to appear nice than to be nice.

Huberty   As a youngster was referred to as 'quiet' and 'nice'.

Knight   Although unpopular with peers at Duntroon, a few found him to be 'nice enough and good-hearted'. Police dealing with him for his firearm's licence recorded, 'has an excellent attitude to police'.

Ryan   Some relatives found him to be a 'kind and gentle boy'. Police interviewing him over firearm registration matters remarked on his politeness.

Vitkovic   People spoke of him as a 'nice, quiet and polite individual'. Helped fundraise for the Australian Birthright Movement and was keen to help underprivileged people.

Gray   Was regarded by some as a sensitive person interested in pottery and painting and despite having meagre resources gave willingly to door-to-door collectors, such as the Red Cross.

Hennard   His sisters' partners regarded him as 'a mild-mannered guy, not at all aggressive', and 'a nice guy'. His girlfriend said he was 'sensitive, with good manners and a caring attitude', when not drinking alcohol. He often helped an elderly neighbour by doing odd jobs around her property.

Hamilton	An overly-polite man who some regarded as a quiet, kind individual. He spoke softly but never laughed.
Bryant	Was spoken of as 'polite, kind and generous'.

Trait: Suffered name calling /taunting/bullying particularly in earlier life

Whitman	Was dominated throughout his life by his father.
Huberty	Was laughed at by co-workers over his extreme views on capitalism.
Knight	Had been assaulted a couple of times at secondary school by what he termed 'ethnics'. Was significantly affected by bullying and taunts at the Duntroon Military College.
Ryan	He had a miserable time at school and because of his isolation and moods he was picked on and bullied by other children.
Vitkovic	Was called 'Vic the prick' at school and though this was intended as an innocuous remark it affected him deeply.
Gray	Was a 'bottom of the heap' kid who was taunted at school because of his glasses.
Hennard	Unknown, but school friends recalled the strange haircut he was given as a punishment. Taunts about it would have been difficult to take.
Hamilton	'Mr Creepy' or 'Mr Ho Hum'. Because of his creepy manner and a habit of talking to himself he was called names.
Bryant	Was called 'Silly Martin' by other children who teased him about his habits and also nicknamed him 'The Shadow' for his habit of suddenly appearing out of nowhere, then disappearing.

Trait: Tended to avoid (especially the gaze of) others

Whitman	There is no evidence of this in Whitman.

Huberty	Mike Mauger said, 'He would never look you in the eye.'
Knight	Whilst not specifically avoiding a gaze, his next-door neighbour said he often said hello to Knight who never replied.
Ryan	Tended to avoid people while on the work scheme and would sit alone at lunch-times.
Vitkovic	Towards the end became withdrawn and did not engage with people and even wrote of becoming alienated from his family.
Gray	Walked with his head down and often crossed the road to avoid people and if forced to speak often grunted.
Hennard	Referred to several times as 'rushing by clutching a backpack and staring straight ahead'.
Hamilton	Always walked with his head down, avoiding the gaze of others. Spoke regularly to Comrie Deuchars, but never looked him in the eye.
Bryant	Often looked to the side of a person's head when talking instead of looking directly at them.

Trait: Personal appearance deteriorated prior to the killings

Whitman	Neglected his muscular physique and became overweight and, on reaching the stage of profound personal dissatisfaction, decided to become a 'bum'.
Huberty	While his personal appearance did not deteriorate his behaviour did, to the point his daughters became frightened.
Knight	While his grooming and clothing had not appeared to deteriorate, an ex-girlfriend felt he totally changed over the final few months. 'He became an inane ocker or yobbo which wasn't like him before.'
Ryan	Unknown if there was any change.
Vitkovic	Put on weight and generally became untidy.

Confessed at the end he was 'fat and ashamed' of his body.

Gray His deteriorating appearance became noticeable leading up to the massacre. Was referred to as emaciated, dirty and unkempt. Had not been feeding himself and when neighbours took him food he refused, slamming the door.

Hennard His paranoia became so great his sister did most of his shopping. Was usually tidy and clean-shaven but became scruffy, unshaven and hyped-up. How near this was towards the end was not established.

Hamilton No reported deterioration in appearance as he was always rather scruffy.

Bryant Before the massacre he grew his hair long and took on a surfer-type appearance. Prior to that he had kept himself neat and tidy.

Trait: Were collectors of some sort

Whitman Kept a large collection of militaria and weaponry.

Huberty Was an avid collector of guns.

Knight As a boy collected thousands of toy soldiers which he carefully painted, and became an avid reader and collector of history books detailing battles.

Ryan Owned an elaborate and expensive collection of antique firearms and swords.

Vitkovic Had a large collection of videos amassed over a number of years.

Gray Collected books on warfare and militaria and had a collection of military models.

Hennard Collected large models of jet fighter aircraft.

Hamilton Collected cameras and over 5,000 photographs and videos of boys in swimming trunks.

Bryant Collected several thousand videos.

Trait: Were not under the influence of drink or drugs at the time of killings

Whitman   Was embalmed before the autopsy, so tests were inconclusive, but his actions in the tower suggest he was not under any influence of drink or drugs.

Huberty   Was clear of drugs and alcohol.

Knight   Claimed to have drunk up to 14 glasses of beer but blood tests and evidence from bar staff suggest he had half that amount. Unlike other mass murderers, he had been drinking but was not unduly affected.

Ryan   Did not drink to excess, nor was he known to use drugs. Was sober at the time of the killings.

Vitkovic   Did take prescription drugs for depression, but was not affected by drink or drugs on the day.

Gray   Had no record of drug or alcohol abuse and had not been drinking on the day of the killings.

Hennard   Occasionally smoked marijuana and drank alcohol, but was not under the influence of either on the day of the murders.

Hamilton   Despised alcohol and there was no evidence of drug use as a cause for his murders.

Bryant   Liked sweet-tasting wines but did not drink to excess. Was not under the influence of drink or drugs.

Trait: Wore unusual clothes or accessories

Whitman   Not established.

Huberty   Not recorded, but wore camouflage trousers to McDonald's.

Knight   Remembered as someone who often wore a military-style camouflage jacket.

Ryan   Often dressed in camouflage-style clothing, with paratrooper boots, and regardless of the weather wore sunglasses.

Vitkovic   Wrote, 'I felt conquering, I felt strong. I could sense people in cars feared me. I looked mysterious, rain jacket pulled over my head, you couldn't see my face.'

Gray   Never seen without a hat or a balaclava - no matter the weather. Refused to take his hat off at a relative's wedding and in a doctor's surgery during examination.

Hennard   Nothing unusual noted about his clothing.

Hamilton   Wore a blue anorak with the hood up in summer and winter. Seemed to wrap himself up in it.

Bryant   Wore clothes that did not match each other the climate or the occasion. While well-dressed, the combinations and styles were described as 'weird'.

PROFILE SUMMARY

It must be noted that while many people share the traits common to mass killers, it does not mean they will have a proclivity towards murder. Millions of people come from dysfunctional backgrounds, choose to live in a fantasy world or lead lonely lives, but they do not go around killing people.

The conclusions that can be drawn from the profiles are that potential mass murderers are, to a degree, identifiable as a group - not all of them, but certainly some. If we accept that most mass murderers will exhibit all, or a large percentage of, the individual characteristics, then that is a starting point to identify potential killers. Society can do two things as preventive measures. One relates to the availability of firearms and the other concerns mental health services.

MENTAL HEALTH

In defence of the psychiatrists and psychologists who were consulted by men who went on to commit acts of mass murder, it should be stated that it is easy to look at situations with the benefit of hindsight. In reality, many people talk to mental health professionals about fantasies or impulses to kill others. Their comments are often 'throw away' lines born from anger or frustration. Usually, the threats are non-specific and are made by people who are often not taken seriously. A classic example is Martin Bryant, who was so ineffective and effeminate people could not believe he was capable of murdering 35 individuals. 'It was a case of Martin saying silly things again'. Perhaps, apart from Vitkovic, amongst the mass murderers profiled in this book there was no clinical reason for compulsory intervention.

However, it should be considered that when people display the profile of the pseudo-commando, and express a desire to kill, then some sort of action is required. If compulsory intervention is not appropriate, and the subject refuses voluntary treatment then, at the very least, there should be some way of ensuring these individuals do not get access to firearms. If they already have them, consideration should be given to revoking their licences.

One might argue that it is impossible to identify these potential killers. Evidence in these profiles indicates there were plenty of warning signs. Thomas Hamilton was palpably paranoid, as was George Hennard. Martin Bryant and David Gray were 'strange' enough to have been quite obvious. The local police sergeant who owned a property at Aramoana, and knew Gray, referred to him as 'certainly an eccentric' as he sped to the incident. James Huberty phoned a clinic for help the day before he murdered. The 'screening' questions he was asked did not reveal any immediate need for action. Perhaps there needs to be a re-evaluation of the initial questioning process to determine if those seeking help - as Huberty did - are potential pseudo-commandos. Using the profile as a guide, mental health professionals might take a more serious view when the likes of the men featured *in Killing for Pleasure* make threats to kill. They are potentially dangerous and should be treated as such.

What we do is a matter for mental health professionals. In 1999 the British Department of Health and the British Home Office issued a paper entitled 'Managing dangerous people with severe personality disorder'. Professor Paul Mullen, responding to the paper, wrote an editorial article published in the British Medical Journal of 30 October 1999. He believed severely personality disordered individuals were over-represented among recidivist offenders - though such disorders do not inevitably lead to serious offending. Professor Mullen felt the proposals put forward were so contradictory they would have no chance in influencing the prevailing system. He was concerned that disturbed and distressed individuals currently attract little interest from mental health professionals and even less from those who fund services. Professor Mullen asks:

What is wrong then with proposals that promise far greater resources for a relatively ignored group of mentally disordered people and at the same time hold out the prospect of increased public safety?

As far as Professor Mullen is concerned:

There is a crying need for mental health services for severely personality disordered individuals.

If anything is clear from the profiles outlined in *Killing for Pleasure* it is that, by and large, the pseudo-commandos involved in brutal mass murder had disordered personalities and that in most cases they had sought help or had intimated their fantasies. Professor Mullen is right. Mental health services need to have a much better capacity to accommodate these people but how it is done is a question the mental health professionals themselves will have to determine.

FIREARMS

Whenever there is a mass killing, there is the inevitable knee-jerk reaction to tighten gun laws, especially those calling for the outlawing of military-style semi-automatic weapons. Just as predictable is the clamour from the pro-gun lobby to defend themselves. They will trumpet their call, 'Guns don't kill people. People kill people.' The anti-gun lobby comes up with a slogan of its own - 'Guns don't die, people die!' The inescapable reality is that all of the men in *Killing for Pleasure* used guns to kill their victims. Each man owned legally-purchased guns. Also unavoidable is the fact that most of the men were not fit and proper people to own guns. The way in which 'Silly Martin' easily procured his lethal semi-automatics is an indictment on the system. Michael Ryan, David Gray and Frank Vitkovic should never have been allowed semi-automatics and unlimited ammunition. We must ask how can people like Thomas Hamilton get access to semi-automatic pistols?

The answers to the dilemma do not come from politicians or the anti-gun lobbyists. The answers come from the killers themselves. On the day of the Aramoana massacre David Gray wrote to a gun magazine suggesting ways the government could prevent the likes of himself from purchasing semi-automatics. His letter was a plea to make guns so expensive he could not afford to buy them.

Frank Vitkovic wrote of society manufacturing time-bombs like himself. 'Today, somewhere, a future time-bomb is being manufactured by society.' Frank Vitkovic was not wrong. Yet when the human time-bomb is primed, society lets him collect unlimited weaponry. Vitkovic must have reflected on this in wry amusement as he bought his M1 carbine, or his magazines 'with extra zap'. He also tells us how to identify potential mass murderers, saying 'look for people with a history of rejection, loneliness and ill treatment, who have a fascination with guns'.

Julian Knight is another with a deep insight into the psychology of mass murder - and he had plenty of time to reflect on the subject. He suggests that everyone applying for permission to own firearms be psychologically tested. Clearly that would be impossible, but Knight, the terror of Hoddle Street, has a point. While psychological testing cannot be an absolute guarantee, it can give an indication to a person's instability. The judge, in summing up Knight's case, said, 'You had a diagnosable, serious personality disorder'. If that was so, should such people be able to access firearms, or has Julian Knight really got a point?

Rather than test everyone psychologically for registration of a firearm, would it not be possible to at least test those who fit the profile of the pseudo-commando? Should not enquiries be made into the backgrounds of people with a predilection to loneliness and paranoia? Or should we simply limit enquiries into those people with violent dispositions? All nine subjects in *Killing for Pleasure* displayed violent thoughts or actions, but they were well-hidden. Obviously violence alone is not the only predictable behaviour that needs examination. The lonely paranoid is potentially far more dangerous.

If societies are not prepared to weed out and stop arming potential pseudo-commandos then we will continue to have incidents where commentators will be forced to say, 'Evil visited us this day and we don't know why!'

CHAPTER ELEVEN
THE GLOBAL PHENOMENON

The nine subjects profiled in *Killing for Pleasure* were selected at random and represent just some of dozens of cases reported worldwide in the past few decades. The United States has had more than its share of these tragic mass killings, but similar events took place in South Africa, Germany, Canada, Sweden, The Philippines, Pakistan, New Zealand, France, Russia, Hawaii and Australia, as well as in several parts of the Middle East. There was only space in this book to detail nine cases. However a brief summary of another five instances, also selected at random, clearly shows that the link between these killers is far from tenuous.

Two of the following summarised cases took place in 1999, a year that has been particularly significant. By providing information on these cases the reader can see two things. Firstly the pseudo-commando profile is significantly exhibited in each of the killers, even allowing for the fact their backgrounds have not been explored in great detail here. Secondly, despite the toughening of gun laws, the rate of mass killings has not diminished. If anything it has increased, particularly in the United States. During 1999 a new phenomenon became apparent where mass killings were carried out by offenders who were not acting alone. Following the Columbine High School incident, police in the US and Canada were faced with numerous actual or potential incidents in schools, often undertaken by offenders who had accomplices.

Brief case studies of a further five mass killers are outlined below.

PATRICK HENRY SHERRILL

Edmond, Oklahoma - 20 August 1986
Victims: 14 dead, 6 injured

Despite having worked in the mail sorting branch of the Edmond Post Office for 18 months, Pat Sherrill was never known to socialise with fellow workers. He grew up a loner and maintained his distance from everyone. At age 44 the ex-Marine was noted for odd and reclusive behaviour. He wandered his neighbourhood at night, often dressed in camouflage clothing; at other times his clothes seemed dated and old-fashioned. When describing Sherrill people use words such as 'odd', 'weird', 'strange' or 'eccentric'. Others found the way Sherrill looked at them disturbing and uncomfortable.

Born on 13 November 1941 Pat Sherrill grew up on a farm 100 kilometres from Oklahoma City. At high school he performed below average academically, but had more success in the sports arena. Team games did not interest him but he did display ability in wrestling. On graduation from high school in 1959 Sherrill enrolled at Oklahoma University on a wrestling scholarship. However his university studies were short-lived and he dropped out after a few months.

In January 1964 Sherrill enlisted in the US Marine Corps and was sent to Camp Lejeune, North Carolina, where he was classified as an expert with a pistol and a marksman with a rifle. Coincidentally, another marine there at the same time, also classified as a marksman, was Private Charles Whitman. Whether Sherrill knew Whitman or made the connection after Whitman's rampage in Austin may never be known. Sherrill told anyone who would listen about his exploits in the war in Vietnam, but he never was involved in that Southeast Asian conflict. He even visited a psychologist who diagnosed him as suffering a 'fictitious post-traumatic stress disorder', an imaginary battle fatigue syndrome.

When Sherrill was discharged from the Marines in 1966 he drifted from job to job, often leaving for no good reason. On one occasion he was dismissed after harassing a female co-worker.

Sherrill lived with his widowed mother in Oklahoma City and was known to abuse her verbally, yet relatives insisted he cared for her. Mrs Sherrill kept the home neat but following her death in 1978 from a dementia disorder, Pat Sherrill lived there alone with his pit bulldog. He was a capable and precise radio technician and avid collector of 'radio ham' spare parts and the house soon became dirty and cluttered with all kinds of equipment.

In October 1984 Sherrill got a job as a firearms instructor with the Air Force National Guard Reserve. When he gained a place on their shooting team he had access to pistols and plenty of ammunition. Sherrill's life at that time was going nowhere and he told people so. While not known for violence he did exhibit paranoid behaviour. He believed people were laughing at him. Children began to refer to him as 'Crazy Pat'. Sherrill's response when angered was to fix people with an intense stare. An associate once described Sherrill as 'the loneliest man I've ever known'.

Eighteen months before the killings, Sherrill was taken on as a part-time postman in nearby Edmond. Before long he was embroiled in trouble and was suspended for seven days after leaving mail unattended. Five months later he was given a 14-day suspension for cruelty to an animal. A customer's dog had growled at Sherrill from behind a fence and the next day Sherrill sprayed the dog with a repellent chemical, then abused the animal's owner. True to his paranoid beliefs, Sherrill determined his suspensions were the management's way of 'getting' at him.

On 19 August 1986 he again got into trouble and was reprimanded by two supervisors. Afterwards he told co-workers, 'They will be sorry.' At 7 am the following day Patrick Sherrill, wearing his postal uniform and carrying two .45 calibre semi-automatic pistols, walked into the mail sorting room and began shooting at the 50 people already at work. Without speaking he walked around methodically shooting people. One woman cried out, 'No Pat, no,' but he ignored her pleas and shot her. Five other women who were huddled together were coldly and calculatingly shot. Sherrill was seen to calmly reload his guns several times and the only time he spoke was to yell at those who begged him to stop.

Police who arrived at the post office could see Sherrill through a window, pacing back and forth. Moments later he shot himself and died. Technical Investigator Rockie Yardley of the Edmond Police Department searched Sherrill's house after the tragedy and reported:

> His residence was extremely dirty and cluttered. He had fixed breakfast that morning, leaving the skillet on the stove with portions of his meal on the plate next to a sink full of dirty dishes.

The thing that struck Officer Yardley as strange - and it was one of the traits common to pseudo-commandos - was that there was something orderly amidst the chaos.

> In a spare bedroom, which was extremely cluttered, he had a shelf running around all four walls. The shelf contained every *Playboy* magazine published. They were all in date order and in a neat row. This seemed very unusual in a house so trashed and dirty.

Sherrill displayed many of the traits outlined in Chapter 10: paranoia, loneliness, grudges, difficulty with employment, relationships, cruelty to animals and odd behaviour. Patrick Sherrill compares closely to the nine main subjects in *Killing for Pleasure*.

MARC LÉPINE
Montreal, Canada, 6 December 1989
Victims: 14 dead, 13 injured

When 25-year-old Marc Lépine walked into Montreal's L'Ecole Polytechnic on 6 December 1989 he plunged Quebec into three days of mourning. Lépine, like George Hennard and Frank Vitkovic, had an intense hatred of women, whom he determined were the cause of his own failings.

Marc Lépine was born Gamil Gharbi on 26 October 1964. He was of Algerian descent and had a difficult early life. The very quiet youth and his older sister grew up in a seriously dysfunctional environment where their businessman father meted out physical punishment to his son and wife. To protect the boy from the unstable and unsafe environment he was removed from the family and placed in several foster homes. When he was seven, Lépine's parents divorced and he returned to his mother, but she was often away studying in pursuit of a career. In the following years he attempted to rid himself of his father's influence and when he was 14 changed his name from Gharbi to his mother's French name, Lépine.

From an early age, Marc Lépine was emotionally insecure, isolated, and lacked social abilities - all problems that would affect him throughout the rest of his life. Despite these disadvantages he was an above-average student and possessed an intellectual potential that should have seen him move along a professional career path. Lépine had only one true friend, but when he and his mother moved to another city when he was 17, he lost contact with his friend and became truly isolated.

Following high school Lépine did a three-year course in pure sciences, a one-year course in electronics, and studied chemistry and computing, developing an avid interest in computers. It was in Lépine's nature to be convinced he would fail in everything and he would then provoke the failure. He once enrolled for a computing and science course but dropped out even though he was progressing well. He intended studying at L'Ecole Polytechnic but never enrolled, perhaps because of his preconceived ideas of failure. In many ways the intelligent Lépine followed a similar path of frustration and failure to that of Charles Whitman.

Rejections were also to feature heavily in Lépine's life. While working in the laboratory of a hospital in Laval he developed an interest in a young woman. The attraction wasn't mutual and she declined his advances. Then, because patients were supposedly horrified at Lépine's acne, he was given a job out-of-sight in the kitchen of the hospital's cafeteria. To compound matters, Lépine was forced to resign following incidents of strange and bizarre behaviour. He couldn't find another job and had difficulty coming to terms with the situation.

One of Lépine's ambitions was to join the Canadian armed forces but again was faced with rejections. His application for the cadet forces was turned down on the grounds that he was asocial. Lépine's inability to make social contact had caught up with him.

As an adult, Lépine lived in a Montreal apartment block with a young man who was also painfully shy. They shared a five-room apartment in a poorer part of town where rents were more affordable. Neighbours saw little of Lépine and felt he was not only introverted and kept to himself, but that he went out of his way to avoid contact. There were exceptions, particularly where women were concerned. His attempts to attract women were often unsuccessful. He could be kind and considerate towards them, but once his advances were rejected he became frustrated and the façade of niceness fell away.

A young woman living close by attracted Lépine's attention. Immediately after she shifted in to her apartment Lépine turned up with curtains for her and although she thought the gesture bizarre, she accepted the gift anyway. She saw him occasionally when he waved to her from his window but it became obvious Lépine was watching her. When she began painting her apartment he suddenly turned up with a ladder for her to use. Two things put her off having anything to do with him. One was a skull, clearly visible through the window, sitting on a bookcase. The other thing was Lépine's laugh - an intriguing, sick kind of maniacal noise. Every night she and other neighbours would hear Lépine's chilling laughter.

Lépine was a disturbed man, but had never sought or been referred for psychological examination. He was unemployed and had been for several months. His young flatmate spent most of his time studying but Lépine focussed on two activities. One was computing and the other interest, which became an obsession, was a fascination with war. He spent a lot of time watching war films - to such an extent that the noise annoyed neighbours as he played the videos late into the night.

Lépine was a familiar sight around gun shops, regularly calling in to look at weapons. A few days before the polytechnic massacre the bearded Lépine purchased a .223 Sturm Ruger mini 14 semi-automatic rifle he said he needed for sporting purposes. On 5 December he was seen, still sporting his beard, but when he went to L'Ecole Polytechnic the next day he was clean-shaven and wearing jeans, a shirt, cap and work boots. At just on 5 pm Marc Lépine, fuelled by paranoia and a deep hatred of women, entered the polytechnic where students were giving oral presentations to classmates. His first victim, a university employee in the corridor, was shot before Lépine calmly walked into a classroom of 60 students. In perfect French, he quietly told the males to move to one side of the room and the females to the other. At first students thought he was joking, but quickly did as they were told when he fired a shot into the ceiling.

'Do you know why I'm here?' Lépine asked his hushed audience. 'I'm here to fight feminism.'

Lépine remained remarkably calm and witnesses later commented on his cool eyes. As the men escaped, Lépine killed six young women lined up against a wall. He then went to the cafeteria and amongst the hail of 25 bullets he fired another three young women died. Lépine moved to the third floor where 26 students were listening to class presentations. Running across the top of the desks Lépine fired down at students who were vainly trying to hide. One of his last victims was 23-year-old Maryse Leclair who was just completing her class presentation when Lépine burst in. He shot Maryse in the back, then turned his attention to the others. After killing another three young women he returned to Maryse who was calling out for help. Lépine took a hunting knife and ended her life by stabbing her three times.

Soon after killing Maryse, Lépine was heard to exclaim, 'Oh shit!' then turned the gun on himself, ending his reign of terror. Although the bullet he used to end his life was the last one in the chamber he did have another loaded magazine in his pocket.

In rare cases, mass murderers have stopped their rampage before they were forced to. Perhaps in these cases the killer suddenly comes to the realisation of the enormity of what he has done and wishes to end the rampage. Even though Lépine ended his life when he did, he had caused tremendous harm to the people of Montreal and Quebec.

In Lépine's shirt pocket police found a three-page suicide note that gave some clues to his motives for killing 14 innocent young women. Lépine claimed the reasons for his actions were not economically-based but political. Feminists, he claimed, had ruined his life and the last seven years had brought him no joy. Lépine mentioned his futile attempts to get into the army resulting from his assessment as asocial. He went on to say he was an intelligent, rational person who had been forced into taking extreme actions. He asked how a clearly disturbed man such as himself was able to obtain a lethal weapon with such ease and that as he began terrorising people, how could he go for so long without being stopped? With the letter was a list of 15 prominent women from the police, union movement, communications area and political life who had, as Lépine determined, invaded a man's world. The women were deemed the enemy by Lépine and only survived, he said, because 'I started too late'. Lépine knew of other mass killings and in his letter mentioned Denis Lortie, the murderer who walked into the Canadian Provincial Legislature five years earlier and killed three men.

Opinions were divided on Lépine's mental state. The De Coster Report, put together to try and explain why this terrible event happened, sought opinions from several psychiatrists. Dr Garneau believed Lépine suffered from a severe personality disorder characterised by schizoid and paranoid traits. As a result of social incompetence he had come to the delirious conviction that feminism was the source of all his difficulties. Dr Montgrain, on the other hand, felt Lépine was not psychotic but did have a personality disorder that could be described as schizotypal.

The composition of Lépine's letter, bearing in mind what he did, is interesting. Twice he apologised, once for spelling mistakes and again for the brevity of his letter. A linguistic specialist said the letter's syntax was almost perfect and the vocabulary was of a high register. But the further one delves into the letter, the more Lépine seems to alternate between the real and the imaginary world. He used numerous Latin terms and mentioned Caesar's Roman Legionnaires, something Julian Knight identified with.

Like many pseudo-commandos, Lépine was a significant loner with very few friends and was regarded as 'odd' and 'strange'. More importantly, he held paranoid beliefs and his views on women developed into extreme grudges. Not only did Lépine fail to form relationships with women, he could not even be friends with them. To Lépine, women and feminists were the same thing, and in his suicide letter talked of a 'declaration of war' against feminists. Lépine's letter and the Vitkovic diaries held strikingly similar views on the changing role of women in society.

To protect himself from the wounds of his childhood Lépine erected an impenetrable wall around himself that made him even more introverted and socially isolated. Because he had more success with machines than people, Lépine tried to supplant his need for relationships with computers and formed an emotional attachment to them. However such 'instruments', as Lépine found out, do not cater to the human need for affection.

Lépine's other obsession, with war movies and anything associated with war, in many ways modelled the thoughts of Julian Knight and James Huberty. Essentially, Marc Lépine was as 'typical' of the pseudo-commando profile as any other man mentioned in *Killing for Pleasure*.

MATTIAS FLINK
Falun, Sweden, 11 June 1994
Victims: 7 dead, 1 injured

Mattias Flink is one of the few mass murderers to survive his rampage. However his capture and subsequent interviews have failed to reveal the reasons for his violent outburst. He claimed to remember very little of what took place.

Born on 8 March 1970, Mattias Flink grew up as an only child in a stable household. He was a calm, relaxed youth who never caused his parents any problems. His early years at school were unremarkable and from the age of seven to ten Flink was a Boy Scout. Just before he turned ten his parents decided to separate and he was given the choice of living in the family home with his father or moving out with his mother. The boy chose to stay with his father and their relationship was a good one. They rarely disagreed and got on well together. Flink's mother lived only a few hundred metres away and he saw her regularly. She remarried and had three children with whom Mattias got on well.

Flink's childhood and adolescent years were harmonious. He was an average student interested mainly in electrical and mechanical courses. If anything, he under-achieved academically, but decided at the midpoint of his studies that a military career was his favoured option. Army life corresponded with his personality type and would satisfy his interest in weapons. He had grown up around guns and seemed quite relaxed about them. His father, and his father before him, had been gunsmiths, so the youth's interest in guns was not unexpected.

Flink had taught himself to shoot with an air rifle and developed a comprehensive knowledge of weaponry. He was not fixated with guns but did enjoy shooting at the rifle range. In the army he rose to the rank of second lieutenant in the same regiment where his father worked as a weapons' engineer. Flink was a smart, well-educated and organised young man, and was regarded as a good soldier. He believed he was a rational man whose emotions were not easily stirred. When 22 he moved out of his father's house and took up residence in an apartment on his own.

Mattias Flink had never been in trouble with the law and little is known as to what led to his murderous attack. But in the weeks leading up to the rampage his behaviour deteriorated markedly. The first indications of trouble came on 29 April 1994, when Flink spoke to his father about feeling psychologically unwell. He said he had behaved like an idiot towards his girlfriend Eva and that he regretted his actions. The previous day, after a drinking session with co-workers, he had told Eva there was something important he had to tell her. To gain her attention Flink said he had placed his hands on her shoulders and forced her to sit down. However Eva's recollection was different. She said Flink put his hands around her throat and began to argue.

Flink's behaviour further deteriorated in mid-May when he was involved in a serious fight with two lieutenants from his regiment. Again, the incident followed a drinking session. Up until the period when he became troublesome, Flink had been a moderate drinker, always knowing his limits. Once or twice a week he would have a couple of strong beers and rarely drank spirits, but during 1994 his alcohol intake increased. For no apparent reason Flink attacked the two colleagues - who were considered his friends - and a serious fight developed. The fight and the assault on Eva worried Flink's father, who had never previously noticed such behaviour in his son. A doctor who was a long-time friend of the Flink family was consulted, and after deliberation she considered that Mattias Flink needed help. Eva also felt he needed psychiatric help.

The week before the tragedy Flink borrowed his father's car so he could go into the woods alone for a few days. Flink's mother had taught her son to appreciate the outdoors from an early age, and he enjoyed nature and fishing and liked the solitude of camping alone in the wilderness. On returning the car he told his father he had broken off the relationship with Eva and that he was feeling better for it. He claimed that prior to meeting Eva he had never felt the violent urges he now had. He also believed Eva did not have the same feelings for him as he did for her, and this produced feelings of jealousy which consumed a lot of his thoughts. He became unsettled and found it difficult to concentrate.

The reality was that Flink had been largely unsuccessful in relationships with young women. As well as fishing, one of Flink's passions was target shooting, but the girls he tried to attract did not share his passion and generally did not enjoy going to a rifle range. Flink was a jealous and possessive young man in relationships with girls and he was clearly jealous regarding Eva.

On 11 June 1994 Flink was not on duty and the day began quite normally. Although he had broken up with Eva, he bought her flowers and wanted to wish her luck for the nurses' examinations she was taking that day. He then attended a church service dressed in his military uniform and carrying a Glock semi-automatic pistol in a shoulder holster under his jacket. Nothing untoward happened, and he said he felt good mentally.

In the afternoon he visited friends in Falun before returning home where he changed into jeans and a jacket. However, instead of returning the Glock pistol to the armoury, he hid it in a clothes cupboard in his apartment. He loaded three magazines with 15 rounds in each and inserted one into the Glock.

During the evening, Flink had a meal and a few beers then went to a couple of clubs where he drank gin and cokes. He was in a cheerful mood until he met Eva in a restaurant, and a row erupted. Flink could not remember what the conflict was about, but thought it might have been because Eva ignored him. The argument was sufficient for a bouncer to throw Flink out of the eatery, but during the melee Flink lost his wallet, so returned to find it. As he re-entered the restaurant Flink met a commander from his regiment and spoke to him. Such was the dramatic change in Flink's appearance the commander did not at first recognise him. After speaking briefly Flink went to approach Eva but saw her sitting on a man's knee. Flink had suspected Eva often flirted with other men and this incident confirmed his belief. Angry and jealous he turned and left the restaurant.

Mattias Flink went home to his apartment and put on his military uniform. Later he would tell police he began looking for something in the apartment but could not remember what it was. It may well have been the loaded Glock but he left the apartment without it. He then went to his regimental headquarters and took an AKS automatic rifle and ammunition. He must have known that he would not be returning as he threw his keys away before jogging towards the Falun town centre.

Flink came across a group of six women from the Swedish Women's Voluntary Defence Service who were in Falun for training and were returning to their regiment. Without warning, Flink opened fire on the women, killing five instantly and severely wounding the sixth. He carried on into the town, discarding an empty magazine as he ran. With a new magazine in place he approached the Falun post office and began shooting at an approaching car. The car came to an abrupt halt and Flink continued firing, killing the sole occupant. His seventh and final victim was a male cyclist.

Flink left the scene and climbed into the cab of a crane on a nearby building site. He began to think over what he had done and decided to wait for the police to arrive, but soon after climbed down and decided to go home. He now felt as if nothing had happened and was calmly making his way towards his apartment when he was challenged by police and quickly captured.

Evidence suggests that Flink's rampage was not planned, certainly not to the stage of most mass murderers in *Killing for Pleasure*. However, earlier in the day, he had loaded several magazines for his Glock. While he didn't use that weapon it is quite conceivable he had already considered, even if only subconsciously, that murder of some sort was inevitable.

A possible reason for Flink's rampage was submitted in his defence. The suggestion was that he had an imbalance of serotonin. Serotonin is a neurotransmitter, a chemical that is essential for sending messages between brain cells. It was claimed this imbalance caused Flink to lose control when drinking. Serotonin has been shown to be a factor in depression, and in a major study it was discovered that serotonin levels were abnormal in males with violent dispositions. However, the links between serotonin levels and violence when drinking alcohol are more tenuous. In any event, Flink's history prior to 1994 had been one of a non-violent personality.

In many ways Flink exemplified the pseudo-commando profile. He came from a partly dysfunctional background because his parents divorced, even though the separation was not dramatic. He had some difficulty maintaining relationships with women, and while he may not have been paranoid about them, he was certainly possessive and jealous. He had a deep interest in weapons and though it is unknown whether he fantasised about warfare or killing, the fact that he was a regular soldier could lead to such thoughts. Many pseudo-commandos dress in military-style clothes when they commit their crimes and Flink purposely put on his uniform before going out on his murderous attack.

Mattias Flink differs from the other killers in *Killing for Pleasure* in that he was not significantly lonely. He did have friends and workmates with whom he got on well, and though he lived by himself, he was not necessarily a lonely or withdrawn person. Of all the pseudo-commandos profiled in *Killing for Pleasure*, Mattias Flink would have been the most difficult to recognise.

MARK ORRIN BARTON

Atlanta, Georgia, 29 July 1999
Victims: 12 dead, 13 injured

Mark O Barton was born in Sumter, South Carolina in 1955. Though he was destined to lead a life marred by some incredible controversy, his early life was unremarkable. Barton's father was employed by the United States Air Force and was stationed for a period in Germany until the family returned to the States when Mark was 11. Mr Barton was reportedly a stern man and strict disciplinarian, and father and son did not get on well. Barton's adolescent years were punctuated with minor scrapes with the law, and when he was 14 was caught breaking into a drug store.

His high school years were lonely times and he tended to keep to himself, unable to fit in with other students. He neither socialised nor had girlfriends. Where Barton showed no interest in sport he did excel at two academic subjects: science and mathematics. After leaving school Barton attended the University of South Carolina, graduating with a degree in chemistry. With an interest and ability in chemistry it was not surprising Barton would choose a career in that field and tried a range of jobs in the chemistry line.

One job in Texarkana, Arkansas, had promising prospects and he began to climb the ladder of success - but near the top rung he had a serious fall. Barton's secretary said he was paranoid about co-workers, so much so that he often retreated to his office believing 'people were out to get him' and even resorted to taping other employees' telephone conversations. Those who got on the wrong side of Mark Barton found they stayed there and he could be very vindictive. In one case, a salesman who fell out of favour with Barton found that Barton had responded by altering the man's sale orders in the company computer. This delayed deliveries to clients.

In September 1990 it was decided Barton's performance in administration did not match his technical skills and he was dismissed. The visibly angry Barton left the building, but returned at night a week later and broke in. After downloading financial data and formulas for his own use he erased the firm's computer hard drives. Although Barton was caught, the firm decided not to prosecute and Barton and his family left for Georgia.

Mark Barton was neither the ideal husband nor father. Outwardly he seemed reasonable, and was actively involved in his son's scout group. On the other hand, Barton killed his small daughter's kitten then pretended to show fatherly concern as he helped her search for it. Barton often ridiculed his wife in front of work colleagues referring to her as 'stupid'. The power-orientated and suspicious Barton had a controlling influence over his wife. Whenever she left the house she had to tell him where she was going and when she would return. Because of his influence the Bartons did not socialise and kept very much to themselves.

Things began to go terribly wrong for Barton in 1993. His wife and mother-in-law were brutally murdered and Mark Barton became the prime suspect. The campervan the women's bodies were found in showed no evidence of forced entry and robbery was not the motive. Just prior to the deaths, Barton had insured his wife for $600,000, $150,000 of which would be divided between his children with Barton pocketing the balance. With insufficient evidence to proceed, police were unable to lay charges. Soon after the death of Barton's wife, a woman he had been having an affair with divorced her husband and moved in with Barton. The couple later married, and in 1999 she was to die at Barton's hands.

The year after his wife's murder, police investigated Barton again following allegations he was sexually molesting his three-year-old daughter. Again there was insufficient evidence to prosecute and he went free. A clinical psychologist who examined Barton said of him: 'He appears to have been irritated by living in a household with a woman he considered brighter than he was and around whom he felt he had to be perfect.' The psychologist also formed an opinion that Barton was capable of homicidal thoughts and actions.

The neighbours in the middle class Atlanta suburb where Barton lived barely got to know him. He kept very much to himself, and when he did speak, conversations were brief and to the point. Some neighbours were unsure of what to make of Barton and one remarked, 'There is something wrong with this man.'

Domestic problems continued when Barton's second wife, Leigh, left him in October 1998 and moved into an apartment. The separation affected him deeply and the following July, in the same month the Atlanta massacre would take place, Barton moved back in with her. If the reunion was to be a happy one it wasn't going to last long.

Barton ran a chemical consultancy business from his home, as well as investing heavily on the hectic day-to-day stock exchange. His dealings had substantial swings of losses and gains, and in the days leading up to the massacre he made significant losses. This, coupled with his separation of nine months, could have been the catalyst for his atrocities. On Tuesday, 27 July 1999, Barton took his son to a scout meeting and showed no outward signs of what was to come, but that night he bludgeoned Leigh to death and hid her body in a closet. The following day he killed his children, put them into their beds and placed a computer game on 12-year-old Matthew's body and a teddy bear on 8-year-old Mychelle's. On all three bodies Barton left notes.

At 6.38 am on Thursday, 29 July 1999 Barton typed out a letter explaining his terrible deeds. The letter confessed to the murders of Leigh and the children, denied implication in his first wife's murder, and concluded by indicating a plan to kill more. The letter read:

Leigh Ann is in the master bedroom closet under a blanket. I killed her on Tuesday night. I killed Matthew and Mychelle Wednesday night. There may be similarities between these deaths and the death of my first wife, Debra Spivey. However I deny killing her and her mother. There is no reason for me to lie now. It just seemed like a quiet way to kill and a relatively painless way to die. All of them were dead in less than five minutes. I hit them with a hammer in their sleep and then put them face down in the bathtub to make sure they did not wake up in pain, to make sure they were dead.

I'm so sorry. I wish I didn't. Words cannot tell the agony. Why did I? I have been dying since October. Wake up at night so afraid, so terrified, that I couldn't be that afraid while awake. It has taken its toll. I have come to hate this life and this system of things. I have come to have no hope. I killed the children to exchange them for five minutes of pain or a lifetime of pain. I forced myself to do it to keep them from suffering so much later. No mother, no father, no relatives. The fears of the father are transferred to the son. It was from my father to me and me to my son. He already had it. And now to be left alone. I had to take him with me. I killed Leigh Ann because she was one of the main reasons for my demise. I know that Jehovah will take care of all of them in the next life. I'm sure the details don't matter. There is no excuse, no good reason I am sure no one will understand. If they could I wouldn't want them to. I just write these things to say why. Please know that I love Leigh Ann, Matthew and Mychelle, with all my heart. If Jehovah's willing I would like to see them all again in the resurrection to have a second chance. *I don't plan to live very much longer, just long enough to kill as many of the people that greedily sought my destruction.* [Emphasis added]

On the bodies he left notes that read:

I give you my wife Leigh Ann Vanderver Barton, my honey, my precious love. Please take care of her. I will love her forever.

I give you Matthew David Barton, my son, my buddy, my life. Please take care of him.

I give you Mychelle Elizabeth Barton, my daughter, my sweetheart, my life. Please take care of her.

After finishing the letters Barton had at least seven hours to change his mind about killing those who 'sought his destruction'. At just after 2 pm a calm Mark Barton walked into the office of a day trading stockbroker in downtown Atlanta. 'It's a bad day for trading and it's going to get worse,' he said.

Barton went into the branch manager's office and shut the door. He chatted to the manager and his secretary, then without warning drew a 9 mm Glock semi-automatic pistol and a .45 calibre Colt semi-automatic pistol and started firing both simultaneously. He began to walk through the building, killing four people and injuring several others. He left the building and walked across the road to a second brokerage firm where he killed another five people. Barton ran from the building and drove away in his van. When cornered by police at a service station 30 kilometres from the scene of the massacre, he pulled out the pistols and fired both into his head.

Police found a total of four handguns and 200 rounds of ammunition in Barton's van, and another pistol at his home. The weapons, the letter and the fact he waited at least seven hours after deciding to commit his massacre suggest a level of forethought and planning. Clearly, Barton had many of the traits that have characterised the pseudo-commandos of the previous three decades - paranoia, isolation, the holding of grudges, cruelty to animals and a general strangeness. Mark Barton was just one of many mass killers to strike in 1999 and is a classic example illustrating that the pseudo-commando phenomenon has not slowed.

ERIC HARRIS AND DYLAN KLEBOLD
Littleton, Colorado - 20 April 1999
Victims: 13 dead, 23 injured

Few people who watched the television coverage of the Columbine High School massacre could forget the images - young people, hands on their heads, streaming from school buildings as armed police covered them - or the seriously-wounded student, covered in blood, falling from a broken window into the arms of waiting police. Television crews flashed the dramatic scenes to a worldwide audience, while two young men went about their deadly business inside. The day, 20 April, was significant, as it was specially chosen by the killers. Firstly, it marked the anniversary of the birth of Adolf Hitler, possibly the twentieth century's darkest figure. The young killers were admirers of Hitler and never tried to hide their interest in the Nazi philosophy. 20 April was also 'senior skip day' where senior high school students across the United States skip class to smoke marijuana.

Somewhere there is a poignancy about where society is heading.

On one hand, young men from stable home environments choose a dictator's birthday to exact terrible vengeance on perceived wrongdoers. On the other, a day is set aside by young people specifically to smoke marijuana to give society the message that 'we can do what we choose'. As the century came to a close, a new twist developed: pseudo-commandos working in pairs with their favourite targets becoming schools. The Columbine High tragedy was the fifth shooting in a United States school over a period of two years and was quickly followed by a further rash of incidents in the United States and Canada. As late as 29 October 1999, an attempted mass killing at a school in Cleveland, Ohio was thwarted. One might ask, 'When will the madness end?'

Like Charles Whitman 33 years earlier Eric Harris was the consummate actor. Although he planned the disastrous rampage at Columbine High School, he never gave anything away or deviated from his character. When he wanted to, Harris could be a comic, a serious student or an inspired writer. He had a contagious laugh and looked towards the future. Although he was an outsider he had a side to his character some found nice, so much so they could not believe he could be responsible for such terrible mayhem.

Eric David Harris was born in Wichita, Kansas on 9 April 1981. The son of an ex-air force pilot, he grew up in a stable home environment with an older brother and parents who were financially well-off. Wayne and Kathy Harris, with their two sons Kevin and Eric, moved around the country depending on where Wayne Harris worked. Eric, the youngest Harris, was remembered as a normal kid, though rather timid and shy. Playing baseball he seemed happier sitting alone in the dugout, and when he did come up to bat, he often let the ball fly past without attempting to strike it. His hobby was playing computer games and he would initiate discussion about that interest, but at other times school friends would have to approach him if they wanted to talk.

In 1993 the Harris family moved to Littleton, Colorado, but by then Eric had attended five different schools. The constant moving left the youngest Harris unsettled. He felt he was always going back to the bottom rung of the ladder to start climbing again. During this time he built up a lot of resentment, especially in the way he perceived others. He felt he was the subject of ridicule as other kids poked fun at his appearance. Despite the mounting rage Eric Harris was, in other respects, just a normal kid growing up in a neighbourhood. In his teens he got his driver's licence and was often seen driving a Honda car around. Unlike a lot of young men, Harris drove sensibly and slowly. He formed a friendship with Brooks Brown, a fellow student, and the two shared a passionate interest in computer games. However, a split in the friendship turned nasty and revealed a more sinister side to Harris. After breaking his friend's windscreen, Harris posted a message on the Internet suggesting that if anyone wanted to commit a murder Brooks Brown would be a suitable target. Although the matter was referred to police, no action was taken as a formal complaint was not made.

In 1996 signs of a strangeness about Harris began to creep in. The tongue-tied youth had taken a girl to a school dance and a few days later she broke up with him. Harris responded by faking suicide. She found him lying with his head against a rock with fake blood spread around. Whatever Harris's motives, the prank was quite cruel.

As Harris matured he became more confident and outspoken, though he didn't fit in at Columbine High. In the tradition of the movies *Grease* and *Revenge of the Nerds* the 'jocks' were the ones to look up to and at Columbine it was no different. The tougher group teased and taunted him, calling him 'fag' and 'pussy'. Harris, basically a lonely youth, took a job at a pizza parlour in 1997 and around the same time another shy boy also began working there. His name was Dylan Klebold and from that point Harris and Klebold were inseparable.

Where Harris was the leader, Klebold was the follower. Some said Klebold had low self-esteem and followed Harris around as his shadow. Born in Lakewood on 9 September 1981 Dylan Bennett Klebold grew up as a normal boy. His parents, Tom and Susan, supported him and his older brother. They were essentially an ordinary family with happy, well-behaved children. Dylan enjoyed being a boy scout and played baseball.

In 1985 the Klebods moved to Littleton and in 1990 bought a very comfortable home from which they ran a real estate management business. For the most part, the early years were unremarkable for the ordinary but rather shy boy. He wasn't an athlete but enjoyed playing in the Columbine Fantasy Baseball League. He was meticulous at the game and was a bright student.

Around the time Klebold and Harris got together their appearance and tastes began to change. Neither had any desire to identify with the sporting elite, the 'jocks'. Instead they joined a group called the 'Trench Coat Mafia' and dressed in black clothes with a paramilitary style - wearing their trademark black trench coats regardless of the weather. Both boys began to identify with the heavier music of the German rock band style and began to use Nazi symbols and expressions to give themselves an identity and shock other students.

As members of an outsider group with a radical appearance and views the duo soon became outcasts and isolated. They were targets for derision and taunts, yet stuck to their belief that it was their right to be different. Harris began to believe that no one liked him and turned more and more to his only true friend, Dylan Klebold. Like Harris, Klebold had also built up a lot of hate and rage but only investigations following the Columbine High tragedy would indicate how intense that hatred was.

As they became entrenched in their new identities, the boys' thoughts turned more towards weaponry and they often discussed guns. Both began to let their Trench Coat Mafia mentality intrude into their school work. They began to write disturbingly violent essays and made videos depicting themselves attacking a house with toy guns, searching rooms and firing at beds. In another video they were filmed in the mountains firing real guns.

At school, when students were asked to write about an inanimate object, Harris wrote that he was a shotgun that fell in love with a shotgun shell. Rather than producing light or happy themes, the duo tended to concentrate on the darker side of life and would shrug off any questioning about their violent essays by saying, 'it's just a story'. However, their habit of spending large amounts of time in the computer lab and making videos with freaky music had an effect on other students. They began to give off 'scary vibes' that caused some students to walk in the other direction when approached. This tended to alienate the boys further and they became more entrenched in their new personas.

In early 1998 Klebold and Harris were arrested for breaking into a van and stealing electronic equipment. Their punishment was to attend a year-long court-ordered diversionary programme and complete an anger management course. They completed their punishment and the course analysis showed Harris was an intelligent, focused achiever who had the potential to be successful in life. Klebold, too, was seen as having good prospects but lacked motivation. A condition of their punishment was the requirement to sign a contract stipulating they would not acquire firearms, but obviously both boys breached that agreement.

As they became angrier at those who put them down, they began to take part in what they called 'pranks' or 'missions'. They considered themselves a gang with many enemies at school and their revenge would be sought through their 'missions'. They began by gluing up door locks or setting off small explosions to get back at the 'enemy', but their level of retribution escalated to dangerous proportions. Harris, who was engrossed with computers, began to use the Internet as a vehicle for his anger. On a website he wrote:

I will rig up explosives all over town and detonate each one after I mow down a whole fucking area full of you snotty rich, motherfucking high strung Godlike worthless pieces of shit whores. I don't care if I live or die in the shootout. All I want to do is kill and injure as many of you pricks as I can.

When authorities found out about the Harris 'pranks' he was warned to watch his behaviour.

In early 1999 Harris and Brooks Brown ended their feud and again became friends. Harris tried to soften his hard line in the Trench Coat Mafia but the 'jock' mentality never let up and he was still subjected to derision and taunts. As he became more depressed, he was prescribed Luvox, a drug used to treat anxiety conditions including obsessive compulsive disorder, panic disorders, social phobias and depression.

Although Klebold and Harris dressed in paramilitary clothing and frequently spoke about weapons, Dylan Klebold was never interested in a military career. Harris, however, was intent on joining the Marines. In his screening interview he did not mention he was taking Luvox and, when this was revealed during the second week of April 1999, his application to join the Marines was turned down.

Dylan Klebold and Eric Harris planned their attack on Columbine High for a year. They knew the day and the hour their attack would take place, and over preceding months the boys monitored students in the school cafeteria to decide when would be the busiest time there. They mapped the school out, noting lighting and possible hiding places and worked out a series of hand signals they would use during their 'mission'. For weeks they gathered together material to make their improvised explosive devices and prepared their weapons. Despite knowing they were sure to die, the boys continued their lives as normal. Both still talked of their futures in the long-term. Klebold even visited the University of Tucson, Arizona to look around his chosen place of continuing education.

In the final lead up to 20 April the boys made a number of videos in an endeavour to explain what they had been planning for the past 12 months. They spoke of their perceived enemies, those who had abused them, and their so-called friends who didn't do enough to defend them. 'I hope we kill 250 of you,' Klebold coldly said as Harris held the video camera.

The two talked of the impending attack and how unbelievably tense it would be. There was no doubt that the boys were resolved on their terrible course of action. Their final video, made on the morning of 20 April, was essentially a suicide note, a time to say goodbye and to put their affairs in order.

'It's half-an-hour to judgement day,' Klebold said as Harris filmed him. They expressed remorse, not for the intended victims but for both sets of parents. 'There was nothing you guys could have done to prevent this,' Eric Harris said.

Klebold's message to his mother and father was to tell them they had been great parents and he apologised for having built up so much rage. The two boys knew their actions were sure to ruin their parents' lives and while they expressed regret, they were adamant the attack on Columbine High would go ahead. Harris, the sometime serious scholar and admirer of William Shakespeare, quoted from *The Tempest*: 'Good wombs hath borne bad sons,' he said.

The boys then bequeathed some of their possessions to friends and the final words came from Harris. 'That's it,' he quickly said. 'Sorry. Goodbye!' They left the video in Harris' bedroom, knowing full well it would be found and viewed after they were dead.

On the day of the massacre the boys met early for their regular practice at a bowling alley and played as normal. If there were any hints as to what might follow, they were carefully hidden. For a couple of days Harris's behaviour had shown flashes of anger and Klebold's father detected a slight tension in his son - but in teenagers such anxiety is quite normal. Only in retrospect did Mrs Klebold realise her son's final goodbye had a slight edge to it. During the morning the boys prepared their weapons, packed them into duffel bags and drove to the school. Somehow the boys had copied a set of the school's master keys, and it was suspected they had been able to hide a large propane gas tank bomb in the cafeteria earlier in the day.

All along the intention had been to cause widespread panic, but the attack did not go to plan. Harris and Klebold were to have taken up an ambush position outside the school buildings. As students ran from the bomb-wracked buildings they would open fire with their semi-automatic rifles and shotgun. While some bombs exploded, the majority failed to ignite, and the gunmen were forced to enter the buildings in their search for victims.

Columbine High School caters for the needs of almost 2,000 students from an affluent part of Colorado, and when Dylan Klebold and Eric Harris attacked, they created intense panic and fear amongst the unsuspecting school population. The boys walked into the school where they had been taunted for so long. They believed they had the right to be different and could be 'strange' if they wished. Why should they have to conform? They had been put down too long and believed those who did it to them had to be punished.

The duo, dressed in their usual black clothing, fingerless gloves, and combat boots, arrived just before 11 am. The normally clean-shaven Harris was sporting stubble and his brown hair was now black. One of the first victims could have been Brooks Brown but, in a final gesture of conciliation, Harris told his one-time friend to get out. 'I like you, go home,' Harris said.

While Brown was granted mercy, Harris and Klebold showed little to other students. 'Jocks' were the primary target, but others also died. The gunmen taunted their victims. 'This is for all the people who made fun of us all year,' they called out.

The execution style of killing categorised by mass murderers was emphasised when Harris killed 17-year-old Cassie Bernall. Reports by witnesses said the giggling Harris grabbed the girl by her hair while holding a pistol to her neck. 'I must be God because I'm in total control,' Harris said. 'Tell me I'm your God.'

When Cassie Bernall refused to answer Harris shot her. To another victim one of the gunmen said 'peek-a-boo' before shooting her in the neck. The duo was heard to laugh as they taunted their victims - not normal laughter but a maniacal cackle.

'All jocks stand up, we're going to kill you,' they called out as they searched for their primary targets.

With an illegally cut-down shotgun, a 9 mm semi-automatic pistol and a 9 mm military style semi-automatic rifle, the boys had tremendous fire power. Police later found eight empty magazine clips, each capable of holding over ten rounds, along with dozens of empty shotgun cartridges. Added to the arsenal were over 30 small bombs, mostly devised from CO_2 canisters fashioned into explosive devices packed with nails, ball bearings and other pieces of metal. Exploding bombs caused small fires and smoke set off alarms, adding to the confusion and panic for students taking refuge behind locked doors.

Within minutes of the rampage starting, around 11.25 am, Sheriff's deputies were on the scene and began exchanging fire with the killers. Had police not arrived so soon it is likely the death toll would have been much higher. Klebold and Harris were forced to remain in one part of the building, though they did fire from windows into the grounds and at paramedics responding to the emergency. They were able to walk into the cafeteria where they began firing indiscriminately, killing a teacher and two students. Security cameras captured the rampage and the boys were filmed entering the cafeteria. At one stage they paused to drink from cups left by students who had fled the scene. After searching corridors and classrooms, the killers made their way to the library where ten students, unable to escape, died. The duo continued to wander the corridors, banging on locked doors as they searched for more victims. Large numbers of terrified students sat huddled in classrooms and offices praying that the attackers would not force their way in.

Some of the actions of Klebold and Harris are inexplicable. They swore vengeance on 'jocks', yet killed girls as well as male athletes. They had written in their diaries of killing up to 500 students, yet let some students walk free. An hour after the first killings, the final shots were heard from the library. Harris and Klebold had returned to the scene where they had earlier killed ten victims and had taken their own lives.

The scene greeting police and ambulance staff was distressing and dangerous. No one knew for sure how many gunmen there were. The killers' bodies were booby-trapped and several unexploded bombs - including the propane tank - were scattered around. One bomb with a timing device went off ten hours after the killings ended. To compound matters, hundreds of traumatised students were still in locked rooms doing their best to hide. The events at Columbine were truly horrific and opened a new chapter on the phenomenon of mass murder.

It is quite feasible that Klebold and Harris found sanctuary in a combined fear of persecution and each may have fed the other's fantasies. Although they worked together, they still exhibited many of the classic traits of a pseudo-commando. Both shared a paranoid sense of persecution, were deemed 'weird' because of their choice of dress and behaviour and meticulously planned their crime. Elements of alienation, isolation and loneliness were dominant themes in both lives, and they clearly got a lot of support from each other. Where those with the 'jocks' mentality regarded them as insignificant wimps, the duo became powerful when armed. Finally, there were strong elements of commando fantasies with paramilitary overtones and a fascination with weapons.

THE TWENTY-FIRST CENTURY

While this book recommends a tightening of gun access for some people, it is not 'anti-guns'. If anything, a neutral stance has been taken and the facts speak for themselves. All of the killers mentioned in *Killing for Pleasure* found lawful and easy ways to obtain their weapons. Furthermore, most of the weapons used were semi-automatics and thus manufactured specifically for killing people.

Not only is there a vibrant market for firearms, but there is also a blasé attitude towards the gun culture. This culture is widespread and is as bad, if not worse, in the United States of America as anywhere else. This complacency and the knee-jerk reactions to mass killings were no better emphasised than in November 1999. Half a world away, in Dunedin, New Zealand, the local newspaper carried a report of the Hawaiian massacre. The *Otago Daily Times* carried a report of a 'nice' but lonely man, who, fearing he was about to be laid off from his job at a Xerox office building, took a 9 mm semi-automatic pistol to work and shot dead seven workmates. Directly beneath that story was a news item about a 13-year-old Texan schoolboy who wrote an essay about fellow students being shot with a 9 mm semi-automatic pistol and shotgun. In the wake of the Columbine High School tragedy, the boy's choice of topic was indiscreet. However it was written as a Halloween horror story. Authorities became aware of the story, charged the boy with making terrorist-type threats, and he was placed in a juvenile prison for a week. One might conclude that here was an over-reaction of enormous proportions.

On the same page of the paper were two other stories relating to guns. One was about a man in Littleton, Colorado who left a loaded gun on the ground. His over-exuberant golden retriever stepped on the gun, pressing the trigger, sending a missile through the man's foot. The other story occurred in Oklahoma when a four-year-old found a loaded gun on his parents' bedside table. Thinking it was a toy gun the youngster put it into his backpack and took it to pre-school. He was suspended for a year.

Somewhere here there is a puzzle. A 13-year-old gets jailed for a story and a four-year-old is suspended from pre-school for playing with a gun he shouldn't have had access to. Yet some people who are regarded as 'strange' or 'weird' can get easy access to unlimited guns and ammunition.

Following the Columbine High School tragedy, Jonelle Mitchell, a Washington High School student, asked President Clinton what was to be done about guns and the rash of school shootings. 'I really don't feel safe anymore,' she said. 'When is the government, when are you, going to do something for the other students out there?'

The answer is not simple, but if efforts are not made to take proactive measures then we will end up with a situation we deserve. The first step is to develop more sophisticated screening techniques to identify potential pseudo-commandos. They are one group of people who should be regarded as being 'not fit and proper' people to own firearms. There should also be a change to the gun culture and those who advocate the right to bear arms need to accept there has to be a balance.

Dunblane's Mick North suffered the extreme trauma of losing his precious six-year-old daughter, Sophie, in the despicable rampage of Thomas Hamilton. He doesn't see the owning of a firearm so much as a right but a privilege, and says that if owning a gun were a right, all rights are not equal.

'There is a spectrum with the right to hold a gun at the bottom and the right to be safe, a right to life and a right for my daughter to be able to grow up at the top. I'm afraid many of those who hold guns get their priorities very distorted.'

The President of the United States and his administration, and governments the world over, need to find the answers. It will be difficult, but minimising these terrible tragedies is possible and the solution is in our hands. Leaders now need to accept the challenge and halt this continuing slide into madness. The world will be watching.

EPILOGUE

A PERSONAL STATEMENT

While *Killing for Pleasure* is essentially about the individuals who perpetrated horrible crimes on their communities it is important to acknowledge the devastation caused to their victims.

For many years I was involved with the formation and administration of victim support groups in New Zealand and in 1994 I attended the Eighth International Symposium on Victimology held in Adelaide, Australia. During the Aramoana massacre of November 1990 I was one of the police officers engaged in the operation to bring to an end David Gray's murderous rampage.

When writing *Aramoana - Twenty-two Hours of Terror* I got to know the families of victims and still maintain contact with many of them. This involvement has given me a close insight and empathy for the victims of these tragedies. Throughout the writing of this book I have become even more acutely aware of the pain and suffering caused to thousands of people when these pathetic killers choose to take the lives of innocent people. In no way have I set out to glorify these murderers or their despicable deeds.

Mass murderers of the type written about in *Killing for Pleasure* create a ripple effect that spreads far beyond the immediate families of those killed or injured. All of us are robbed of our ability to feel safe, be it lunch-time in Luby's Cafeteria, in the safe confines of a Scottish primary school at 9 am or in a peaceful seaside settlement on a stunningly pleasant summer's evening. We should be able to go to work or school or walk the streets without the possibility of a

Martin Bryant or Michael Ryan suddenly confronting us. When these people let loose their anger they create confusion and terror in whole communities. Their sudden ferocious attacks tear at the fabric of our societies. The hardest thing to comprehend is the indiscriminate nature of the attacks. Rarely does the murderer know his victims, making even more poignant the question why?

As a retired police officer once involved in the aftermath of a mass murder, I also need to acknowledge the role of the emergency services personnel who are thrust into these terrible tragedies. While researching material for *Killing for Pleasure* I read hundreds of statements from police officers, ambulance paramedics and many others. I have been amazed at the courage, professionalism and dedication of these emergency services personnel as they performed their tasks amid unimaginable carnage. The average person could not comprehend the scene that faces those who are tasked with cleaning up these tragic events. I must confess, although I have seen many graphically disturbing things, little compares to the sight of so many people senselessly killed in this way. The immediate scene of these tragedies is dangerous and deeply disturbing, but also distressing is the work ahead for police, paramedics, pathologists, funeral directors, counsellors and so many others who are society's representatives faced with the task of cleaning up the effects of these senseless rampages.

In acknowledging the role of the emergency services, the following encapsulates for me the essence of being a helper and a victim. While collecting information on Marc Lépine's rampage at the Montreal Polytechnic I made contact with a colleague in Canada. He passed my request for assistance on to a senior police officer of the Montreal Police Department who responded to the scene of Lépine's terrible attack. Pierre Leclair was then the officer in charge of the police public relations section and rushed to the scene to help with the police operation and to control the media. Pierre wrote to me, and in part said:

'When I arrived at the scene I wanted to know exactly what had happened, to be able to talk about it. I went inside and visited all the classrooms where the young women had been killed. In the last classroom I found my own daughter Maryse, lying dead on the podium, where a few minutes before she was addressing her classmates about a project when Lépine arrived and shot her in the back. She did not die immediately. She was crying and asking for help. Lépine shot to death three other women, came back to my daughter, stabbed her three times and finally shot himself. This is what I saw when I arrived there.'

So to Pierre, and all of those involved in responding to these terrible crimes, I salute you. To Pierre, his family and the countless family and friends of the victims, those who were injured, witnessed or were otherwise affected by these ghastly events, I offer my sincere condolences. This book is about the murderers, but in no way do I try and minimise or excuse their behaviour. To me, they and their actions are despicable.

It is therefore appropriate that the last word in *Killing for Pleasure* belongs not to the killers, but rather is dedicated to the 215 people who died at the hands of these 15 men:

Name	Age	Name	Age
Karin Alkstål	21	Steven Curnow	14
Winifred Aplin	58	Melissa Currie	5
Thomas Ashton	22	Barbara Daigneault	22
Anuncia Avignone	18	Therese Danielsson	21
Marcus Barnard	31	Kriemhild (Kitty) Davis	62
Leigh Barton		Dean Delawalla	52
Matthew Barton	12	David Delgado	11
Mychelle Barton	8	Judy Denney	42
Walter Bennett	66	Corey DePooter	17
Geneviève Bergeron	21	Joseph Dessert	60
Cassie Bernall	17	Kevin Dial	38
Elsa Borboa-Firro	19	James Dickson	45
Robert Boyer	33	Steven Dody	43
Maths Bragstedt	35	Catherine Dowling	28
Roger Brereton	41	Charlotte Dunn	5
Rodney Brown	32	Thomas Eckman	18
Russell Brown	42	Anne-Marie Edward	20

Rewa Bryson	11	Richard Esser	38
Nicole Burgess	17		
Francis Butler	26	Dusan Flajnik	53
		Kelly Fleming	16
Neva Caine	22		
Michelle Carncross	18	Patricia Gabbard	47
Patricia Carney	57	Mark Gabour	16
Jimmy Caruthers	48	Elva Gaylard	48
Patricia Chambers	41	Myrtle Gibbs	66
Sou Leng Chung	32	Victor Gibbs	66
Kenneth Clements	51	Susan Godfrey	34
Victoria Clydesdale	5	Gloria González	24
Simon (Chris) Cole	61	A1 Gratia Jr	71
Hélène Colgan	23	Ursula Gratia	67
Maria Colmenero-Silva	18	Debra Gray	33
Victor Crimp	70	Karen Griffith	17
Nathalie Croteau	23	Michael Griffith	48
Emma Crozier	5	Stewart Guthrie	41
Zoe Hall	28	Mhairi MacBeath	5
Johnna Hamilton	30	Julie McBean	20
Kevin Hasell	5	Michael McGuire	38
Jamshid Havash	45	Brett McKinnon	6
Maud Haviernick	29	Abigail McLennan	5
Venice Henehan	70	Lena Mårdner	30
Omar Hernández	11	Vesna Markovska	24
Blythe Herrera	31	David Martin	72
Matao Herrera	11	Noeline (Sally) Martin	69
Sandra Hill	22	Roland Mason	70
Garry Holden	38	Sheila Mason	64
Jasmine Holden	11	Pauline Masters	49
Elizabeth Howard	27	Daniel Mauser	15
Mary Howard	57	Gwen Mayor	47
Mervyn Howard	55	Alannah Mikac	6
Clodine Humphrey	65	Madeline Mikac	3
Patty Husband	49	Nanette Mikac	36
Ross Irvine	5	Connie Miller	41

Magnus (Tim) Jamieson	69
Betty Jarred	34
Ronald Jary	71
Helle Jurgensson	22
Thomas Karr	24
David Kerr	5
Matthew Kechter	16
Abdur Khan	84
Sylvia King	30
Tony Kistan	
Barbara Klueznick	31
Maryse Laganière	25
Marguerite Lamport	
Maryse Leclair	23
Anne-Marie Lemay	27
Leslie Lever	53
Paulina López	22
Sarah Loughton	15
Zona Lynn	64
Ross Percy	42
Vanessa Percy	26
Claudia Pérez	9
Ruben Pérez	19
John Petrie	5
Leroy Phillips	42
Ian Playle	34
Russell Pollard	72
Ruth Pujol	55
Jerry Pyle	51
Janette Quin	50
Edward Quinn	58
John Romero Jr	29
Su-zann Rashott	36
Carlos Reyes Jr	8 months

William 'Billy' Miller	30
Andrew Mills	49
Robert Mitchell	27
Kenneth Morey	49
Judith Morris	19
Emily Morton	5
Vadewattee Muralidhara	44
John Muscat	26
Peter Nash	32
Gwenda Neander	67
Mo Yee Ng	48
Anthony Nightingale	44
Mary Nixon	60
Sophie North	6
Jenny Österman	23
Margarita Padilla	18
Gina Papaioannou	21
Glenn Pears	35
Sonia Pelletier	28
Dion Percy	5
Billy Speed	23
Warren Spencer	30
Glen Spivey	55
Nancy Stansbury	44
Kenneth Stanton	21
Aleki Tali	41
Olgica Taylor	45
Allen Tenenbaum	48
Royce Thompson	59
Björn Tollsten	27
John Tomlin	16
Lauren Townsend	18
Edna Townsley	47
Annie Turcotte	21
Megan Turner	5

Michèle Richard	21	Marianne Van Ewyk	38
Victor Rivera	25	Eric Vardy	51
Mike Rockne	33	Arisdelsi Vargas	31
Daniel Rohrbough	15	Kyle Velázquez	
Joanna Ross	5	Hugo Velázquez-Vázquez	46
Claudia Rutt	18	Aida Velázquez-Victoria	70
Dorothy Ryan	63	Laurence Versluis	62
Annie Saint-Arneault	23	Miguel Victoria-Ulloa	74
Helene Salzmann	50	Douglas Wainwright	67
Robert Salzmann	58	Harry Walchuk	38
William Sanders	48	Scott Webb	30
Roy Schmidt	29	Patti Welch	27
Hannah Scott	5	James Welsh	75
Kate Scott	21	Lula Welsh	75
Rachel Scott	17	George White	52
Thomas Shader	31	Kathleen Whitman	24
Kevin Sharp	68	Margaret Whitman	43
Raymond Sharp	67	Juanita Williams	64
Isaiah Shoels	18	Leo Wilson	6
Thomas Simmons	33	Jason Winter	29
Tracey Skinner	23	Jackie Wright	18
Paul Sonntag	18		

GLOSSARY

antisocial personality disorder A type of personality characterised by habitual, impulsive antisocial behaviour, often marked by emotional indifference and an absence of guilt. In the past, individuals classified as having antisocial personality disorder were sometimes referred to as psychopaths or sociopaths.

asocial 1. Without regard to society or social issues. This meaning is used to describe situations, events, behaviours or people which operate independently of (although not in opposition to) social values and customs. An asocial person is one who is withdrawn from society. 2. Lacking in sensitivity to social customs. This meaning is closer to 'anti-social' because the connotation is that such insensitivity can be potentially harmful to a group or society.

Asperger's disorder A less severe condition of social withdrawal than autism, in which language skills are present and curiosity about the environment is preserved.

attention deficit disorder A disorder characterised by inattentiveness, impulsivity, increased activity and restlessness, resulting in impaired social behaviour and poor school or work performance.

autism Describes abnormal or impaired development in social and communication abilities. Activities and interests are often severely restricted as a result. Behaviour can seem extremely odd to an observer.

beta blocker A drug used to reduce blood pressure and/or anxiety.

delusional disorder A term used to describe a mental disorder characterised by delusion. A delusion is a belief, or set of beliefs, that bear no resemblance to reality are present for one month or more, and are not accompanied by other schizophrenic symptoms.

depression A disorder characterised by intense sadness and feelings of hopelessness and worthlessness.

depressive disorder Major depressive disorder is distinguished by the occurrence of at least one major depressive episode, defined as at least two weeks of depressed mood with at least four other symptoms of depression. (Eg, feelings of hopelessness, guilt, eating or sleeping problems, loss of interest in formerly pleasurable activities or suicidal thoughts.)

depressive psychosis Mood disorder accompanied by psychotic symptoms (eg delusions or hallucinations).

disordered personality Personality characteristics that are inflexible and maladaptive and cause significant impairment and distress either for oneself or others.

dysfunctional Behaviour, thoughts or feelings that hinder rather than help adaptation.

forensic psychiatry(ist) A branch of psychiatry dealing with legal questions such as determination of sanity, issues of mental responsibility for acts committed, whether an individual should be committed to an institution, and treatment of anti-social and/or criminal people.

forensic psychology A specialty that focuses on the evaluation and treatment of criminals.

hypochondriasis(cal) A condition characterised by imagined sufferings or physical illness or, more generally, an exaggerated concern with one's physical health.

insular Remote, detached, aloof.

mythomania The tendency to lie, exaggerate, or tell incredible imaginary stories as if they really happened.

narcissism An exceptional interest or admiration of oneself (especially physical appearance).

neuropsychological Relating to the relationships between brain function and behaviour.

obsessive compulsive disorder An anxiety disorder with two essential characteristics: recurrent and persistent thoughts, ideas and feelings, and repetitive, ritualistic behaviours. Attempts to resist a compulsion produce mounting tension and anxiety which one typically relieves by behaving in a stereotypical manner.

paranoia An intense fear or suspicion that is usually unfounded and most commonly involves delusions of jealousy, grandeur or persecution. In paranoia, intellectual functioning is often unimpaired and the paranoid person may be quite capable of coherent behaviour within the delusional system.

paranoid A person who shows the behaviour patterns associated with paranoia.

paranoid schizophrenic A person with schizophrenia who has persecutory-type delusions.

pathological Abnormal functioning.

pervasive development disorder A class of childhood disorders characterised by a serious distortion of basic psychological functioning. Problems tend to occur across the board and may involve social, cognitive, perceptual, attentional, motor or linguistic functioning (eg, infantile autism).

predatory aggression In relation to pseudo-commandos, this is not strictly a psychological term, but refers to aggression which is predatory as opposed to emotionally-driven. Predatory violence is characterised as 'an attack mode of violence that is accompanied by minimal autonomic arousal, is planned, purposeful and emotionless'. This contrasts to other forms of violence which are accompanied by high levels of physiological arousal in response to a perceived threat and is marked by feelings of anger or fear. (Meloy, 1997)

psychological Relating to the mind and behaviour.

psychopath More recently called 'anti-social personality' or 'sociopath'. A person who is indifferent to the feelings of others, is impulsive, and has little concern for the future or remorse about past behaviour.

psychopathology The scientific study of mental disorders.

psychosis The most severe mental disorders in which a person's thoughts and actions no longer meet the demands of reality. Characterised by extremely odd and upsetting perceptual and/or thought disturbance.

reactive depression Depression that typically results from negative events occurring in one's life.

schizo-affective disorder A disorder characterised by symptoms of schizophrenia and a period of disordered mood, preceded or followed by at least two weeks of delusions or hallucinations without mood disturbance.

schizoid Relating to or characteristic of schizophrenia.

schizophrenia A group of severe mental disorders characterised by at least some of the following: disturbance of thought, withdrawal, inappropriate or flat emotions, delusions and hallucinations (ie seeing or hearing things that are not actually there).

schizophrenic A person diagnosed with schizophrenia.

schizophreniform disorder A disorder with symptoms similar to schizophrenia lasting less than six months which may not result in major problems in day to day life.

sociopath See psychopath.